RUNNING
A LOVE STORY

RUNNING
A LOVE STORY

DOM HARVEY

ALLEN&UNWIN
SYDNEY·MELBOURNE·AUCKLAND·LONDON

Allen & Unwin
Level 3, 228 Queen Street
Auckland 1010, New Zealand
Phone: (64 9) 377 3800

Email: info@allenandunwin.com
Web: www.allenandunwin.co.nz

83 Alexander Street
Crows Nest NSW 2065, Australia
Phone: (61 2) 8425 0100

A catalogue record for this book is available
from the National Library of New Zealand.

ISBN 978 1 98854 703 9

Design by Kate Barraclough
Printed and bound in Australia by Griffin Press

Cover photograph: Running the Waterfront Half Marathon on
Auckland's Tamaki Drive in April 2018.

1 3 5 7 9 10 8 6 4 2

MIX
Paper from
responsible sources
FSC® C009448

The paper in this book is FSC® certified.
FSC® promotes environmentally responsible,
socially beneficial and economically viable
management of the world's forests.

For my mum, Sue Harvey—if it wasn't for you being a runner, I may never have become one myself.

And for the late Arthur Lydiard—if it wasn't for this incredible New Zealander, none of us would run.

CONTENTS

INTRODUCTION

WHEN THIS BOOK WAS first published, I had recently run the Berlin Marathon: a course of 42.2 kilometres through the city's streets that ends under the world-famous landmark, the Brandenburg Gate. Berlin is one of the six World Marathon Majors, and at that time was the fifth I had been fortunate enough to run. I'd done Berlin, New York, Chicago, London and Boston; the only Major I had left to tick off was Tokyo. Now this book is in its second edition, and I've since completed Tokyo as well.

I have the finisher medals from all six of the Major runs I've done hanging on the wall right next to where I sit in my home office. A bit show-boaty? Yeah, maybe . . . but I don't care. I worked bloody hard for every one of them, so I'm not going to keep them in a box or out of sight. Every time I look at them, they take me right back to that city on that day—each medal reminds me of the sights, sounds and smells from each run.

There was a sort of void in my life in the wake of finishing the Berlin Marathon. For almost a whole year, it was my main focus and I worked my arse off to train for it. I took a decent break after it, although that didn't mean I stopped running altogether. I just didn't do anything too serious, and I focused on getting out running for the sheer love of it.

One afternoon, not long after I'd returned from Berlin, my then thirteen-year-old son, Sev, got home from school just as I was putting on my running gear. As I always do when I'm heading out for a jog, I asked if he wanted to join me. Ninety-nine times out of a hundred he says no, but on this day he said yes. I love jogging with Sev. It's a time when we are both totally in the moment with each other. No screens, no devices, no Wi-Fi. We went out for a 5-kilometre jog, and less than 2 kilometres in Sev got the stitch and had to stop. We walked and talked for a bit, and he asked about Berlin. He seemed in awe of the fact I was able to run that far without stopping. For a moment, I was like a Marvel hero in his eyes—not a common thing, as most of the time he thinks I'm the lamest, most embarrassing adult on earth.

As we chatted, I realised that this is one of the reasons you run marathons: for respect. From others, sure, but mainly for yourself. It takes a lot of self-respect to put all that effort into training your body to run a distance that isn't really all that natural . . . and maybe just a bit of self-loathing, as well!

YOU MIGHT ALREADY KNOW of me, but I bet it's because of my job rather than because I'm a runner. I'm a radio broadcaster on The Edge's morning show, and I guess I'm a little bit famous. Not *famous* famous like an All Black—those guys are A-listers.

I'm probably more of an E- or F-lister. You might even call me a 'shit-lebrity'. I've done my job for the past sixteen years, and even after all this time I still bloody love it.

I also happen to run marathons. I'm not a bad runner, and I'm not a good runner. I'm just a runner. There will always be people in front of me, and there will always be people behind me. And, actually, I wouldn't even give a shit if there was nobody behind me. I love running so much that I'd rather be dead-last than not doing it at all. Running is when I am at my happiest, and the feeling of contentment I get after a run is unreal.

NOW I CAN HONESTLY SAY THAT I THINK RUNNING IS FUN. YEP, THAT'S RIGHT. I *LOVE* IT.

I come from a bit of a running family. My parents both ran marathons, and Mum, who's in her sixties, still does them now. I ran long distances as a kid, and even completed my first full marathon at the age of fourteen. Then I stopped . . . and didn't run for over a decade. I only took it up again when, in my late twenties, I tipped the scales at 115 kilos. My motivation then was simply to be able to stand naked in front of a full-length mirror and not be grossed out by what I saw. (I once read in one of those 'fun facts' lists somewhere that running is the second-best form of exercise for weight-loss. What was number one, you ask? The rather inconvenient cross-country skiing.)

When I started running again in my late twenties I *hated* it. Every step hurt. It sucked! But somewhere along the way something pretty cool happened. I stopped hating it. Even after I had reached a weight I was happy with, I kept doing it. Now I can honestly say that I think running is fun. Yep, that's right. I *love* it. If I go for more than two or three days without running, I start to get a bit irritable and feel as though something is missing from my life. Is running the most fun thing to do in the world? No. I can probably think of 50 activities that would be way more fun than going for a run—and none of them involve exercising. But not one of those things would give me the health benefits or the same outstanding feeling of calm, clarity and wellbeing. The feeling of being alive.

I am not some running expert, so this is not a how-to book full of pro-tips and advice (there are plenty of those out there already, not to mention hundreds of great articles online). I'm not qualified to teach anyone anything. I am just a regular guy who drank too much alcohol and ate too much shitty food, then fell in love with running and turned his life around. Also, let's face it, the majority of people have a strong dislike of running, so reading a book about it probably sounds about as appealing as getting stuck in a lift with Donald Trump.

What you will read in this book is a sort of love story about running. It's about how I got back into running, and my love affair with marathons in particular. It's also the story of my mission to break the three-hour mark in a marathon, first in Berlin then, later, in Tokyo.

When I first started writing this book, I was busy training for Berlin. I had no idea if I would achieve my goal or not—and I knew it was a big-balls goal that I really had no business setting. Before I set my sights on Berlin, I used to follow marathon training programmes that I had found on the internet, and my times were always around 3 hours and 20-something minutes. Different training programme each time, but pretty much the same outcome. So I teamed up with a coach, and with his expert advice I managed to run a personal best time of 3 hours and 10 minutes in the 2015 Chicago Marathon. I was blown away. I was 42 years old and had just run the fastest marathon of my life! That's what made me wonder if I was capable of going even faster. If I wanted to run under the mouth-watering three-hour mark in Berlin, I would need to shave another ten minutes off my personal best.

As I got further and further through writing this book, I grew terrified I might have an absolute nightmare in Berlin and end up finishing somewhere between the couple running together in a horse suit and the bloke running the entire way with a fridge strapped to his back. (I have literally seen both of these things in the starting area before!) Reading about a semi-serious runner being beaten by the novelty participants wouldn't be very inspiring, I thought.

So I made a promise to myself: I would arrive on the start line at Berlin having left no stone unturned. Then, no matter what time showed on that giant digital display when I crossed the finish line, I knew I'd be able to honestly write the words 'I gave it my absolute best'. You'll have to read the rest of this book to find out how I got on in Berlin—and then, later in Tokyo—but I can tell you now that I stand by those words.

Of course, the book you're now holding in your hands is the second, updated edition. I've added several chapters to the end to tell you what's happened since this book was first published. More than a year elapsed between the original edition and this one, and it was an especially dramatic year in my life. A lot happened, and while much of it was really great there was also a lot that was really tough, most notably the fact that Jay-Jay and I separated after eighteen years together. It was bloody hard (and still is), but the one thing that remained constant through it all for me was my running. As it has done more than once in my life, running came to the rescue to help me ride out the tough stuff.

If nothing else, I hope you'll find my running story motivating and encouraging. If you're not already a runner, it might inspire you to buy some shoes and give running a whack. Actually, that would be the coolest thing ever! If you came up to me in a pre-race Port-A-Loo queue and tapped me on the shoulder to tell me that reading this book had convinced you to give running a shot, I'd be stoked. And, if you're already a runner, I hope my story might give you the motivation to go further or faster than you have ever gone before.

CHAPTER 1
MY EARLY RUNNING DAYS

I REMEMBER RUNNING EVERYWHERE with my friends when I was a kid, and I never thought of it for a moment as exercise—it was just living. I see my young nieces doing the same thing now. Whenever they're excited and happy, they don't walk from place to place; they run. Sometimes I'd get puffed or get the stitch, but running around never felt like a punishment. P.E., on the other hand, did. Our lazy teacher would send us off to run laps of the school field or around the block. Come to think of it, that's probably where the deep hatred of running starts for so many people . . .

I eventually began running as a sport because my mum was (and still is) a runner. Running is in Mum's blood, actually: a few of her brothers are bloody quick too. Uncle John once ran a 2 hour 41 minute marathon, and Uncle Matt ran one in 2 hours 45 minutes. My Uncle Luke, who is possibly the fittest

52-year-old man in the Pacific Rim, still runs half marathons in around 1 hour 20 minutes, which is motoring. Luke has never done a full marathon, but if he ever did it would be a bloody quick one.

When I was a kid, we had a copy of Jim Fixx's famous *The Complete Book of Running* sitting on the wall-unit at our house, next to the dining table, so that it was always in sight and within easy reach. I'll never forget the cover: a runner's legs, red Onitsuka Tiger shoes and red shorts against a red backdrop. This book helped spark a jogging revolution. Before it was published in the late seventies, hardly anybody was running for pleasure. It was like a bible for runners. It was also right next to our actual family Bible. The actual Bible was hardly ever flicked through, though; it was the running book that was read religiously.

So, even without taking any active interest in the sport, I was constantly surrounded by running chat. Dad dabbled in running too, but he was a far more talented tennis player. Dad ran a few marathons, but he was never that quick. This means I have half my mum's genes, which want me to go fast . . . and half my dad's genes, which mean I won't go bald on top, but also that I'm not running anywhere in too much of a hurry.

Until my siblings and I were old enough to have a say in how we spent our weekends, we were dragged around the lower half of the North Island against our will to either watch Dad play tennis or Mum participate in runs. I gave tennis a crack myself and played it for a couple of years. When I retired from the sport at the age of eleven, I was yet to secure a win. Dad, trying to be glass half full about my appalling record with the racquet, told me I shouldn't be upset—I was the best at being the worst, so in a way I was still the best, he said. I can see now that this isn't really a compliment, but back then it made me feel pretty good about sucking.

The big problem was my coordination. I simply didn't have any. This caused problems with most of the sports I attempted during my childhood. Rugby, cricket, soccer, volleyball, golf: you name a sport, chances are that I gave it a go. Thanks to this coordination handicap, I retired from all forms of team sport by the time I was twelve. I was OK with letting myself down though (not that I really had a say in the matter), and I even got a tiny bit of enjoyment out of seeing how much pleasure my lack of talent gave my opponents. It felt like I was helping them out.

In the end, team sports just became too difficult. Kids can be cruel, and competitive kids can be the cruellest of the lot. It got so bad with some of the teams I played in that even the coach, who was usually just a school teacher or one of the other kids' parents, would restrict my involvement to the absolute bare minimum just to keep the competitive, sporty kids happy. In cricket, I would always bat last and rarely got to bowl, and—just to make extra sure I had no chance of fucking up the outcome of the game—I would be put so far out to field that the ball would never come near me. Some teams caught on to the fact that there was this kid with an inability to catch, throw or even stop a ball standing out near the boundary, so they would deliberately hit it in my direction. You cannot imagine the panic and fear I felt whenever a ball was hurtling through the air towards me and my teammates were yelling, 'CAAATCH IT!' . . . almost always followed by a chorus of disappointed groans when I inevitably missed it. In rugby, I would either be a reserve or placed out on the wing. I would often go the entire game without touching the ball. Some Saturdays, I would get home from my rugby game and Mum wouldn't even have to wash my uniform. That was the upside to having a dreadfully uncoordinated child.

After a while it became apparent that individual sports were the only option for me. That's where the running started. I should point out that I even battled with this. I am pretty sure there are not many people who can claim to have tripped themselves up with an ankle tap once, let alone doing so on numerous occasions. But I can! I would be running along and somehow my legs would get tangled and I'd fall over. In its own way, it's a kind of skill; most people wouldn't be able to do it even if they tried really hard. I'm still not sure how I managed it, but I vividly recall finding myself lying on the ground in a slightly confused state, looking around for obstacles, like tree roots, that could have caused my fall, and thinking, *How did that just happen?*

MY LACK OF COORDINATION WAS SO BAD THAT I HAD A STUBBED BIG TOE FOR ABOUT 70 PER CENT OF MY CHILDHOOD.

I once managed to show off this skill in front of an audience larger than just my siblings or a couple of mates. It was at the Riverdale Primary School sports day in 1983, and I was taking my run-up for the long-jump event. Just before I reached the little white strip of paint on the grass where you are supposed to launch yourself into your jump, my left ankle tapped my right ankle. I went flying through the air and landed awkwardly—but softly—in the sandpit, recording a jump of 87 centimetres. Not enough to make it through to the finals, but a legal attempt nonetheless.

My lack of coordination was so bad that I had a stubbed big toe for about 70 per cent of my childhood. It was always bloody painful, stubbing a toe. It would happen on the usual uneven surfaces, like steps and gutters, but incredibly I also managed to stub my toe more than once walking along on perfectly flat surfaces. You might think that, after it had happened a few times, I would start to make a habit of wearing shoes. But I was a slow learner as well as a bad walker.

In a cruel and ironic twist, my younger brother, Daniel, who was a gifted sports-kid and totally awesome at whatever he had a crack at, was the one who suffered the most embarrassing sports-related injury of any member of the Harvey family. One weekend, Palmerston North Boys' High School held a hole-in-one golf fundraiser on the school field. Anyone from Palmerston North could turn up and pay a couple of dollars for a shot, and whoever got a hole in one or their ball closest to it won a life-changing prize, like a meat pack or something.

In an attempt to grease his way into one of the coveted school-prefect roles, Daniel volunteered to help out at the fundraiser, and because of his sporting prowess the organising committee had no issues giving him the job of standing near the hole with a tape measure to mark the distance of any ball that came close. It was while he was standing there, tape measure at the ready, that he got hit on the head with a golf ball in full flight. The ball knocked him over, but didn't knock him out. It didn't split the skin or bleed, but it did leave a lump on his head that was exactly the same size and shape as the ball that had done the damage.

The other students in the area on ball-retrieval duty ran to Daniel's aid, and after a couple of Panadol and an hour in the sickbay he was good as gold. Naturally, the school was apologetic about the freak accident. Not that apologetic, though—Dan still missed out on being a prefect.

As for the stranger who was responsible for the stray ball? I don't think he stuck around to offer an apology. My guess is he was pissed off that he wasn't going to win the meat pack.

I'm pleased to say that my coordination has improved as I have got older. I have not stubbed a toe in over 20 years, and these days I can run without the ever-present fear of tripping myself over. I can even participate in social team sports. It's not like my colleagues are begging me to be part of the starting line-up for the mid-week indoor netball team or anything, but when I do play they can pass the ball to me with a certain degree of confidence that the ball will be caught . . . most of the time.

WHEN I WAS NINE, I took part in an annual fun run from Feilding to Palmerston North. The distance between the two towns is 18 kilometres, and most of it is on the open road. I did this run in bare feet and pyjamas. True story. Here's what happened: I was watching *What Now?* on TV when Dad, without any sort of advance warning, instructed all four of us Harvey kids to get in the car. While I'd been fully engrossed in my favourite TV show, I'd failed to notice Mum wandering around in running clothes and getting prepared for this run. I was totally oblivious to what had been going on around me in the house. I loved *What Now?* so much that the whole house could have been on fire and I wouldn't have noticed—unless the flames came between me and the screen.

So our entire family of six packed into the car, which was definitely *not* designed to transport that many people in comfort. I sat squished into the back seat with my older sister, Bridget, and my younger siblings, Daniel and Charlotte. I was devastated. This was before we had a video recorder, so I was missing the last bit of *What Now?*

We made it to Feilding and got out of the car. Mum started stretching and doing warm-up exercises with the other runners. I was furious! I was already missing out on my TV programme and now, because Dad hadn't bothered to tell me where we were going or what we were doing, I was going to have to spend the rest of my morning being driven slowly back to Palmerston North so that we could cheer Mum on along the way.

This was turning into the worst day of my life.

I started whining.

This was a risky move on my part. Whenever any one of us whined too much, Dad would eventually reach his breaking point and then the child responsible would get a love-tap on the bum or thigh. Illegal now, but perfectly acceptable parenting in the eighties. If you were lucky, you might just be warned that you were travelling at a very high speed towards spank-town—and usually this warning came in the form of Dad's favourite line: 'Stop whining or I will really give you something to whine about.' Other times, though, we'd drive Dad so swiftly to boiling point that the discipline would come without the warning.

Now, sitting grumpily in the back seat, I made some peevish comment about preferring to run back to Palmerston North than spend the morning stuck in the car. My whinging must have been right on point, because Dad made the executive decision then and there to let his nine-year-old son attempt to run further than he had ever run before, without any sort of training, on the open road, in pyjamas *and* without shoes, just so he wouldn't have to put up with me sulking and being negative. I think he was just hoping to teach me a lesson, show me a bit of tough love. Thankfully, it was summer so I had my cotton PJs on. Unlike my flannelette winter pyjamas, these ones didn't have the diddle-slit in the front. It would have been a traumatising sight for the poor other runners and race volunteers to see a child jogging along barefoot with his undersized genitals sporadically popping out of the hole like the little bird on a cuckoo clock.

THE SOLES OF MY FEET WERE BRUISED AND BATTERED AND TORN TO SHREDS BY THE GRAVEL. IT LOOKED LIKE THEY HAD BEEN MASSAGED WITH AN ORBITAL SANDER.

So I got out of the car and I started running. Every couple of kilometres Dad and my three siblings would drive past and cheer me on. Every time I saw them, Dad would ask if I was ready to get back in the car yet. I was more than ready. But I was a stubborn little bastard, and getting back in the car would have meant admitting that I was wrong, so I kept running. I walked and ran my way to the finish line in Palmerston North in a little bit over two hours. My feet were reasonably tough, because we were used to running around and playing in bare feet, but the road was definitely the winner on the day. The soles of my feet were bruised and battered and torn to shreds by the gravel. It looked like they had been massaged with an orbital sander. I was in agony that night, but I had to bite my tongue because I knew if I so much as squeaked about pain Dad would just say something like, 'Well, you should have just stayed in the car with your brothers and sisters!'

By the next morning the heels of my feet had developed massive blood blisters. They were huge. I had to tip-toe around until Mum found a needle and popped them for me.

Each one contained about a shot-glass of fluid and the watery red liquid came out with such force that it squirted her in the face.

Unfortunately, my battle scars were not considered severe enough in the Harvey household to get me a sick day from school. Mum was generous enough to drive me instead of making me walk. As I walked gingerly into the school gates, she yelled some words of encouragement after me: 'It serves you right for being cheeky to your father yesterday!'

I actually ran that race another five or six times in subsequent years. But I learned a valuable lesson that first time, and when I did the race again I made sure I was dressed more appropriately for the occasion—always shoes, never pyjamas.

I'm not even sure if something like this would even be allowed these days. But back then there was no minimum entry age. These days, of course, things are a bit stricter when it comes to entry criteria. There are far more rules and regulations. The Auckland Marathon, which is New Zealand's largest, has age restrictions of sixteen for the half marathon and eighteen for the full marathon. I'm doubtful that many of these long-distance runs would let a nine-year-old participate . . . and they definitely wouldn't be OK with a kid running in bare feet and shorty pyjamas!

IT WAS THREE YEARS later, not long after my twelfth birthday, that I ran my first half marathon. I didn't do any sort of formal training. I just winged it on the natural fitness and energy of a kid. I actually kept a diary that year. My favourite book at the time was *The Secret Diary of Adrian Mole, Aged 13¾* by Sue Townsend, so I decided it would be cool to keep my own diary, the sort where you write a bit about what you got up to each day. I had forgotten all about this thing until it turned up in a box in the shed during a spring clean last year. I'll let twelve-year-old me step in here.

Saturday, 2 March 1985
I am running a half marathon tomorrow so here is a prayer of hope: Dear Lord, give me strength to complete the 13-mile course in good health and shape. I am planning to do 2.10. Amen.

Sunday, 3 March 1985
I completed the half marathon with sour [*sic*] legs in 2.12. I came 144 out of 160. We also went to church today.

Monday, 4 March 1985
Ouch! My legs were killing me today. I missed out on P.E. I also finished my project and watched *Riptide*. It was grouse.

Yep. I actually used the word grouse.

Many more half marathons followed that first one. This was in the very early 1980s, when jogging first became a mainstream sport in New Zealand. Ten-kilometre fun runs had started popping up all over the country. There are still a handful around these days—Round the Bays in Auckland pulls huge numbers each year—but most of them died off when people realised that the concept of a fun run was way less fun than the name suggested. Mum often participated in these 'fun' events, so my brother, Daniel, and I would sign up as well. We didn't do a lot of training. We'd put on our little white commando sneakers from Para Rubber, which offered about as much support as a slice of processed cheese, and get into it. We never thought anything of the distance or whether there might be any sort of long-term damage to our growing bones and joints (and neither did our parents or the race officials, apparently). We didn't really think of it as sport either. It was just something to do. Our focus was never on our times. All we cared about was who would beat who— and, more often than not, my younger brother would kick my arse, which was humiliating.

I still have some of the certificates I was awarded at these runs. One was for 'The fourth annual Steinlager Manawatu Half Marathon', which I ran in 1 hour 38 minutes. In hindsight, it is probably no surprise that lots of these events ended up being canned. I was raised in Palmerston North and I love the place, but there are not too many landmarks or awe-inspiring sights to take in that can help ease the pain involved in running any sort of distance. Plodding through the residential streets of New Zealand's eighth biggest city for a couple of hours is a surefire way to complete a half marathon but feel like you ran a full.

I eventually worked my way up to the full marathon distance, and completed my first marathon in Whanganui at the age of fourteen with the help of a middle-aged man wearing undies and a tank-top—but that's a story for later. Little did I know then that it would be another 21 years before I even made it to the start line of another marathon.

I BEGAN RUNNING 'COMPETITIVELY' at high school when I joined the school Harriers team. I use the c-word tentatively because, even though I trained bloody hard and always tried my best, I just wasn't very good.

Back then, Palmerston North Boys' High School was a very sporty school. In fact, it still is. When I was there in the late eighties, it was a place where the boys who were brilliant at cricket or rugby could get away with the secondary-school equivalent of murder. As far as 'cool' sports went, being in the Harriers team was way down the list—possibly sandwiched in between badminton and small-bore shooting.

In the summer of my fourth-form year, the act of hoicking on the asphalt courtyard in front of the tuck shop became so popular that it was officially decreed a detainable offence—unless you were the top try-scorer in the first XV, of course. We all did it. I'm not sure why. Maybe we thought it looked cool? Anyway, by the end of every lunch hour, the courtyard would resemble a seabed of big green oysters. There were piles of mucussy saliva everywhere. It was like a minefield of repulsive globules of teenage-boy DNA. If you didn't watch where you were putting your feet, you ran the risk of feeling your foot slide out beneath you as it made contact with the spit.

Hoicking wasn't restricted to outside the tuck shop, either. Another popular spot was the ceiling of the toilet block. It was reasonably high, but with a decent ball of phlegm you could hit the roof *and* get your goo to stay there. It would be in good company up there with the dried-up balls of wet toilet paper that had been thrown up by other students. It must have been the most unpleasant task imaginable for the poor school caretaker to clean up during the holidays. He must have wished in those moments that he had spent more time in school when he was younger so that he didn't have to spend so much time in school now.

As well as having a free-pass to hoick, the school's sports stars could also break other school rules without fear of repercussion. There were some teachers who didn't buy in to this bullshit, but even they were overruled when the coach of the cricket or rugby team intervened to sweep whatever the issue was under the carpet. I'm not talking about anything major here—just minor stuff like wagging, wearing your socks down, talking in assembly, or riding your bike through the school grounds. And, if I'm really honest, I'm only calling it unfair because I wasn't one of the school's VIPs. Sadly, any leniency towards the school's sporting elite did not trickle down to the Harriers. And, even if it had, I doubt it would have given me an easy path through school, since I was still the worst of the best—and I was also still OK with this, because there were some remarkably talented guys in the squad.

HE WOULD TURN UP WEARING A FLANNEL SHIRT AND SHOES SO OLD THAT HE MIGHT AS WELL HAVE RUN WITH SLICES OF BREAD ATTACHED TO HIS FEET.

There were two adults in charge of the Harriers team: Mr Wigglesworth, who was the school's most terrifying P.E. teacher, and an elderly man known as Sport. Sport's real name was Peter Jowett, but he got his nickname because it was what he called everybody he met. He must have been in his sixties or seventies at the time, but he would still get out and go for these ridiculously long runs with us every weekend. He never had flash gear either—and most of the time he wouldn't even be in running gear. He would turn up wearing a flannel shirt and shoes so old that he might as well have run with slices of bread attached to his feet. He also wore his clothes inside out when he was running. It looked pretty odd—fat seams and tags popping out everywhere—but it made some sense when he explained his logic. Wearing his gear inside out meant that the nice, smooth side of every garment would be rubbing against his skin and he would be chafe-free.

Sport used the money he saved by not buying fancy running gear to upgrade his motor vehicle. He loved the feel and the smell of a brand-new car, but unfortunately his wife didn't agree. She thought it was a big waste of money to go getting a new car every couple of years. Sport came up with a plan to get around this: he would, he figured, simply stick to the same make, model and colour of car by trading his current car in whenever a new model was released. His wife would never know! Despite the fact that this plan was flawed and full of holes (new car smell, for starters), every two years Sport would pull into his driveway in a brand-new cream-coloured Nissan Pulsar sedan. And do you know what? His wife never suspected a thing! Or at least, if she did, she never said anything. Sport's not particularly sophisticated scam was eventually exposed when he made a rookie mistake: he forgot to get the new Nissan Pulsar in the same colour. It could probably be blamed on old age, or poor eyesight. Or overconfidence. Whatever the cause, as soon as he pulled up in a blue Pulsar, his cover was blown. Everyone in the Harriers team could see the hilarity in all of this immediately. Not Sport, though. It was several years before he was ready to laugh about it. As for his wife, I am not sure she ever saw the comedy in the situation. And the big loser in all of this? The Palmerston North Nissan dealership. Once Sport's scam was uncovered, he was banned by his wife from upgrading ever again.

Mr Wigglesworth was in his mid-forties, and was probably the fittest person at the whole school. He definitely wasn't the best dresser, though; he was a big fan of those snug-fitting Adidas tracksuit pants with those strange stirrup things on the bottom. Those pants left nothing—*nothing*—to the imagination. From 30 metres away, you could count the amount of loose change he was carrying in his pockets.

Everyone at school feared Mr Wigglesworth. The only thing he loved more than his nightly ritual of 500 sit-ups was putting people on detention. I used to wonder if he ever ended up with writer's cramp from filling in so many green slips. The one perk of being a harrier, however, was that Mr Wigglesworth would show you a little bit of leniency—even if none of the other teachers did. Under Mr Wigglesworth's hawk eye, we were allowed to get away with stuff that non-runners wouldn't even dream of—like crossing the road at a point other than the pedestrian crossing, or having your shirt untucked. Probably not hoicking in the courtyard, though. I don't think Mr Wigglesworth would have even let Usain Bolt get away with that. This favouritism didn't go unnoticed, of course. Non-runners at school didn't really refer to us as Harriers; instead, they gave us the flattering nickname 'Wigglesworth's bum chums'.

Twice a year, the Harriers team would travel to the New Zealand Secondary Schools Athletics Association's road-race and cross-country competitions. At these events, the absolute best runners from schools all over the country would get together to compete, and more often than not one of my teammates would end up with a podium finish. Luckily for me, our school had a policy that if you turned up to all the training sessions and followed the intensive training programme, then you got to go to the competitions—no matter what.

And the training we did was *hard*. The cross-country and road-race events we were working towards were known as 'middle-distance events', which meant they were about 5 kilometres long. A couple of days a week, we would have training after school where we would do either a long, slow run, or a speed session, depending on where we were at in the programme. Then, on Saturday mornings, we would meet outside the school gates and pile into a few different cars to travel somewhere in the countryside for a long two-hour run over some rural roads. The thinking behind these real long runs was that, if you could comfortably run for a couple of hours, then running a much shorter distance would seem easy.

Some of the boys on the team were already naturally fast and then just got faster with training, like my mate Shawn Retter. Shawn was head-hunted by Mr Wigglesworth, who had spotted his untapped natural ability, and Shawn went from good to great really quickly. Others were mediocre runners who became pretty damn good with coaching, like my best mate, Matt Cherri. Then there was me: a blemish on the otherwise impeccable Harriers team. Mr Wigglesworth must have groaned under his breath at the start of every year when he realised I had signed up again. Despite being the slowest, I still enjoyed the runs and the camaraderie. Even though running is very much an individual sport, we all felt like teammates.

Waiting at the start line of these national events was nerve-wracking for all of us. They came at the end of months and months of hard slog, and we only had one chance to achieve the results we'd trained so hard for. Shawn would probably be hoping for a top-five finish, and Matt for maybe a top-ten or top-twenty finish. My goals were always far less ambitious: 'Don't finish last!' The entry fields for these races were always quite small—no more than a couple of hundred of New Zealand's fastest high-school runners—so this was not an idle concern. There was always a real threat that I could end up being that poor bastard who finished dead last. It had to be someone, of course, but I just didn't want it to be me. Thankfully, that never happened—though I came close.

At the New Zealand Secondary Schools road race in Hastings when I was fifteen, I got tripped up during the start of the race. I ended up on the road in a pile of lean and lanky teenage bodies. I still remember looking up and seeing everyone else sprinting off down the road. I was grazed, but otherwise uninjured, so I immediately leaped back on to my feet and bolted off. The adrenaline was pumping through my veins. I knew I was almost in last place. There had been three or four other runners involved in the pile-up—maybe five, max. I couldn't be sure. All I knew is that most of the field was already a long way up the road. *Bugger.*

PEOPLE SAY YOU SHOULD ALWAYS THINK POSITIVELY, BUT IN THIS CASE I RECKON MY NEGATIVE THOUGHTS ARE WHAT SPURRED ME ON.

As I started running, the sickening thought occurred to me that maybe some of the other kids in the pile-up might have had to pull out because of injuries—and that would *definitely* make me last. People say you should always think positively, but in this case I reckon my negative thoughts are what spurred me on. I was so afraid of being last that I ran like I had just stolen something from the dairy until I caught the tail end of the pack and was sure that I was no longer in last place. Phew! The relief!

From there, I continued to pass the slower runners all the way to the finish line. It was actually a good feeling to be passing people for once, rather than being passed. I finished in place one-hundred-and-something: safe from both the back *and* the front of the field.

I was bent over with my hands on my knees, staring at the

ground and panting when I felt a hand on my back. I looked up. It was Mr Wigglesworth.

'Well done, Dom,' he said. 'Good on you for getting back up and keeping going. You did great.'

He was right. And wrong. Finishing in the back half of a competition is nothing to do cartwheels over. But it had been one of my best-ever runs.

Mr Wigglesworth's comment was all it took for me to start crying. Not just a little cry, but a proper burst-into-tears sob where I could feel myself struggling to catch mouthfuls of air. He pulled me in for a hug. A proper two-armed job. The type of hug that would be inappropriate for a teacher to give to a student in almost every circumstance imaginable, especially when the teacher is wearing tracksuit pants so tight that his genitals look vacuum-packed. But it definitely felt like a good Dad hug.

Through my tears I explained why I was upset. 'I started at the back and passed people the whole way. I could have done so much better if I hadn't tripped!'

That was a lie. The reality was that the trip had cost me maybe ten seconds of time, twenty seconds at a very generous stretch. A time difference that would not have made much difference in my overall placing. The real reason for my sadness was the realisation that I was simply not a good runner. I was doing the same work as all my mates, but I wasn't getting any pay-off for my effort. I was the best that I could be . . . but it was nowhere near good enough.

Apart from the sense of disappointment I inevitably had after each of these school trips, I always enjoyed them immensely—a couple of days off school, the feeling of importance of wearing the school tie and blazer as the school rector farewelled us and reminded us of the school's expectations. (This had become a standard speech to all travelling sports teams after a kid had pulled a brown-eye out of the back of a mini-van while on a trip. The motorist in the car behind, who caught an eyeful of this teenage butthole, called the school to complain. The school was fuming, and the student was made to pull his pants down again—this time to be caned. For the rest of his years at school, he had the nickname 'Brown Spot'. After a while, everybody forgot his real name—even some of the teachers.)

The Hastings trip was the last one of those NZ Secondary School trips I went on with the Harriers. I couldn't keep doing all that work only to end up disappointed. It was embarrassing. At the age of fifteen, I retired from all forms of sport. I am pretty sure that after I told Mr Wigglesworth I was quitting his Harriers team I heard the plastic cork pop on a bottle of Bernadino sparkling wine.

I stopped running altogether after that, for a very long time.

CHAPTER 2
WHY I'M IN LOVE WITH RUNNING

I AM A ROUTINE kind of guy, a creature of habit. Maybe that is just a nice way of saying I am bloody boring. I tend to find a way of doing things that works for me, and then stick with that. If it was socially acceptable to do so, I would eat the same meal every evening: a vegetable and a meat. Broccoli for the vegetable—*always* broccoli—boiled in a pot of water with chicken stock. And either salmon or steak for the meat. If I could I would just go for salmon every single night, but I find that after a few days in a row the oil gets a bit much; I suppose it's my body's way of letting me know it's reached its omega-3 limit. When I get to that point, I'll get a bit crazy and switch to steak for a couple of meals.

The only problem with this approach to eating is other people. Specifically, people who crave variety and get bored easily. You know, people who eat for the taste and to be social, rather than simply as a means to fuel their body. The way I see it, as long as my body's got the nutrients necessary to keep it chugging along then I've done my job. Oh, and I also have remarkably immature tastebuds, which means I'm often unwilling to try new or fancy things. I'd happily eat broccoli and salmon for pretty much every meal. Not surprisingly, this has cost me a number of dinner-party invites over the years. While it's acceptable for vegetarians and gluten-free eaters to flag their dietary requirements before they go round to a friend's for a meal, people like me are simply referred to as fussy eaters—and that's to our faces. Behind our backs, I suspect we probably just get called a pain in the arse.

My friend Corinna hasn't had me back to her place since the salad incident. She invited Jay-Jay, my wife at the time, and me round to her house for dinner one night, and she served a salad. For *dinner*. Nothing else. Just salad.

When the 'meal' was finished she asked how it was.

I (unwisely) answered honestly. 'Well first of all, Corinna,' I said, 'salad on its own is not really a meal, is it?'

'It was a big salad,' Corinna replied defensively. 'And I didn't do meat because Jay-Jay is vegetarian.'

Jay-Jay was giving me a death stare from across the table, but I ignored her. I wasn't finished.

'And secondly,' I carried on recklessly, 'I'm not so sure about those bits of fruit in there.'

As well as the usual salad ingredients, like lettuce, feta and tomato, this salad also had bits of apple, pear, strawberries and watermelon in it.

And I didn't stop there, either. I dug deeper. 'I mean, there is a salad and there is a *fruit* salad. Salad is made with vegetables and is what you have as *part* of a main meal. Like, on the side. *Fruit* salad is what you have for pudding. I don't think the two belong together.'

Cue around three seconds of a silence so heavy that it felt like a whole minute. Corinna didn't know what to say. I think deep down she must have known I had a valid point.

BUT I HAD BIGGER CONCERNS AT THIS POINT— I HAD FINISHED DINNER AND I WAS STILL SO HUNGRY THAT I THOUGHT I WAS GOING TO FAINT.

Jay-Jay stepped in. 'Dominic!' she chided. 'You can be a real dick sometimes.'

The cheek of it! Corinna asked me for feedback. I gave some. And suddenly I'm the world's worst human. How does that work? I guess I should have been concerned about Corinna's feelings. But I had bigger concerns at this point—I had finished dinner and I was still so hungry that I thought I was going to faint.

We did the dishes then left. The good thing about going to someone's house and only eating a salad is there are very few dishes to be done.

My honesty earned me an ear-bashing from Jay-Jay on the drive home. Her abrasive lesson on manners only stopped when we made it to the McDonald's drive-through—a necessary pitstop before I passed out!

I'm still not convinced I did anything wrong. Sure, I may have sounded like the uncouth bogan version of a *MasterChef* judge, but I somehow mistakenly thought my feedback would be appreciated.

The salad incident was six years ago. I have not been invited back since.

BEING A ROUTINE GUY extends to other areas of my life as well, and especially to running. I don't ever get bored with running the same routes, and I like that my runs give structure to my day. As with food, I tend to get into the habit of doing things a certain way and then, if it works for me, I stick with it.

For instance, last summer when I was training for Berlin I developed something of a post-run ritual, just some little habits that I noticed had crept into the end of my runs and gradually became regular things. In a perfect world, according to just about any running book or article you will read, when you finish a run you shouldn't just stop when you get home. You are advised to jog slowly for a few minutes, walk for a bit, and finally follow that up with some stretching. Bugger that! After a hard run, the last thing I feel like doing is more bloody exercise! Plus, who has the time for all of that admin? It's this slightly defiant attitude that often makes me feel like I am different from most other runners. I run . . . but I don't necessarily feel like I am a 'real' runner. If that makes sense. I still eat crappy food and drink a lot of wine. And my motivation for taking up running as an adult in the first place was just so I wouldn't be grossed out by my own naked body. Anyway, my after-run ritual developed as a consequence of what had been a particularly humid New Zealand summer. Here's how it went:

Remove my iPod shuffle, Garmin watch, shoes and shirt— leaving me wearing nothing but my shorts and a glistening layer of sweat.

Unlock the back door and call my dog's name.

Grab a bottle of cold water from the fridge.

Go outside and lie on the deck for a few minutes, while the dog feverishly licks the sweat from me.

It sounds gross, I know. And it truly was. Since it had been such a hot and humid summer, I was getting home from my hard runs involving speed work absolutely drenched. I was so wet you could be forgiven for thinking I got caught in a downpour.

But the dog loved it.

And it was a chance for me to spend a small period of time reflecting on my run as I allowed my heart to return to its resting rate.

The dog's name, by the way, is Kanye. We named him after the American rapper, Kanye West. Kanye seemed like a cool name when he was a tiny puppy; we didn't want something 'doggy' like Benji, Buddy, Max or Oscar. What we didn't take into consideration, though, was just how awkward and embarrassing it would be at the park. Shouting 'KAAAAAAAANYEEEEEEE!' at the top of your lungs while a disobedient little dog invades a field where a game of touch rugby is in full swing is, I have discovered, a fantastic way to draw attention to yourself. Benji, Buddy, Max or Oscar would have been far less original, but also far less embarrassing. Kanye is a toy breed, a Sydney Silky terrier, and weighs maybe 5 kilograms, tops. He can run fast—he would beat me over 100 metres—but due to his tiny size, and his habit of stopping to sniff every bush, tree, post, fence, gate, pole and other dog, he would be a hopeless companion for anything longer than a sprint distance. So he doesn't get to come for runs with me, but he does get to lick my sweat off me. Some dogs have all the luck.

ONE OTHER ROUTINE I have is preparing the playlist on my iPod shuffle for long runs. These long runs can be the stuff of absolute dread—they can be tedious and boring and can take up to three hours of your Saturday or Sunday morning. But, if you are training your body to run 42 kilometres, they are a necessary evil. The night before these runs, I will prepare a brand-new playlist with around a hundred songs, which is way more than what I will ever need, but it means I can skip any song I don't feel like listening to when it comes up.

I find the act of compiling this playlist, then getting my running gear all laid out and ready to go, is something that gets me mentally prepared and excited about my upcoming run. When I wake up, I get dressed and have a quick bite to eat. Always the same thing: a sports drink, a slice of toast with honey or peanut butter, and a banana. Then, without procrastination, I hit the road. The sooner I start, the sooner I'm finished. Where possible, I will start running so early that it's still dark outside. There is something pretty special about being out running while most people are still sleeping, and having the streets all to yourself. Catching a good sunrise is always a nice way to help to take your mind off the suffering too! Getting started early also means I get home in time to go out for brunch with the family or some friends.

I tend to stick to the same routes, too. It's a comfort thing. I like the familiarity of it. I know where the spots are that I can get a drink of water. I know where the public toilets are. And I also know where there are bushes that will do as an alternative to a public toilet if I absolutely have to go!

EVEN THOUGH I LOVE my routines, I also love getting to run in new, different locations. It's a fantastic way to see things that you might otherwise miss out on when you're in a new place. In the pre-smartphone days, running in an unfamiliar city was a bit more difficult than it is now. You used to need landmarks and an amazing memory to remember where you had been and where you were going. Now, as long as you have Wi-Fi or a data plan that won't send you bankrupt, you're away laughing.

In 2011, after I'd run the Boston Marathon, Jay-Jay and I took the train down to New York to do some sightseeing for a week. The day we arrived, we went to the observation deck of the Rockefeller Center, which is 70 storeys up. The view was incredible—a sea of skyscrapers as far as the eye could see and bang smack in the middle this huge green space. *Central Park*. I decided then and there that the next morning would be the perfect time to go for a little run around the park to loosen my legs, which were still a bit tender from running Boston a few days earlier.

We were staying at a hotel in the Times Square area. I had an iPhone at the time, but the previous year I had been stung with a phone bill for roaming data that was big enough to make Bill Gates sweat and, as a result, I was incredibly cautious about using my phone unless I was in a Wi-Fi area. Using the maps app on my phone while I was running was simply not an option, but I was confident I could find my way without it. Before leaving the hotel, I looked up the route. It seemed easy enough: just run from our hotel on to Sixth Avenue then keep running along it until I get to Central Park. Boom! Happy days.

I got on to Sixth Avenue and started running. Central Park was only a couple of kilometres away, but I soon discovered that my watch battery was flat so I had no way of knowing how far I had gone. I ran along Sixth Avenue. And ran. And ran. Central Park sure felt a lot further away than it had looked from the top of 'the Rock' . . .

Eventually, I reached the end of the road and made it to the park.

But it wasn't Central Park.

It was the much smaller and less well-known Battery Park.

I had turned *right* on to Sixth Avenue when I was supposed to turn *left*, and had ended up all the way down in the financial district of New York. The good news is I got to see the Statue of Liberty (way smaller than you think she will be). But the bad news is I never made it to Central Park.

I also had to run/walk all the way back to the hotel. By the time I hobbled back into our room, way later than I had predicted, I was also in trouble with Jay-Jay. She said she thought I had been stabbed, but I think she was really just mad because I got back after 10 am, which meant we missed the amazing buffet breakfast that was included in our room price.

I'VE NEVER BEEN STABBED while running in foreign places. Actually, I have never found myself in any sort of unsafe situation at all. Mind you, the sorts of foreign places we tend to go to are more likely to be advertised in the window of House of Travel than featured on the New Zealand Government-endorsed SafeTravel website.

There's only one time when I felt a bit uneasy, and that was when I went running in Detroit.

I was sent to Detroit for a work assignment in 2013 to interview Taylor Swift because it was about to be announced that she was bringing her 'Red' tour to New Zealand. It was a bloody long way to go for a ten-minute interview, but the concert promoters were paying for my travel and I got a few days off work, so I was over the moon about it. And, if I am being honest, I am way more of a Swizzler than I would ever admit to my mates. (Swizzler: I think that's what us Taylor Swift fans are called, right?)

When it came to Detroit, I really had no idea what to expect. I didn't know anybody who had ever even been there. All I knew was that it looked like a bit of a shithole in Eminem's music videos and it was apparently bankrupt. I always found this last one a bit strange. Firstly, how could a whole city be bankrupt? And, secondly, what the hell did that even mean?!

I flew from Auckland to Los Angeles then jumped on another flight to Chicago, where I checked in for my flight to Detroit.

'Are you sure you want to go to Detroit?' the lady from American Airlines who served me said. 'There are plenty of nicer places we fly to.'

I laughed.

She didn't.

I never did figure out if she was making a joke or not. I assume she was serious, since making any sort of a joke at an airport in the United States is frowned upon.

My first impression of Detroit was from the windows of the taxi that took me from the airport to the city. I saw lots of burned-down and abandoned houses and entire deserted suburbs. It was like something you might see in a Will Smith movie where he is the only human still alive. And it got grimmer the closer I got to the city. There were big, abandoned high-rise buildings everywhere, including a former hospital and train station.

'Why haven't those buildings been demolished?' I asked the taxi driver. 'An empty lot would surely be far easier on the eye.'

'They can't be torn down,' he told me. 'The city doesn't have the money to pay for demolition.'

Ahhh. Now I understood: *that's* what it means when a city is bankrupt.

I was booked into a hotel called MGM Grand, which was right in the middle of the city, and it is one of the flashiest hotels I have ever stayed at (and I am a bit of an accommodation snob). The juxtaposition of this luxury, five-star casino and hotel, with its impeccably manicured grounds, nestled alongside old, abandoned buildings with high fences and razor wire around them was quite surreal.

The room was beautiful and had unnecessary-but-awesome features like a waterproof TV in the shower. The amenities included a big indoor beach-pool area and a fully equipped and staffed gym, which was free for hotel guests. When I went to the gym for a quick workout, a super-helpful attendant magically appeared from nowhere to offer me a fresh bottle of water the moment I finished the bottle I had. He also gave me a fresh towel.

Taylor Swift's concert was held at Ford Field, a 70,000-person stadium, and it was completely packed out. I'm not sure who these middle-class Americans were, but with tickets going for between US$100 and US$300, they had obviously found a way to keep their heads above the water despite the area's recession.

The interview with Taylor was unremarkable. These things usually are. You get given a very short, super-strict time slot, and on this occasion my list of questions had to be submitted for prior approval by the publicist. I asked all my pre-organised questions and Taylor gave the expected answers.

Me: 'Tell us about what the fans can expect this time round.'

Taylor: 'This show is so much bigger and better than the last one . . .'

Then I got to watch the show from the comfort of a small VIP area that was next to a smaller stage near the back of the stadium where Taylor came to play a few acoustic songs during her set. As it turned out, Taylor's predictable answer to my generic question was spot on: as promised, the show *was* amazing.

Also in this little VIP area were Taylor's parents, Andrea and Scott, who were both lovely. Scott and I got chatting and, after a couple of minutes, he reached into his pocket and handed me a fistful of guitar picks branded with his daughter's name. It was a lovely gesture, but I later learned these picks were excess stock. Out-of-date picks that should have been disposed of because they were from the previous tour—the one that was smaller and not as good as this one.

Then I felt a tap on my arm, followed by an English voice saying, 'Hello, mate. Fancy seeing you here!'

It was bloody Ed Sheeran.

Ed had been in New Zealand a couple of weeks earlier and had spent quite a bit of time on our radio show. He and I chatted about Detroit and the other places he had been to since leaving New Zealand. Then he excused himself . . . and walked out on to the smaller stage next to the VIP area. He was there as part of the show; he and Taylor performed their hit duet together, 'Everything has changed'.

It was a surreal experience and one of those moments where I was reminded of just how lucky I am to call this my job.

The morning after the concert, I decided to go for a run outside. I wanted to see some of the city before I had to leave again. (That's the only downside of these work trips when you are lucky enough to land them—you often spend more time in the air in a plane than you do on the ground.) I asked the concierge if he could suggest some routes. He gave me a map, then drew a 3-kilometre loop on it that went through the central city.

'That area's recently been upgraded to include CCTV cameras everywhere,' he told me. 'If you stick to that area, you'll be safe.'

Fuck that! I thought. Chances were I'd never be coming back to this place. I wanted to explore. I wanted to see some of Detroit—the *real* Detroit. I decided to ignore the concierge's instructions and just follow my nose. First off, I wanted to run around 15 kilometres and that would have meant doing five laps of the new, improved, nice-looking, tourist-friendly central-city area. A part of Detroit that looked nothing like Detroit. *Boring!* But mostly I wanted to get a closer look at some of those broken buildings, those tall towers that were the victims of the area's economic downturn, buildings that had once been impressive but were now reduced to broken-down and boarded-up shells.

CHANCES WERE I'D NEVER BE COMING BACK TO THIS PLACE. I WANTED TO EXPLORE. I WANTED TO SEE SOME OF DETROIT—THE *REAL* DETROIT.

After only ten minutes of running in the opposite direction to what the well-meaning concierge had suggested I crossed a busy four-lane highway and everything changed instantly. There was barely any traffic, very few people, and lots of abandoned, graffiti-covered buildings. The only businesses visible were liquor stores and pawn brokers. Even the grass had gone from green to brown. The grass literally had been greener on the other side. I began to see the concierge might have had a point.

The road I was running along looked like it must have once been bustling, but it was now so deserted I could have run down the middle of it unhindered. Up ahead, I saw a group of five guys loitering outside one of the bottle stores that were the only operating businesses I saw in this part of town. There was no one else in sight. I began to feel a bit uneasy. These guys didn't do or say anything, but as I approached I could see them watching me and chatting. I began to imagine that this group was planning to mug me or stab me. *They'll be so disappointed when they find that they've killed me for no cash and two energy gels*, I thought. As I got nearer, I slowed down so I could make sure that I'd have enough energy for a surge of speed to shoot past them.

'Shit, Dom,' I muttered to myself angrily, 'you've really cocked it up this time, mate!'

I contemplated crossing the road to avoid the guys—the way I do to avoid Greenpeace collectors at home—but then I thought that would look too obvious. I was by now convinced that they were scheming something, and I was sure I was only about seven seconds away from finding out what.

I sped up just a touch, so that I was going fast enough that they (hopefully) wouldn't be able to catch me on foot. Since they were leaning or squatting in a sort of circle formation around the liquor-shop door, I also moved towards the outer edge of the footpath. I figured that if I ran a couple of metres clear of them they wouldn't be able to grab me or trip me up.

I kept looking nervously ahead, with one eye on them in my peripheral vision. They were still staring at me. Then one of them nudged his mate. He stepped out into the middle of the footpath, faced me and screamed, 'RUN, FORREST! RUUUUUUUUUN!!!'

His mates burst into hysterics. By the time he'd finished getting his hilarious joke out, I was already 10 metres up the road. I didn't bother to look back or to stop and exchange some witty banter. Instead, I put both my arms up in the air and threw them the thumbs up over my head. It was my unspoken way of saying, 'I heard you, and I appreciate the joke, even though it *is* from a movie that's over twenty years old. Oh, and thank you for not popping a cap in my ass.'

After that brief interlude of panic, the rest of my run around Detroit was rather uneventful. It was even a bit sad and lonely, to be honest. As I ran along the residential streets, I was blown away by the bizarre sight of abandoned houses with boarded-over windows sitting right next to family homes with tricycles, toys and trampolines scattered outside across the front lawn. To see homes filled with love and life next to empty dishevelled buildings was a contrast, to say the least.

A STABBING WOULD HAVE BEEN BAD . . . BUT NOWHERE NEAR AS SEVERE AS THE 'I TOLD YOU SO' EAR-BASHING THAT I WOULD HAVE GOT FROM THE WIFE AS A RESULT.

I eventually found myself at a big bridge that had a sign on it showing a big maple leaf and arrow. If you have your passport with you, or rate yourself as a strong swimmer, you can escape Detroit at this point and get to the town of Windsor in Canada in just a few short minutes. I ran along the river and ended up back in the nice town-centre part that the bloke at the hotel had told me about. It was lovely. Clean and busy, nice sculptures, and not an empty building or vagabond in sight. I suppose when you have a whole city that is on its knees you have to start rebuilding it from the centre and work your way out.

When I got back to the hotel, I told the concierge where I had run and described the abandoned buildings I'd seen. I also mentioned the guys hanging around outside the liquor shop, and told him how I had been shitting myself but all they did was crack a not-very-original running joke.

The concierge told me I was foolish. 'Almost everyone along that stretch of road is a crack user,' he said—meaning where the liquor store was. 'Most of them are armed with guns or knives. You're lucky you didn't get stabbed.'

As I walked across to the hotel lifts, I breathed a sigh of relief. A stabbing would have been bad . . . but nowhere near as severe as the 'I told you so' ear-bashing that I would have got from the wife as a result.

THE FIRST TIME THAT Jay-Jay and I went to London together was in December 2013. We had been about to leave our jobs at The Edge to take up another job, but part of the reason we decided to stay where we were was because we got offered a two-month sabbatical over December and January. Now, finally, at the age of 40, I was getting to visit the place most Kiwis go to in their early twenties. Because Jay-Jay and I had both been busy building our radio careers, we had missed out on the chance for a Gap Year or OE, so we decided to use this sabbatical to cram in as much of Europe as we could. We started in London. We only had a few days there, and there were some touristy things that I wanted to do which I knew Jay-Jay would have absolutely no interest in. Top of my list was to go to Abbey Road to see the famous studio where The Beatles recorded their iconic album with the same name. So, early on our first morning, still jet-lagged, I got up first thing and threw on numerous layers of running gear. Since it was just before Christmas, it was bloody freezing and I rugged up in gear that I would never run in in Auckland: jacket, beanie and gloves. I worked out the route from our hotel—6 kilometres all up. I could shoot there, get some selfies at the pedestrian crossing made famous by The Beatles, then be back in time for breakfast. Easy!

There's just one obvious thing that I failed to factor in: by the time I arrived at Abbey Road, I was sweaty and red-faced from the cold. I managed to get a few selfies but I looked horrible in all of them—if anybody looks good during or just after a run, they are doing something wrong! Another disappointment was that it was impossible to get a good photo on the famous pedestrian crossing. You wouldn't know it from the legendary album cover, but Abbey Road is a real busy stretch of London road, with commuters who lack the patience to be held up on their way to work by some dick from New Zealand who is trying to take a photo for Instagram.

I got to go on some incredible, breathtaking, unforgettable runs on this trip, always first thing in the morning while the rest of the city slept. On our first morning in Rome, a fairly compact city, I shared the Trevi Fountain with only a handful of other people, got to run the Spanish steps and made it to the Colosseum in time to see it bathed in a blood-orange sunrise. At the time I rued the fact I didn't have my phone with me; it was a picture that would have rivalled those of some of the smuggest people I follow on Facebook. But I still have the mental picture of it, and it is something I won't forget. Anyway, I doubt the camera on my phone would have given it the same respect that the human eye can.

Then there are the bridges I have been lucky enough to cross on foot: London Bridge, San Fransisco's Golden Gate Bridge, Queensboro and Verrazano–Narrows bridges in New York, Queenstown's Old Shotover Bridge, the Sydney Harbour Bridge, and of course the Auckland Harbour Bridge (something that can only be done once a year during the official Auckland Marathon). Once I even ran past the New Zealand Member of Parliament Simon Bridges in Tauranga. Unlike the other bridges I mentioned I was not left in awe of his magnificence . . . but I'm sure he's a lovely bloke.

ONE OF MY FAVOURITE things about running—especially long runs—is that it gives you time for your mind to wander. It's not like there's much else to do! People often ask me what I think about when I run, and that's a hard question to answer. If I am doing any sort of speed work, I am usually so buggered that all I can think about is the act of running. *How's my form, my technique, my pace? Can I keep this speed up or should I slow down?* I'm constantly listening to my body for feedback. For all the runs that don't require any specific speed target—my favourite sort of run—I don't necessarily think about especially important stuff. Often I don't think about anything in particular at all—or at least not anything important enough for me to remember it afterwards. Usually there'll just be a collection of fleeting thoughts passing through my brain. I may be in the zone, listening intently to the song that's playing at the time. Or my mind may be darting around, lingering on whatever subject pops up before wandering to the next.

If there's a problem in my life or something going on at work that I need to think about, running is a good chance to do that in a clutter-free headspace. While I was working on writing this book, memories and ideas often bubbled up to the surface while I was out running for things I may be able to incorporate. But the majority of the time what I'm thinking about is any old thing at any old time—just whatever happens to pop into my head. Not really the answer people want to hear, but there you have it.

Early last year, when I'd just decided that I was going to go for the Berlin Marathon, I set off on a weekend training run. At 15 kilometres, it was my longest so far for the year, and even though I ran it at a bit of a challenging speed I still felt pretty good when I got home, and that was mostly because my mind had been busy mulling stuff over while I'd been out running. This run had been one of the ones where I did find myself thinking about something—or, rather, someone— in particular: David Bowie. He'd recently passed away, so I had loaded my iPod shuffle (which I almost always run with) up with a playlist of his songs. Though he'd been diagnosed eighteen months earlier with the liver cancer that eventually killed him, he hadn't announced anything publicly so the news of his death came as quite a shock to lots of people. I'd bought a couple of his albums over the years, but I couldn't tell you the last time I had actually listened to them. Running with his songs playing in my ears reminded me just how good he really was.

It also got me thinking about death. (Good times!) This subject consumed my thoughts for the entire run. The thought of dying sucks. As I ran, I wondered what his last moments were like. Was he sad because he was leaving this brilliant career and life behind? And a teenage daughter who he gave up touring for and walked to school every morning? In his final weeks, did he ever feel scared to close his eyes in case he fell asleep and never woke up again? Was he in so much pain that he didn't have the energy to think about anyone but himself? Or was he so stoned on pain-management drugs that he was breathing and existing without actually thinking of anything or anyone?

It's such a ghastly thought, considering what you would leave behind and what you would miss out on if you died tomorrow. For me, I'd miss out on watching Sev, our son, who we have raised since he was four, grow up. Sev's biological father is Jay-Jay's brother, but not long before Sev's fifth birthday his father was sent to prison so this frightened little boy was sent to live with his aunty and uncle who he barely knew. Truth be told, we were probably almost as terrified as he was! We had no children of our own and no clue about what the fuck we were doing. For the first few years, Sev just called us by our names. Then one day, out of the blue, he started calling us Mum and Dad. (I think part of his motivation was because he was embarrassed when kids at school asked why he lived with his uncle and aunty; the curiosity of kids can be so cruel.)

IT'S SUCH A GHASTLY THOUGHT, CONSIDERING WHAT YOU WOULD LEAVE BEHIND AND WHAT YOU WOULD MISS OUT ON IF YOU DIED TOMORROW.

If I died tomorrow, I wouldn't get to live vicariously through Sev as he—hopefully—makes good life decisions. I wouldn't be there to—hopefully—help him to make those good life decisions. I also wouldn't get to be there for him if he ever needs help after he's made bad decisions (which all of us do eventually). I wouldn't be around to make sure my parents are taken care of as they age . . . Mind you, I'm notoriously useless at keeping in touch with Mum and Dad so I'm probably not the best offspring for that role, anyway!

Ordinarily, death is something I try not to dwell on too much. I don't think I'm scared of it; it's just not something I want to happen. Then again, it's easy to say you are not scared of something if you're not imminently facing it. Maybe the fear would kick in if I was told I had a terminal illness?

When you really zero in on it, though, it's a bit strange that death is such a taboo subject. It is one of the few things in life that will happen to each and every one of us. I think the best we can all wish for is that we go out like my nana did. She was in her late eighties and had been ready to go for years. As she used to say to me, 'I'm in God's departure lounge, just waiting for my name to be called.' It's not that she was bored with life or had some sort of death wish; she was just comfortable in the knowledge that, at her age, she was unlikely to outlive her houseplants. In the end she spent a few days in hospital and ended up dying at home, surrounded by family. A beautiful death. I suppose she was one of the lucky ones.

Grandad's death was the polar opposite. He was a school headmaster for most of his life. He loved a drink and a smoke. When he retired at the now relatively young age of 60, he spent his extra free time just drinking and smoking more. He ended up getting really sick and dying what seemed to me like quite a prolonged and painful death. Here he was, this funny, charming and articulate man, who spent his last couple of years unable to leave the house for more than a couple of hours at a time. He needed help getting in and out of the car, and his voice in the final months was reduced to an almost inaudible whisper.

If you had any choice as to how you were going to spend your last moments alive on this earth, I'm pretty sure everybody would go with Nana's ending. None of us knows how long we have, of course. Luck of the genes comes into it, and then there are unforeseen tragedies that can cut a life short. But, if I am lucky enough to make it to an old age, I want to give myself the best chance I can to remain fit and healthy and strong—and, deep down, I think this is why I run. It's not about living forever or trying to out-run death. It's all about making the time I do have the best it can possibly be. As the saying goes, if you don't have your health, you have nothing.

IT'S ALL ABOUT MAKING THE TIME I DO HAVE THE BEST IT CAN POSSIBLY BE. AS THE SAYING GOES, IF YOU DON'T HAVE YOUR HEALTH, YOU HAVE NOTHING.

ON OUR SECOND DAY back at work at the start of last year, we all sat down with our new boss, Ryan Rathbone. Ryan had his year planner out. He had called this meeting to discuss annual leave and when we would be able to take it. This might seem like a slightly odd thing to do at the beginning of the year, especially when your staff are fresh back from a three-week break, but breakfast radio works a bit differently to other jobs. You get to take your leave at the times of the year that fit around ratings periods, or surveys as they are known. Much like school teachers, we get told exactly when we can take our annual leave—although, unlike school teachers, we get fewer weeks off! In this particular meeting we were told that there were two weeks in June where we could take time off, but that was it for the year. It is important that all the regular on-air staff are working during the ratings periods to give the station the best chance of getting a good result. Even if you get ill, you are encouraged to try to work through it.

I mentioned to Ryan that I would be off for a full week in late September for the Berlin Marathon, something that had been green-lit before Ryan had started. This was a big call, because the Berlin Marathon happens to fall during one of these survey periods. It had taken a hard-sell on my part

. . . and maybe also a touch of begging and sulking. After a lengthy email exchange in which I pulled out phrases like 'life goals' and 'bigger picture' and 'work–life balance' it was agreed I could go FOR ONE WEEK ONLY. Which doesn't leave a lot of time for jet-lag or adjusting to a new time zone. And leaves no time whatsoever for sightseeing.

Ryan was cool with the leave, but what he struggled to get his head around was why the hell anybody would want to spent 27 hours on a plane to go and run 42.2 kilometres, only to get straight back on the plane afterwards and head home again.

'Didn't you just do one last year?' he asked. Ryan is a big Australian bloke. He likes beer, league, cricket and skateboarding. 'You went to Chicago or somewhere. Why do you want to do another one?'

I explained to him my goal of trying to break the three-hour mark.

He didn't look any more convinced. 'Why don't you just do one in New Zealand? It would save you thousands of dollars, you wouldn't have to fly all that way *and* you could save up that leave and use it for an actual holiday.'

Ryan wasn't trying to talk me out of it. He was just trying to get his head around why, exactly, I was doing what I was. He thought it was a waste of a week of leave—when you only get a certain amount of it—to go all the way to Europe only to come straight back again. In fairness, he probably had a point.

I also told him about my dream of running the six marathon majors. 'So far I've ticked off Boston, London, New York and Chicago,' I said, marking them off on my fingers. 'Next on the list is Berlin. Then the final of the big six is Tokyo.'

Ryan chewed on his pen, shaking his head in disbelief.

'Fucking hell. You're mad, mate. You must either really hate yourself or love pain to keep wanting to do those things.'

This is something that all marathon runners encounter from time to time from non-runners. When you tell people you are training for a marathon (or *another* marathon), you hear this kind of stuff a lot. People will tell you they think you are mad. I actually quite enjoy this. I reckon most runners do too. We must. Otherwise we would be more selective about who we told about our marathons. Instead, most of us will tell anyone who asks. We may even tell those who don't ask. We talk about it on Facebook, and share details of our long training runs, which are often done smugly in the dark hours of Saturday or Sunday morning, when all the people who tell us we are mad are still sleeping.

But what Ryan said got me thinking. I don't feel either of his theories are true for me. Yes, there are days when I think I'm a pain in the arse, but I don't hate myself. And I can't say I enjoy the pain that is guaranteed to come when you sign on to do a marathon. Actually, the prospect of the inevitable pain is something that makes me nervous in the week leading up to a marathon and especially on the morning of the run itself. Regardless of how much or how little I have trained, I get anxious, because I am well aware of just how much it hurts to push yourself to go as fast as you can across such a long distance. It's only a small consolation to know that almost every other runner will start feeling the same discomfort when they pass the sign that says 35 kilometres. By that stage 80 per cent of the marathon distance has been covered, and almost every fibre of your body aches.

It's not the pain or any kind of self-loathing that I run for. The feeling I find addictive is when the run is over and that pain goes away: the endorphin rush. Also, it's worth it, because I experience these endorphin rushes every time I run. The longer or harder the run, the bigger the rush I get to enjoy once I finish. This is especially true on the day of a marathon. I'll spend months working towards what happens on just that one day. As soon as I finish a marathon, the agony I have been in disappears. What I'm left with is this overwhelming feeling of joy and satisfaction—a feeling that only a marathon finisher can truly understand. It doesn't matter if I achieve the time I hoped to do or not. I mean, of course my elation is increased if I score a new personal best or do a better time than I expected. But even when I run a personal worst (I suppose that is a PW instead of a PB, but nobody ever talks about their PW . . .), it is still a greater feeling than not running a marathon at all.

CHAPTER 3
USE IT OR LOSE IT

AS I'VE MENTIONED, MY mum is also a runner. She actually ended up getting quite good at it, too. It all started with a jogging group in the late seventies. After she gave birth to Charlotte, the youngest of us four kids, Mum decided she wanted to do something to lose the baby weight she had gained. Since she'd been busy raising a young family throughout the seventies, she'd had very little time to herself for anything like exercise. And, anyway, even if she had had time to exercise I'm not sure what she would have done—this was an era long before gyms, boot camps, aerobics, Jazzercize, Pilates, Zumba, yoga or power-walking. There were spinning classes, but not ones that had anything to do with stationary bikes or Lycra pants; these ones were for women who were so keen on knitting that they made their own wool with a spinning wheel! (Sounds like a hassle to me, but apparently heaps of people did it.) The only women who ran at this time were competitive runners, and the jogging craze didn't really hit its tipping point until sometime later in the eighties.

Anyway, one morning every week, Mum would meet up with a bunch of other young mums at a hall in the middle of Palmerston North's Esplanade and they'd head off for a jog together. Then, afterwards, they would spend way more time sitting around gossiping, drinking cups of tea and eating Krispies and Vanilla Wine biscuits than they'd actually spent running. It was through this jogging group that Mum developed her love of running. Being the competitive sort, she did notice that she was faster and better than the other women in the group. Mind you, that is possibly nothing to do a fist-pump over— I'm pretty sure a lot of these women were mainly in it for the gossip and affordable biscuits.

Before long, Mum decided to run a marathon. In 1980, she had gone to Rotorua with Dad to support him running the marathon there. He finished it in 4 hours 26 minutes. It was his fourth marathon and a long way off the fastest time he eventually managed of 3 hours 45 minutes. On the drive home, Mum suggested that she might like to try running a marathon too. I think she had this romantic idea of her and Dad going out for long training runs together every other weekend. At the time, my sister Bridget would have been nine—which, in the eighties, was thought of as definitely old enough to look after her three younger siblings if Mum and Dad decided to go off running for a few hours!

Apparently, Dad laughed at Mum's suggestion, and even made some throwaway comment about how he didn't think Mum would be able to do it. That was just the challenge and motivation that Mum needed. I'm guessing that proving Dad wrong would have been almost as satisfying to her as completing her first marathon.

At the time, Dad was what is known as the family's

'breadwinner'. This word sounds cringey now, but it was thrown around a lot back then, and Dad would often use it as a punctuation point to win an argument. Most nights, Dad would come home from work and take control of the TV set. He would put it straight on to Channel One to watch the six o'clock news. At the same time, on Channel Two (there were only two channels in total), there was a show called *M*A*S*H* that all us kids wanted to watch instead.

'Daaaad!' we'd collectively whinge. 'Why do *you* always get to decide what channel is on?'

His answer? 'Because I'm the breadwinner.'

THIS WAS A PIVOTAL MOMENT IN SUE HARVEY'S LIFE: THE MOMENT SHE GOT THAT NEW PAIR OF SERIOUS RUNNING SHOES, SHE BEGAN TO TRAIN FOR WHAT WOULD BECOME ONE OF MANY, MANY MARATHONS.

Dad's breadwinner status also afforded him the power to decide how the money he earned for his family was spent. So, when Mum said that she would quite like a new pair of proper running shoes to train for this marathon that Dad had said she probably wouldn't be able to do, Dad decided she would have to work for it—just to make sure it wouldn't be money wasted.

'All right, you can get some new shoes,' he said. 'But! Only once you're able to run for thirty minutes without stopping.'

Thanks to her feisty attitude, and also the base fitness she'd built up from her jogging group, Mum hit this 30-minute mark after only a few runs.

This was a pivotal moment in Sue Harvey's life: the moment she got that new pair of serious running shoes, she began to train for what would become one of many, many marathons.

Mum ran her first full marathon in Rotorua in 1981. She finished in 3 hours 51 minutes. I'm not sure how Dad felt about her smashing his time from the year before. Knowing my dad, I'd say he was just pleased that the shoes he had agreed to buy had not been a waste of money. Fast-forward almost four decades and Mum has run a total of 39 marathons. Her personal best was a blistering 3 hours 9 minutes at the Christchurch Marathon in 1987 when she was 37. That time was fast enough to earn her first place in the 35–40 age group, and she won a $500 shoe voucher—a prize that probably had my dad howling tears of happiness.

Mum reckons she could have gone faster that day if it wasn't for Dad. The day before a marathon, you are supposed to rest as much as you can. The only exercise you should do is some casual walking or a little jog of a few kilometres to keep your legs nice and loose. Since Dad wasn't running, he was quite keen to do some sightseeing. He encouraged Mum to join him as he climbed the north tower of the Christchurch Cathedral. The views of Cathedral Square, the city centre and the Port Hills were spectacular once you made it to the top of the narrow spiral staircase, but it's probably not the greatest thing to do the day before you run a marathon.

After catching the marathon bug, Mum started to take her running a bit more seriously. She signed up for as many events as she could find. On the weekends when Dad didn't have tennis, we would get in the car and go road-tripping, usually around the lower North Island, supporting Mum in whatever the latest run was that she'd entered. To her, the smaller these runs, the better—it increased her chances of winning one of the prizes. The furthest we went was Te Kuiti for a half marathon. I remember this day because it was horrible: four hours of driving, four hours for the run and prize-giving, then four hours for the drive home again. We left at 7 am and didn't get home until it was pitch black. And, to make things worse, Mum didn't even win a prize *and* the fish 'n' chips we got for dinner in Ohakune on the way home gave me the shits.

One run which became an annual event for Mum was a 15-kilometre race that started and finished at the Ohakea air-force base about 25 minutes out of Palmerston North. My brother, Daniel, and I always liked going to support Mum on this run, because it was one of the only occasions that civilians like us could ever get on to an actual air-force base. We thought that was pretty cool. While we cheered Mum and the other runners on, there would be these Skyhawk fighter planes taking off and landing just metres away from us.

Sadly, though, all good things must come to an end. As the result of an incident that caused our parents a great deal of embarrassment, Dan and I were banned from ever going to the Ohakea run again. I was eleven and Dan was nine. In our defence, it was actually all just a naïve misunderstanding (but it's not like Mum or Dad gave a rat's arse about that excuse).

After the Ohakea run finished, there was always a prize-giving ceremony and some post-run drinks held in a hall known as the Officers' Mess. I'm not sure how long this after-run function actually lasted, but we were kids and we both had really short attention spans so it felt like it lasted for weeks. On this fateful day, while the MC was calling the runners up, Dan pulled a golf ball out of his pocket and started bouncing it on the corner of a table.

'Where did you get that from?' I asked. I couldn't believe he had been holding on to something that could be used as a boredom buster and had failed to mention it.

'I found it on the grass outside just before,' he told me.

'Let's go outside and play with it, then,' I said.

We headed out of the hall and started bouncing the ball on the road. We'd bounce it as hard as we could, then step back to watch in wonderment at just how high in the air it would go. Because of the rough surface of the road, the bounce of the golf ball was a bit unpredictable, and that soon became annoying. It meant we spent more time chasing after the ball than we did marvelling how high we could bounce it.

That's when Dan had the greatest idea ever. 'I know where there's a real smooth surface we can bounce it on!'

I followed Dan between some buildings and various offices, then we made our way through an open gate and out on to one of the biggest and smoothest surfaces I have ever seen in my life. It was magical! It stretched out on either side, flat and perfect and just begging to have a golf ball bounced on it.

THAT'S WHEN DAN HAD THE GREATEST IDEA EVER. 'I KNOW WHERE THERE'S A REAL SMOOTH SURFACE WE CAN BOUNCE IT ON!'

Boy, we had a blast, Dan and me. All alone. No other person as far as the eye could see. We would bounce that golf ball and it would travel for days.

After getting bored of the golf-ball game, we ran over to get a closer look at some parked-up fighter jets. Dan was busy giving me a leg-up to get inside this thing, when we suddenly discovered we were somewhere we shouldn't have been.

'Oi! What the HELL do you think you're doing?'

We froze in our tracks.

'We just wanted to look at the plane,' I said.

Then Dan added, 'I promise we weren't going to steal it or anything.'

A terrifying man in a uniform, with the loudest voice we had ever heard, appeared. 'How did you get in here?' he barked.

Dan and I jumped away from the plane. We looked at each other.

'Um, over this way,' Dan said, and the two of us nervously led the man back to the unlocked gate. It was probably about 700 metres away, so it was a very long way with the man firing questions at us as we walked.

'What are you boys doing on base?'

'Our Mum's running in the fun run.'

'Do you know it's illegal to walk on to a tarmac?'

Tarmac?

Up until that moment, we'd had no idea that tarmac was even a thing. It might seem obvious to you now, as a grown-up reading this, but we were just kids. We had no idea about tarmac, or about the fact that it was strictly forbidden for little boys to be running around on it and seeing how high they could bounce a worn-out Spalding golf ball.

When we finally reached the gate, we found a huddle of air-force staff waiting for us there. While all the adults stood around discussing the gate and what had happened, Dan and I slunk away and walked briskly back to the Officers' Mess and the post-run drinks. We were both pale white, and probably acting a little sheepish, but since all the adults were busy drinking and mingling neither Mum nor Dad picked up that anything was wrong.

'What have you two been up to?' Mum asked.

'Erm . . . just playing,' we replied. Which was the truth. Sort of.

We scurried off to sit at the end of a faraway table, in an effort to make ourselves scarce.

Then the door to the Officers' Mess suddenly swung open. There stood the angry guy who had found us at the plane. Everyone fell silent. The man furiously scanned the room. Then his eyes landed on me and Dan, and he locked us in his gaze. He pointed at us, then wiggled his finger, motioning for us to go over to him. It was just like one of those scenes in a movie where someone gets busted, and everyone else goes quiet to see what's going to happen. We probably should have been embarrassed, but we were too scared about how much trouble we were going to be in for that.

'Are your parents here?' Lieutenant Grouchy McGrouchface barked.

Dad was already walking towards us, so we didn't even have to answer. Grouchy walked over to Dad, and they started having what was very obviously a serious chat. Mum joined them to see what was going on. Dan and I sunk down in our chairs as far as we possibly could, wishing we could somehow make ourselves invisible.

The serious chat was very serious. It took whole minutes, which seemed like hours to us.

When Mum and Dad finally came back over to us, their faces glowered with a look that screamed, 'You two are in so much trouble when we get you away from this crowd.'

'What's going on?' one of Mum's club mates from Kia Toa asked.

'Apparently, these two were out there on the runway, bouncing a golf ball around,' Mum said, still glaring at us. 'The officer found them trying to break into one of the fighter planes.'

We cringed, but Mum's mate burst out laughing. 'Hey, guys!' he yelled to the others. 'You won't believe it! Sue's kids were out there, bouncing a golf ball on the tarmac!'

All the other grown-ups within earshot burst out laughing too.

We knew we were in the shit, but we also had a feeling that this reaction from other 'responsible' adults might help to soften the blow. Luckily for us, we were right. Our punishment was nothing more than a lecture that lasted the entire car trip back to Palmerston North about how bloody stupid we were. Oh, and we were banned from Ohakea—not by the Royal New Zealand Air Force, mind. The ban was put in place by Mum and Dad, and it was *steep*: a strict lifetime ban. That was fine by us, though. We'd found the only decent surface to bounce a golf ball, only to learn it was out of bounds.

MUM IS NOW IN her mid-sixties, and she's still running marathons. Her motto is 'use it or lose it', and she practises what she preaches. She is definitely giving herself every chance of living not only a long life, but a quality one as well. She's an inspiration.

Dad, on the other hand, has not run in years. In 1984, he and Mum went to Honolulu on a running holiday to do the Honolulu Marathon with a few other couples from Palmerston North. Dad didn't want to be the only person on the trip who wasn't doing the run, so he decided to come out of running retirement for this one event. He even devised his very own running plan. He never claimed copyright on it, so you are welcome to steal it if you wish. It was pretty simple: run a mile, walk a mile, run a mile, walk a mile . . . You get the idea.

He reasoned that he could easily run one mile—he would just struggle to run 26 of them in a row. Makes sense, right? And, because his plan required just as much walking as running, his training would be nowhere near as intense as if he hoped to run the whole thing. He was playing competitive tennis at the time and was fit from that, so he just did a handful of 30-minute runs around our neighbourhood for training. That was it. He was ready to implement his run–walk marathon plan. He crossed the finish line in 5 hours 23 minutes and vowed to never run again. Ever. He has kept this promise to this day.

Remarkably, the marathon was not even the most horrible thing to happen to Dad on this holiday. A couple of days after the run, Mum and the others in the group went out for a short jog to try to loosen up their tired legs. Dad's legs were more sore than anybody else's and the last thing he wanted to do was any more running, so he stayed back at the motel unit and watched some sport on TV while chowing down on a complimentary bowl of macadamia nuts. Within minutes, his face had ballooned up so badly that his eyes shut from the swelling. Alone and freaking out, convinced he was minutes away from dying, Dad felt his way around the room until he found the phone—but, since he couldn't see anything, he couldn't even dial 911. Fortunately, Mum and the others weren't gone for long. Was Dad happy to see them! Well, not *see* them, but you know what I mean. He was raced to hospital and fixed in no time at all. Fortunately, this expensive hospital visit was covered by their travel insurance. Dad had survived the run and the macadamias, but I reckon a surprise medical bill could have killed him.

A couple of years ago I took Mum to Chicago to run the marathon with me. There is something pretty cool about being in your forties and participating in the same marathon event as your mum. Many guys my age have already lost their mums, so to still have my mum around *and* be able to run marathons with her is incredible. In Chicago, Mum finished the distance in an impressive 4 hours 28 minutes, beating a lot of men and women half her age. However, at over an hour slower than her fastest-ever time, this erosion of speed is not something she is finding it easy to accept with dignity. I remind her how remarkable it is that she is still running at all, given that so many people reach her age and can't run for more than a couple of minutes without difficulty. She knows this to be true, of course, but still finds it frustrating. I guess it's the competitor in her.

I can understand how she feels. I'd like to think that as I get older and my times start to get slower, I will be grateful that I can still participate at all, but who knows how I'll react? I'm sure I'll feel a bit annoyed too. That's how runners' brains work. We always want to be beating ourselves. It's always the same goal: just try to be the best you can be. Much like Ernest Hemingway once said, 'There is nothing noble in being superior to your fellow men. True nobility lies in being superior to your former self.'

After Chicago, Mum and I travelled to Los Angeles, and stayed there for a couple of days before flying back home to New Zealand. From where we were staying, we could see the famous Hollywood sign on the hill. It looked pretty close. So Mum and I set off to take a look. On our way, we found out that it wasn't close at all. By the time we made it back, we'd been gone for almost three hours of fairly brisk and pretty steep walking. Remember this was two days after running the marathon in Chicago, so our legs were still burning and heavy with lactic acid. Oh, and it was also 30 degrees Celsius outside, with the sun beating down.

Since it was so extremely hot, Mum used a bit of classic Kiwi number-eight-wire ingenuity to keep the sweat from dripping down into her eyes: she got some toilet paper from a public loo we passed, folded it over until it was the width of a headband, then tucked it into the frame of her glasses.

I couldn't believe what I was seeing. 'Mum!' I cried. 'You can't do that. It's embarrassing. And it looks ridiculous. Take it off.'

Mum was far more concerned about stopping the perspiration from dripping in her eyes than she was about my feelings, though. 'No, I will *not* take it off,' she told me. 'We don't even know anybody here—and it works.'

My only solution was to up the pace so that we could get the walk over and done with.

Remarkably, Mum never complained or said a word about our brisk pace, the distance or the heat.

I CAN BE A BIT OF A RUNNING ANARCHIST, AND THIS IS DEFINITELY A TRAIT I'VE INHERITED FROM MUM. I'VE NEVER SEEN HER STRETCH OR DO ANY SORT OF PROPER POST-RUN COOL-DOWN EXERCISES.

MUM HAS OBVIOUSLY BEEN a huge influence in my life when it comes to running. She's the reason I grew up knowing it was even possible to go and do something crazy like run a marathon. And I suspect she is probably where I get my determination and stubbornness from. Thankfully, though, I have not inherited her love of cask wine.

As I've mentioned, I can be a bit of a running anarchist, and this is definitely a trait I've inherited from Mum. I've never seen her stretch or do any sort of proper post-run cool-down exercises. Until quite recently, she was also a heavy smoker. She quit the fags a few years ago, but when she was still smoking she would go out for a long training run then get home and sit on the deck, still in her running gear, flick off her hot and sweaty shoes, and light up one of her Winfield Reds. This was totally fine in the privacy of her own backyard, but it got some sideways glances at places like marathon prize-givings where you have all these runners in peak physical condition sitting on the grass with their hard-earned medals around their necks. There Mum would be, also with her medal around her neck—but, instead of a banana or Powerade, in her hand she would have a ciggie. If she was ever self-conscious or embarrassed about it, she did a fantastic job of hiding it! She only gave up in her late fifties, after my sister Charlotte gave her an ultimatum: 'Quit the fags or don't even think about putting my kids in your car or in your apartment.' Tough love? You bet. But it worked.

It's hard to know what damage, if any, the cigarettes have done to her lungs. She seems in pretty good nick now and her medical check-ups are always as breezy as taking a new car in for a warrant. The way she looked at it was that any damage the ciggies were doing would be cancelled out by her running. She isn't a trained medical professional (obviously). I'm pretty sure everything she knows about medicine has come from watching *Shortland Street* and *Grey's Anatomy*.

CHAPTER 4
SHIT HAPPENS

I AM IN LOVE with running, but I'll also be the first to admit that there are definitely some highly unlovable things about it. One thing in particular that you get *very* used to as a runner is the need to go toilet when you're running. It's not always dignified, but it is unavoidable. The Port-A-Loo spot at the starting area of any marathon is always hell. The bigger the event, the more hellish it is. Obviously, you want to start a long run as hydrated as possible, but you also don't want litres of water sloshing around inside your bladder. So it's a good idea to use the facilities before your run commences. Add in the pre-run nerves, and you'll most likely end up having to go back for a nervous wee as well. I have a mate who spends the entire time before every run either in the loo or back in the line waiting to go again. No lies! Often these lines are so long that he gets in line even if he doesn't have to go; he figures that he'll probably have something to deposit by the time his turn comes round to use it again. Ewww.

When I did the Chicago Marathon, all the runners had to be in their starting pens (known as corrals) for around half an hour before the run even started. I was stressing out. I made a couple of visits to the Port-A-Loo before I headed to my corral as late as possible. I was filled with a sick feeling that I would need to go again. The more I thought about it, the more I felt like going. I was penned in on all sides by anxious and excited runners and there was nowhere to go. *Nowhere*. I resigned myself to the fact that I would have to start running then just peel off to the side of the road at the first opportunity and go discreetly against a tree or something. Not an ideal way to start a marathon. I wasn't concerned about the non-runners who might find themselves the unfortunate witnesses of my public urination in broad daylight. Oh no, my main concern was that I would lose 30 to 60 seconds of time when my run had barely started.

Then I saw them.

Two women right next to me. They were just another pair of runners among the thousands crammed into this corral, but my ears couldn't help pricking up when I heard one of them say, 'For goodness' sake, Jenny! Just do it. No one will notice. And, even if they do, no one will care.'

The other woman—Jenny, I assume—looked around at the sea of faces. None of them was looking at her (apart from me, but she didn't know that because I was being very sneaky and using my peripheral vision). All the other runners were in their own world, mentally psyching themselves up, totally oblivious to what anyone else was doing.

Then Jenny's friend said, 'Here, use this old jacket. Wrap it around you like a skirt.'

At the start of these big runs, a lot of the participants wear old gear over what they'll run in so as to stay warm during the long wait before the start. They'll then peel this old gear off in the minutes before the starter's gun goes and throw it to the side of the corral. Then, after the runners have left, the useful gear is swept up and donated to charities. Jenny's friend had found some stranger's jacket on the ground and picked it up and offered it to her.

Out of the corner of my eye, I saw Jenny wrap this jacket round her waist as instructed. Then she squatted down in the gutter on the side of the road . . . and she peed. I was so jealous. It was genius. Her pal was dead right too: nobody noticed, and nobody cared. Well, I mean, I noticed—but only because I was in the exact same predicament and was eager to learn how I too could take a wee in the starting corral without causing embarrassment or offence.

OUT OF THE CORNER OF MY EYE, I SAW JENNY WRAP THIS JACKET ROUND HER WAIST AS INSTRUCTED. THEN SHE SQUATTED DOWN IN THE GUTTER ON THE SIDE OF THE ROAD . . . AND SHE PEED.

Jenny doesn't know it, but she gave me all the courage I needed. I remembered something a mate of mine who played a bit of rugby had told me. He said that if a player ever needs to go during training it often takes too long to run back into the changing rooms, so they'll just get down on one knee on the grass and stretch out the other leg. At the same time, they'll discreetly pop their penis out of the side of their shorts and bingo! So that's exactly what I did, in the gutter, in the streets of Chicago, surrounded by thousands of strangers. If anyone was watching, I don't think they would have been fooled by my sudden urge to stretch out my right hamstring, but I didn't care. The relief was indescribable. As Jenny's wise friend had said, nobody noticed and nobody cared.

THE NEED TO PEE—or a Code Yellow situation—is something that occurs in training runs as well as races. If you're going out for a couple of hours, it's to be expected. It is always way less stressful on a training run, though, because you're not worried about losing valuable race time. It's also often a good excuse to catch your breath for a second. I know exactly where all the public toilets are on the routes I usually run at home, so I'll just hold on until I make it to one of them. Sometimes this is simply not possible, so I'll just shoot into a bush or some other suitable place where I can be sure I won't be seen by anybody. This may be an unfair advantage of being a male, but I would guess there are also many female runners who have found that desperate times call for desperate measures.

The worst, though, is when you are faced with a Code Brown.

OK, guys: time for some real talk. This is something that all you runners will already know, but many of you not-yet-runners may be shocked to learn. When your feet are pounding the concrete footpath around 160 times every minute, it does tend to jar your body a fair bit. Imagine picking up a nearly empty box of scorched almonds, with just a couple of the little oval chocolates left at the bottom of the box, then tapping the side of that box 160 times a minute for up to three hours. Eventually the chocolates are going to fall out, right? Analogies have never been my strong point, but I think you get the idea. What I'm trying to say is that constipation is one of the few conditions a runner will never have to battle through!

My good mate Andy Rowe made it on to the famous red-chair segment of British host Graham Norton's chat show with a story about an emergency defecation situation he witnessed when he was out on a run with another friend of ours, Duncan Hyde. For those of you unfamiliar with Graham's red chair, the idea is that an audience member gets given the opportunity to take a seat and share a story with Graham and his celebrity guests. There's a giant lever that Graham sometimes controls, and sometimes he'll pass the power to one of his guests. As soon as whoever is controlling the lever loses interest in the story, they'll pull the giant lever, which flips the storyteller backwards off the red chair. It takes an impressive story to earn the right to finish your story and stand up and walk away from the chair.

'I was out for a run with my friend Dunc,' Andy started. 'We were running past a park, and Dunc really needed to go for a poo. So we saw a toilet block and we ran over to the men's side. He was busting—he really needed to get this thing out of him—but the men's was closed. By this stage he didn't even care. He ran round to the women's side, but that was closed as well. He started frantically looking around, muttering, "Where can I go? Where can I go?" So he ran over to this bush and crouched down behind it . . . and he went. About thirty seconds later, I saw this big German shepherd come bounding over. Dunc pulled his shorts up and jogged off, just as the dog's owner came over and was like, "Ooooh, Roy! You naughty boy!" She pulled a plastic bag out of her pocket, put the plastic bag over her hand, and scooped up Dunc's poo. She then tied the bag to her shorts and wandered off with his poo swinging from her belt.'

Graham Norton, his celebrity guests and the studio audience erupted in laughter. Andy became one of the lucky few to walk away from the red chair.

Something far less hilarious than that happened to my old dental hygienist, whose name has most definitely been changed in the story that follows. I bumped into Dianne at Auckland Airport back in 2010. It turned out we were both flying down to Christchurch to take part in the marathon that was on the next morning. We did some seat swapping so we could be seated next to each other for the plane ride. Our goals were very different—I hoped to run under 3 hours 15 minutes, a time which would have been a personal best for me and, more importantly, qualify me for the Boston Marathon; Dianne, on the other hand, was trying to win the women's division. To do that, she hoped to run the marathon in around 2 hours 45 minutes. Just as the flight was beginning its descent and the lollies were being handed out, Dianne confessed to me that she would be running with an adult nappy underneath her running shorts. She explained that in the last marathon she had done, a few months earlier, she had started feeling unwell but didn't want to stop running because she was in the lead. If she'd popped into one of the Port-A-Loos, she would have risked losing the race. So she soiled herself. She ran the last few kilometres with a mixture of faecal matter and perspiration dribbling down her legs. She won—but she didn't bother to frame the victory photo.

The next day, I caught up with Dianne after the marathon. She hadn't had a great run (by her standards) and had finished in 3 hours 2 minutes. But, on the bright side, she hadn't had to use the adult nappy for its intended purpose. That, to me, sounds like a victory in itself.

Before this plane ride during which Dianne opened up and shared the poo story with me, I had been in her dentist's chair maybe a dozen times as a patient, and I had never paid any attention to whether she was wearing latex gloves or not. After Christchurch, that all changed. There are just some things you don't need to know about the person who is going to have their fingers in your mouth for an hour!

IN ALL MY THOUSANDS of hours out running there have been a ridiculous number of occasions where I have urgently needed to stop for a defecation situation but have been nowhere near one of my known toilet stops. It is mortifying at first, but after a while it's just something you get used to. I always make sure I kick some dirt or foliage over it afterwards. I couldn't bear the thought of some earnest dog owner finding one and bagging it by mistake.

The worst thing that happened to me was during a long training run while I was on holiday in Rarotonga. It was a two-hour run in 26-degree heat. Somewhere into the second half, I suddenly and urgently needed to go. That's the problem with these jog-logs: the amount of warning you get is not usually sufficient. I stopped in front of a church with a well-mown lawn and manicured gardens. I wandered around the back, hoping to maybe find an unlocked toilet block. There were no toilets . . . but there was some thick, jungle-like bush, which would be perfect for privacy.

I went a couple of metres into the bush. I squatted down. I was flooded with a sense of relief. But this relief was closely followed by intense panic and sheer terror. I was bent over and had just started to pull my shorts back up when this bizarre cold feeling touched my right buttock. Then the cold was replaced with a hit of warm air against my exposed bottom.

With my shorts still halfway up my thighs, I whirled round and found myself face-to-face with the biggest wild pig I had ever seen in my life. This thing was a monster. It probably weighed a couple of hundred kilos—not that I was waiting around to get him on a set of scales. With my shorts still clinging on to my thighs, I scuttled the few short paces out of the bush and back on to the church grass, terrified that me old mate would be in hot pursuit.

Back in stark daylight, I abruptly pulled my shorts all the way back up (I was outside a church, after all), then I ran as fast as I could as far away from that pig as I could.

It's lucky I'd just gone. If I hadn't, I'm certain the fright I got from Porky breathing on my bum definitely would have caused me to shit myself!

I WAS BENT OVER AND HAD JUST STARTED TO PULL MY SHORTS BACK UP WHEN THIS BIZARRE COLD FEELING TOUCHED MY RIGHT BUTTOCK.

A LOT OF RUNNERS crave variety in their run routes, but I'm not fussed. I'm a routine guy, remember? While I love running as a way of exploring when I'm overseas, when I'm at home I run any one of a selection of favourite loops that I've worked out. One of the loops I do often takes me down underneath the Auckland Harbour Bridge and along a boardwalk beside Westhaven Marina, with a backdrop of the Sky Tower and the Auckland city skyline. I use this area for a lot of my speed-work runs—it's the perfect place due to the lack of traffic and absence of traffic lights, so I can run without stops or delays. On speed runs, I am usually so busy keeping an eye on what I'm doing that the stunning scenery disappears altogether, but when I'm not doing speed work it's usually an enjoyable route, with the salty air and the scenery.

I say 'usually' because every now and then running can

jump up and bite you on the arse when you're least expecting it. You can be out on a run you've happily done a million times before and suddenly hit a wall. This is exactly what happened to me on this loop a while back.

I'd set out to do a training run of 14 kilometres all up, but before I even reached the waterfront boardwalk I turned off and cut my route down to 8 kilometres. Some days, you head out for a run and it feels like there is a strong tail wind pushing you along and you think you could keep running forever. These days don't come often enough, sadly, and this was definitely *not* one of those days. This was instead one of the days where just putting one foot in front of the other is hard work. These are days when that imaginary tail wind becomes a strong head wind *and* there's also someone behind you, pulling on the back of your shirt. Sometimes you'll have a reason for feeling like shit—like a hangover, or stress, or illness—and knowing that makes it bearable. But sometimes there is just no reason or excuse. Out of the blue, you'll just get handed a day where running is really hard and not all that enjoyable.

In a way, these kinds of days are probably necessary for you to be able to appreciate the days where running feels effortless; gotta take the bad with the good, as they say. But, if I'm really honest, when I'm training, the unexplained bad days make me nervous and scared. What's to say that when I finally make it to race day I won't start running and find out that it's a day where my body doesn't want to run? It's a real fear for me.

Nevertheless, there is always something positive that can be taken away from a bad run. Often, it's as simple as getting home, kicking your shoes off, and sculling a glass of cold water. As you lie in the shade on the back lawn, feeling your body cool down and the sweat begin dry on your skin and turn to salt, you'll start to feel it: the runner's high. That rush of endorphins that makes every run—even the worst ones—worth it. I have regretted missing runs but I have never, ever completed one and regretted going out and doing it.

ONE THING THAT CAN make a bad run even worse is cramp. Last year I headed out for one of my longest training runs—over 30 kilometres—and it was a perfect storm. The whole way, I felt like shit. I struggled. Badly. I started out running at the pace I was meant to do, according to my training programme, but it became clear about ten minutes into the run that I would be unable to keep it up. So I dropped back to a slightly more comfortable pace. I thought if I could keep to this slower pace, then I might be able to pick up my pace at the end of the run and finish fast. But it was not to be. I just kept feeling worse and worse. When I reached the 26-kilometre mark, I made a feeble attempt to run faster, which lasted all of 300 metres before I said to myself, 'Nah, fuck that' and went back to the more comfortable cruising pace. The run took me *a lot* longer than it was meant to and, to make things worse, when I got home I started to cramp up! It seemed no part of my body was exempt from excruciating pain. That run left me feeling pretty gutted.

I met Mum for lunch later on in the day and told her my frustrations about the run.

'I don't think there would have been too many forty-three-year-old guys who got out of bed this morning to run thirty-four kilometres,' she said to me. (She's clever like that, throwing my own advice back at me.) 'So, even though you felt bad, you've still done something most people could never do.'

It was the reminder I needed to pull my head in and not lose perspective. Regardless of time and personal goals, it's so important to remember that simply being able to run a marathon in the first place is a privilege.

Marathon training is funny like that. You have great days, and you have shit days. I guess you just have to learn to take the good with the bad, and hope like hell that when you wake up on the morning of an event it will be one of the good days. It's a little bit like life, really.

IT'S SO IMPORTANT TO REMEMBER THAT SIMPLY BEING ABLE TO RUN A MARATHON IN THE FIRST PLACE IS A PRIVILEGE.

WHEN I DECIDED THAT I wanted to run the Berlin Marathon in my fastest-ever time, I also decided that I'd need some help. So I got a coach on board, called Coach Ian. I'll introduce you to him properly a bit later, but for now suffice to say that he got me to do some pretty whacky technical things in my training that I'd never done before. At one notable session, he had me go out to a fancy sports complex in Pakuranga in South Auckland to run around a 400-metre track with a bunch of plastic pods the size of Tim Tams attached to various parts of my body. There was even one attached to one of my shoes. He also made me run wearing a backpack that contained an iPad that fed data back to another iPad that he had in his hands. It was all part of some kind of speed-testing exercise, apparently.

So off I went, racing as fast as I could round the track with my backpack and my Tim Tam pods. The track's surface felt kind of firm and rubbery at the same time. This surprised me, because I'd always imagined those tracks to be like asphalt or something. Running on one of these tracks also makes you feel magically faster . . . Until you stop, that is, and get told your lap time, which brings you back down to earth with a hard thud and reminds you that you really have no place being there.

When you usually run much longer distances, you would think a few short runs like this would be easy. But when you are running as fast as you possibly can, one lap of a 400-metre track starts to feel like a bloody long way. By the end of this whole exercise, I was buggered. It was hard.

As we went through some stretches and warm-downs together, Ian explained the purpose of this rather odd session to me. I nodded as I listened, but really I had no idea what it all meant. If you want to know, you'll need to ask Coach Ian.

'You just need to tell me what to do,' I said to him, 'and I'll do it.'

In my car on the way home, though, I was flooded with all sorts of thoughts and self-doubt. *Is this all really worth it?* I asked myself. *The effort. The pain. The hassle. After all of this, how fucked off will I be if I don't even get close to the time I'm aiming for? All this effort will be for nothing.*

Much like how bad runs make me nervous, hard sessions also make me fret.

You're finding it hard now, I berated myself, *and you're not even into the hardest part of your training!* The marathon was still seven whole months away at this stage.

I find it fairly common for this kind of self-doubt to creep into my thoughts. I don't know if it's the same for everyone or just me, but it actually happens quite a lot. When I become aware of this, though, I try to change my thoughts and think of something more positive. I try to turn any self-doubt into a motivational tool—something to remind me to work harder to try to overcome whatever it is I'm afraid of having happen when it really counts.

So I took a deep breath and flipped my thinking. *How lucky am I?* I reminded myself. *I can afford to pay someone $100 a month just to help me try to achieve my goal.*

Honestly, I don't even know if this 'positivity' strategy works or not. But I do know that life is definitely more enjoyable with a positive attitude than it is with a negative one. I am a reasonably motivated person—I think anybody who runs a marathon is—but I'll also admit there is no way I would have had the desire or motivation required to do all the stuff Coach Ian got me to do on my own. In that moment, I reminded myself of how lucky I am to have a job and a family that allow me to give my goals a decent crack.

Then my thoughts veered off in an entirely different direction altogether. *Man, I am starving!*

And, coincidentally, this thought came to me around the same time as my fuel light pinged on. There was a Caltex just a few hundred metres up the road. I could have easily made the trip home without running out of petrol, and when I got there I could have had a banana or a protein smoothie—some sort of healthy snack appropriate for someone training for a marathon. Instead, I flicked the indicator on, got some petrol . . . and shouted myself a Diet Coke and a Bounty Bar. Probably not the sort of post-run meal the experts (or Coach Ian) would recommend but, shit, it tasted amazing.

THE OTHER THING WITH training for a marathon, or any kind of running event, is that your programme doesn't take a break if the weather is crap. Often, your weekly long run will fall on a blustery Sunday—the sort of winter's day that is really good for staying indoors and binging on Netflix, and not a lot else. If you're a runner, though, it's highly likely that there will be days like this where you find yourself outside doing, say, a one-hour hill run. Fortunately, I don't actually mind bad weather that much. I'll just chuck on a thin pair of gloves and a beanie and get into it.

Hill runs on the other hand . . . hill runs are tough. For everyone. No matter how fit you are, or how often you run hills. As well as getting me to run around with gadgetry stuck to me, Coach Ian also got me to incorporate hill runs into my training. So, one winter's morning, I drove to Mount Eden, where I was to run several laps round the hilly inner-city volcano.

Before starting out, I double-checked the notes he had given me: *Run for 50–60 minutes on a hilly course. The purpose of this session is just to run on hills and have some fun.*

Have some fun?

Are you fucking kidding me?!

There is nothing fun about running up a hill. Ever.

Running up one hill once is not fun.

When you do it over and over for an hour, it gets less fun with each climb to the summit.

There are activities in life that most people would agree are fun. Things like watching hilarious YouTube videos of people stoned on anaesthetic after a visit to the dentist.

Then there are activities in life that most people would agree are completely unpleasant. Things like taking your seat on a long-haul flight and realising you are next to a person with a hacking cough and a tendency to hog the armrest.

Well, let me tell you, even that long-haul flight next to a punishing stranger would be more fun than running up a hill for an hour. I can think of so many things that are more fun than running up a hill for 60 minutes: doing a big shop then having your card declined at the supermarket checkout; running out of hot water in the middle of your shower; going to the doctor to get shards of glass removed from your sphincter. OK, that last one may be pushing it—but I think you get the general idea.

I felt like texting Ian the definition of the word fun: *Enjoyment, amusement, or light-hearted pleasure*. He was clearly confused. Despite his instruction, and needless to say, I did not have fun running around Mount Eden that day.

But the thing is that the run did go well. And the hot shower I had when I got home felt amazing. It's not often you shower and actually think about how good it feels, but this was most definitely one of those occasions. That's the funny thing about running: the harder it is, the more satisfied you feel when it's finished.

WHILE IT'S TRUE THAT, for the most part, I'm not bothered by the weather, there's one thing that can play havoc with your running, and that's wind. It's happened to me more than once when I've set off for a weekend training run, and felt amazing for the first half. It's one of those good days, where you feel like you've got that tail wind pushing you along, and you're pacing well. You're feeling pretty good about things . . . until you turn around, and realise that the tail wind really was there, and it's just rudely become a head wind. If it's really windy, you'll usually be able to tell because the trees are shaking around; but sometimes it's more subtle and it's not until you've turned around to face it that you even know it's there.

This kind of wind can be a real drain on your energy, especially if you're already feeling generally fatigued.

However, the good thing about wind—and, actually, about anything that makes running hard—is that it provides the challenge you sometimes need to push yourself. You get to choose whether you'll dig deep and embrace the pain or not. If you do, you'll need to ignore your brain suggesting to you that it might be a good idea to slow down or take a walk. It's that voice in your head that tells you to back off when you start pushing hard on a run. Usually, the longer and harder you push yourself, the louder this voice becomes.

When you look at it like this, you realise running isn't just about training your body; you also need to train yourself to ignore this voice. Some people have no trouble doing this. Unfortunately, I am not one of them. This voice sounds like he has my health and wellbeing in mind, so I'm often tempted by his suggestions.

THERE IS NO DENYING the fact that running, and especially training for a marathon, is a big demand on your time.

My job as a breakfast-radio announcer probably sounds like a pretty fun and easy gig—and, for the most part, it is. But it's also really mentally demanding. Even though the show itself is only four hours a day, by the time it's over I sometimes find myself exhausted from talking, thinking and just being 'switched on' all the time. Plus there is actually a lot more to it than the four hours we spend on-air. By the time you incorporate the planning, show meetings, emails and other parts of the job, it ends up being as many hours as—sometimes even more than—any other job. And, because of the 4 am starts it kills any chance of a social life.

I try to be in bed by nine on weeknights, and the only people we will have dinner with are really good friends, because they understand and tolerate our need to eat dinner before 7 pm. I'm lucky that I work from home in the afternoon, which gives me the flexibility to run whenever I like and to fit my work around it, rather than the other way round.

But there are still days where things are so busy with work that it can feel like I don't have any time left over for anything else. The way I see it though, running is an important partner to my job, so I always make an effort to find time for it. In fact, the mental demands of what I do are part of the reason I fell back into running as an adult in the first place. I find it's the perfect way to clear my head after a show. The liberating feeling of running outside in the fresh air and not having to talk to anybody or think about anything is amazing—like a form of mindfulness, I suppose.

RUNNING IS AN IMPORTANT PARTNER TO MY JOB, SO I ALWAYS MAKE AN EFFORT TO FIND TIME FOR IT. IN FACT, THE MENTAL DEMANDS OF WHAT I DO ARE PART OF THE REASON I FELL BACK INTO RUNNING AS AN ADULT IN THE FIRST PLACE.

When I first started running, there were no rules. I'd head out for twenty minutes or two hours—it didn't matter. I was governed only by how my body felt and when my next commitment was. I ran simply for joy.

When I'm in the midst of a rigorous marathon training, I sometimes miss that kind of freedom. It definitely feels great to train hard towards a goal, and to see yourself making gains and going faster, but I've also come to realise that it's not necessarily the progress I make that I love about running. I've learned that the love I have for running is wrapped up in the act itself; it has nothing to do with my speed. I know that, as I get older and my times erode, I will be happy to just run, no matter what the pace.

CHAPTER 5
HOW RUNNING SAVED MY LIFE

WELL, THAT'S JUST BLOODY brilliant, isn't it? I remember thinking, as I lay in the back of the ambulance with an oxygen mask strapped to my face and paramedics fussing about me. The sirens were bleating and every now and then the driver blasted the loud air-horn as well to let other road users know they had to get the fuck out of the way. I was lying down, of course, so I have no idea what speed we were doing, but I know we were flying. Way faster than the 50 kilometres an hour that everyone else was forced to stick to in this residential area. My head was spinning and, besides being swamped by the surrealness of my predicament, I was also a bit scared we could be involved in some sort of road crash.

I even tried to sit up at one point. I wanted to get a look out of the tinted window on the ambulance's side, but before I could even get close one of the paramedics in charge of keeping me alive pushed me back down.

Shit was serious.

This was the first time I had ever been in the back of an ambulance as a patient. I live in a city, so I'd seen ambulances in beast mode a thousand times before, with their lights flashing and sirens screeching. Whenever I saw an ambulance travelling like this, I always assumed the poor patient in the back must be fighting for their life.

Now *I* was that person. But I didn't feel like I was dying or as though my life was in any sort of jeopardy. I mean, I felt like utter crap—but it wasn't any worse than how I'd felt a dozen times before over the previous couple of years. I was pretty sure I could have just as easily driven myself to the hospital, or at least caught a taxi. I was a little bit embarrassed by my starring role in this whole real-life hospital drama.

We arrived at Auckland's North Shore Hospital in a few short minutes, and I was immediately rushed in on my stretcher. I lay there in the emergency ward while the incredibly hard-working and professional medical staff raced around me. It was all very overwhelming. Lots of noise. Lots of shouting. I've never had so many hands on my body at once. Someone was on my left side, checking my blood pressure; someone was on my right side, filling these little vials full of blood; someone else was about to cut off my 60-dollar running T-shirt with scissors. That's when I panicked and tried to sit up.

'Wait!' I cried. 'That's a very expensive T-shirt. I'll just take it off.'

That was not an option.

I was pushed back down and the cutting commenced. *Fuck*. Perfectly good (and pricey) shirt ruined. As soon as it was off, someone else stuck these ECG pads to my chest. My heart rate would have been nuts on that first reading—I was stressed about the T-shirt!

After a few of the most intense and frenetic minutes of my life, and once it had become clear I was not *likely* to drop dead then and there, the bulk of the staff dispersed with their bloods and data and whatever else they had collected. Things finally simmered down.

It was still early on a Sunday morning, and the ward seemed rather quiet. It was now just me and a couple of nurses, who wandered around doing paperwork and keeping an eye on me. I propped myself up on my elbows and even cracked a couple of jokes. I felt I needed to do this to demonstrate that I was really fine, that there was nothing to worry about.

I STARTED MY EXPLANATION WITH WHAT IS PROBABLY ONE OF THE MOST PANIC-INDUCING SENTENCES OF ALL TIME: 'I DON'T WANT YOU TO PANIC . . . BUT I'M AT THE HOSPITAL.'

I was allowed to use the hospital phone, and I tried to get hold of Jay-Jay. This wasn't as easy as it sounds, because she was running in a 10-kilometre race and didn't have her phone on her. Eventually, she answered. She was naturally confused. At that precise time, I should have still been running the Auckland Marathon, with a long way left to go.

'Where are you?' she said, trying to work it all out. 'Why aren't you running?'

I started my explanation with what is probably one of the most panic-inducing sentences of all time: 'I don't want you to panic . . . but I'm at the hospital.'

Poor Jay-Jay went from the happy high of running her race in a faster time than she had expected to the low of having to drive to the hospital to find out what the hell was going on with her husband. She arrived still wearing the clothes she had run in. As soon as I saw her, I burst into tears. I'm not usually much of a crier—Jay-Jay could probably count on one hand the number of times she has seen me blub in the seventeen years she has known me. I think it all just got a bit overwhelming at that moment; seeing the face of someone who loves me looking so concerned just broke me. We hugged. My face was salty with dried sweat. I was still in my running clothes and shoes. My shirt was missing, but let's not dwell on that. (Did I mention it cost 60 bucks?)

Marathon running had almost killed me. But in a funny sort of way, it had saved my life at the same time. It was only due to a series of meaningful coincidences, all of them centred on running, that I had ended up in hospital that day.

THAT MORNING HAD BEEN a crisp one. It was late 2005, just before the start of the Auckland Marathon. I was feeling pretty good to have made it to the start line injury free. This is a big thing for a marathon runner. The actual marathon event is a bit like a victory lap. It's the reward for all the hard work that you've put into getting your body ready for this one day—the long runs, up to three hours at a time and often all by yourself; the sacrifices made to your social life; the winter runs on cold, dark, windy, wet mornings. Despite their best efforts, some people don't even make it to the start line—injuries flare up and stop them in their tracks, or life simply gets in the way so they don't get enough training done. But I had made it. Sure, I had a couple of black toenails and one of my knees was a little bit achy, but I was confident it would carry me through the streets of Devonport and Takapuna, over the deceptively steep and long Auckland Harbour Bridge, then out along the stunning Tamaki Drive waterfront until I arrived at the affluent suburb of St Heliers, where I (and a few thousand others) would turn and run all the way back along the waterfront to the finish line at Victoria Park, 42.2 kilometres and however many hours later.

The loud starter's gun went off, causing hundreds of birds resting in the surrounding trees to scatter at the same time as the runners. Packed tightly into the starting area, we shuffled our way towards the start line, then the pack started to thin out over the early kilometres. Many runners fly off far too quickly at the start of a marathon—a bad mistake and one that usually catches up with them in the final stages of the run. It's hard not to do this, with so much excitement and nervous energy in the air.

I wasn't wearing a watch, so I had no idea of how fast I was running. My plan was to just run the race according to how I felt. A nice, conservative start to ease into it, then I'd pick it up to a steady but controlled pace. If I was feeling good when I hit 35 kilometres, I'd cut loose for the final 7 kilometres. Easy peasy. Smart plan, I thought.

But after only a couple of kilometres, I was feeling like crap. When you are only 2 kilometres into a marathon, it is less than ideal to be feeling exhausted. You can expect to feel wrecked in the second half of the run, ideally sometime *after* the 30-kilometre mark, but if you're battling only ten minutes after the starter's gun goes off then you're staring down the barrel of a day that will be more unpleasant than having your wisdom teeth removed. Without anaesthetic. By a dentist with atrocious halitosis.

The discomfort I was feeling was not foreign to me. My training for this marathon had presented me with a few challenges. At the time, we lived at the bottom of a fairly steep and long hill, so every run started with a climb of a few hundred metres. On a few occasions, I had left home and started out a bit faster than I should have, then found myself feeling sick by the time I got to the top of the hill—just a few minutes after leaving home. Sometimes, I would end up doubled over in crippling agony at the top of this hill, with severe stomach cramps and vomiting up that ghastly bile stuff. I would be grey in the face and have a headache so intense that it felt like my skull was being squeezed in a vice. I'd feel so physically drained and ill that the mere thought of turning around and walking down the hill and back home felt like it might not be possible.

It was not pretty.

I WOULD BE GREY IN THE FACE AND HAVE A HEADACHE SO INTENSE THAT IT FELT LIKE MY SKULL WAS BEING SQUEEZED IN A VICE.

Jay-Jay had urged me to get checked out. She told me that this was not normal and that I needed to be seen by medical professionals. As usual, she was right, but I was a bit more flippant about things. I was 32 years old and had only just started getting back into running again. I chalked it up to me not being as fit and able as I had been when I was younger, and I blamed the hedonistic lifestyle choices I'd made during my twenties for catching up with me.

These incidents only ever happened when I tried to push myself a bit hard; if I was just jogging at a conversational pace, I was fine. And, whenever these episodes did occur, they would last for only fifteen or twenty minutes before everything returned to normal. I was reluctant to go and spend money on a doctor or specialist, because I figured it wouldn't do any good unless they could check me out when the attacks actually occurred, and that was only one in every twenty runs. (Later I learned that cardiologists have treadmills in their clinics so that they can do tests that simulate what happens to a patient's body during exercise. Duh! Of course they do.)

NO SELF-RESPECTING RUNNER EVER WANTS TO BE BEATEN BY THE GUY DRESSED AS DARTH VADER OR THE LASS WHO'S GOING TO JUGGLE THREE TENNIS BALLS THE ENTIRE DISTANCE.

Now here I was having one of these attacks really early in the actual event. Bugger! But I knew how these things played out: I'd feel like I was on the cusp of death for ten minutes, maybe throw up the pre-race breakfast I'd eaten a couple of hours earlier, get goosebumps and a cold sweat and have to walk for a little bit, and then I'd come right and resume running again. I was just pissed off, because I knew that even a few minutes of walking so soon into the run would give me a very slow finish time. I could even be beaten by one of the novelty runners! No self-respecting runner ever wants to be beaten by the guy dressed as Darth Vader or the lass who's going to juggle three tennis balls the entire distance.

I walked as briskly as I could, to avoid losing as much time as possible. Then I saw that right next to the very first water station, just 4 kilometres into the run, there was a St John Ambulance and the paramedic crew. I went over to them and asked if they could spare a minute to check me out. I explained what was happening. The junior ambulance officer sat me down on the stretcher in the back of the ambulance, asked me a few questions, and then slapped a black blood-pressure band on my arm and pumped it up with air.

He looked at his figures. 'Let me try that again,' he mumbled. 'I must have done something wrong.'

He removed the band and started over. He got the same results. He excused himself and went to speak to his supervisor, who was outside the ambulance. I could hear them chatting, but couldn't make out what they were saying. I was starting to get agitated. I was still too crook to start running again, but I would rather have been walking up the road than sitting in the back of an ambulance while these guys faffed around with no sense of urgency.

The supervisor then came in to the ambulance to test my blood pressure himself. He got the same result.

At that precise moment, my life was turned upside down. It was synchronicity. It was the moment that running saved my life.

My blood pressure was so high that I was having what is known as a 'hypertensive crisis', meaning that I required emergency medical care. A blood-pressure reading has two numbers. A healthy person's blood pressure should be above 90/60 but below 120/90; my results on the roadside were 290/230. Later, the paramedics who treated me said it was the highest reading they had ever seen. A compliment, I suppose.

I WAS KEPT AT North Shore Hospital for observation overnight, then the next day I was back in the ambulance and on the move to Auckland City Hospital and the coronary ward for further testing. In the heart ward, I felt embarrassed by the wonderful attention I was getting. Even though I felt fine, I had a team of staff paying close attention to me. I had a heart-rate monitor and any sudden change would cause alarms to sound and staff to come running from all directions. Little things like getting out of bed and walking to the loo or brushing my teeth were enough to make my heart rate change and send the staff into a panic.

After a couple of days of TLC from the coronary team, my tests came back. There was nothing wrong with my heart. This was a cause for celebration—until I was yanked from the luxurious care I had grown accustomed to and thrust into a general ward that I had to share with three other people. One of them was a snorer, and another was a sleep groaner. Just my luck.

I spent my days there sitting on my bed and feeling 100 per cent, while also knowing there was something not quite right going on inside me. In between assuring friends and family members that I was feeling great, I would read and watch movies. Once or twice a day, I'd be taken away for another batch of tests to try to work out what exactly was wrong with me. I had blood tests, ultrasounds, ECGs, an echocardiogram, MRIs . . . You name it, I had it.

Then, after five nights in hospital, the problem was discovered.

It was a big bitch of a tumour called a pheochromocytoma in my abdomen.

The surgeon who had first suggested the possibility of this and subsequently confirmed it was pretty excited. He had heard about these at a conference some years earlier, but had never come across a patient who actually had one. I guess I should feel special.

As I learned, a pheochromocytoma is a rare type of tumour that is, for all intents and purposes, a big ball of adrenaline. It results in the release of too much of the hormones that control your heart rate, metabolism and blood pressure. As soon as I was told all this, everything made sense. As well as the running incidents, there had been other alarm bells that I had successfully managed to ignore. If someone gave me a fright, or someone cut me off in traffic, for example, I would start shaking and sweating profusely. I'd thought I was just being jumpy, but now I knew it was all because of this bloody tumour flooding me with adrenaline.

It was a beast of a thing: the size and shape of a really big grapefruit, 12 centimetres long and 6 centimetres wide. I remember wondering how, if it was that big, it had taken so long to find the fucking thing. Turned out the problem was that all the early tests and MRIs had focused on my upper chest area; nobody had thought to look in my stomach area. I didn't have much of a belly on me, but it had still managed to successfully hide itself, so there wasn't even a lump or any visible sign of it.

As soon as the tumour was located, I was given a date a few weeks away for surgery, and in the meantime I was allowed to go home. This came with strict instructions. No exercise of any sort was top of the list. So, for almost a month, I lived the life of a senior citizen in a retirement village. I even pulled the no-exercise card to get out of doing some light housework.

THE DAY OF THE surgery finally arrived. The surgical team warned me about how serious this operation was. There was, they told me, a huge scope for things to go wrong, because just touching the tumour could cause adrenaline to flood my bloodstream. In the worst case, that could result in me having a stroke or even dying on the operating table.

Geez, guys, I thought. *No need to be so melodramatic*

about all of this. I felt so perfectly healthy that it was hard to imagine how I might die.

As you have probably worked out from the fact you are reading this book, the operation was a success. After seven hours on the operating table, one night in intensive care, then another few days recovering in a general ward, I was good as new—apart from a 20-centimetre-long scar running the length of my stomach, that is.

A few days after the operation, as I lay in my hospital bed recovering, I got some more bad news. Devastating news. I knew it was bad at the time, but it wouldn't be until years later that I'd find out just how bad it was.

THE SURGEON HAD COME in to see me and make sure I was recovering well. I was. I had begged the nurses to take my catheter out at the earliest moment possible. Man, that thing felt so weird. I would be lying there with a full bladder, pretty much busting to go for a wee, then all of a sudden—without any sort of sensation or feeling—I would no longer need to go. Might sound like an ideal situation to you, but I hated it. I wasn't really up to getting out of bed and walking to the toilet yet, though—every tiny movement took considerable effort and caused crazy pain! But I much preferred to go to all that effort over having that uncomfortable tube shoved down the eye of my penis.

The surgeon and I bantered a bit, and I joked about how he was the first man to be that deep inside me. Jay-Jay and my mum were there, listening and chortling. Then joke time was suddenly over: he put on his more serious demeanour, and asked Jay-Jay and Mum if they could step out for a minute to give us some privacy. The girls left.

My surgeon pulled the curtain around my bed. Then he came and stood next to me.

'I have to tell you that, as a result of the operation and the tumour removal, there's a possibility you have a new medical condition,' he said to me.

'OK . . .' I replied, wondering what it could possibly be this time.

'It's a condition called retrograde ejaculation,' he said.

Well, that came from out of nowhere (excuse the pun). The operation had been in my tummy, nowhere near my junk. How could that have happened?

'Often, with surgery such as this,' he explained, 'the male patient can be left with a condition that means that, during intercourse, when he has an orgasm, the sperm shoots back into the bladder instead of out of the tip of the penis.'

As he stood there chatting about my testicles, I slowly turned bright red. I was acutely aware that my wife and my mum were standing just outside the very light and certainly not soundproof nylon curtain. I sat there nodding, thinking and just trying to process it all.

He filled the silence with more words.

'Everything will still work and feel the same,' he assured me. 'It's just that it could be an issue if you wish to have a family. But fertility treatment is very easy these days. You'll just have to urinate into a cup immediately after sexual activity, then the sperm will be harvested from your urine and inserted directly into your wife's uterus, and boom! Here's a baby!'

I may have used a bit of creative licence on that last bit. I can't remember his exact phrasing. But he did make it sound as though it was as easy as deciding what to have on your sandwich at Subway.

FOUR WEEKS AFTER THE operation, I nervously and cautiously went out for my first run. Just a couple of real slow kilometres around home. I felt fine.

After that, I slowly started running further.

All I wanted was to be confident that these attacks were a thing of the past. And they were. Running suddenly became an enjoyable experience again. I mean, it still hurt sometimes—it does for any runner—but I could leave the house and know I'd make it back home without leaving a puddle of stomach acid on some poor stranger's berm.

I was back to running without limitations, running because it made me happy, just like when I was a kid.

In 2006, the year after the tumour was out, I just ran according to how I felt. I didn't train or enter any events. Every step I ran was purely for the love of running and of being alive. It was only after I realised that I'd survived that it dawned on me just how serious things had actually been. In the lead-up to the tumour being discovered and then removed, I hadn't really had time to process anything that was going on. Even though other people had told me I could die, I'd struggled to believe it because I mostly felt fine. I guess I was putting on a brave face to put those around me at ease. And maybe, subconsciously, I had been trying to trick myself into believing that everything would be sweet.

After a while, I reached a point where I knew it was time for me to accept that I was going to be fine. Time to stop dwelling on the fact that I'd had a close call with death. Time to make plans for the future. I decided to live life the same way I run: instead of looking back, I had to look forward. And the best way to do that, I decided, was to start by going back to ground zero.

At the end of 2007, I signed up for the Auckland Half

Marathon. A half, I thought, was a good way to ease myself back into running, to grow a bit of confidence. I felt OK. It was only other people—those who care about me—who felt apprehensive. It would be exactly two years since that memorable day when I went for my first ambulance ride. Since the half marathon and marathon start and finish at exactly the same place, I would get to retrace my steps from two years earlier. I would get to finish what I hadn't been able to that day.

When the starter's gun went off, I felt no nerves. For me, that's really the difference between running a half marathon and a full marathon. Even now, I get butterflies and crazy nerves at the start of a marathon. A half marathon is still a bloody long way—and an epic achievement for those for whom it's the longest distance they'll conquer—but the full marathon is a different animal altogether. Lots of people can bluff their way through 21.1 kilometres by going for just a few training runs; it'll be a tough day and they might require a few walking breaks, but they'll get through it. The full marathon, on the other hand, is far less forgiving. With a marathon, you pay her the respect she deserves—or don't, at your own peril.

I thought this half marathon would be almost like a religious experience, one of those things where you are so overwhelmed that you cry. It turns out it wasn't. Not at all. I was running and smiling. Happy to be back on these same streets, healthy, fit and alive. The first time I even thought about the events from two years earlier was when I ran past Takapuna Grammar School on Lake Road and saw the same drink station up ahead. Once again, there was a St John Ambulance and its crew of paramedics alongside. As I ran past, I yelled out, 'Keep up the great job, team!' I know they probably weren't the same paramedics, but I wanted to acknowledge their presence and the work they do. They'd saved my life.

IT WASN'T UNTIL TEN years after my operation to remove the tumour and almost as many rounds of IVF later that Jay-Jay and I finally gave up on our dream of having our own children. The cost was just too high—financially definitely, but even more so emotionally. It was draining. Every new round came with a glimmer of hope, a chance. But with every call from the fertility clinic to say, 'I'm so sorry. It didn't work this time', it just got more and more painful. Everyone has their breaking point, and we knew when we had reached ours. We were both exhausted. We were drained and we had started to become cynical.

It was time to give up.

We took part in a few TV documentaries about IVF and our own personal struggle. We're both fairly open books on our radio show anyway, so we figured it would be a good opportunity to give others an insight into what IVF and infertility is really like. I think most people probably, like my surgeon, assume it is fairly straightforward. Magazines are full of stories about celebrities getting pregnant in their fifties, and this makes it seem like it's a sure thing.

After we did the documentaries, lots of guys who had found themselves going through a similar thing started to reach out to me. Usually they had questions; sometimes they just wanted someone else to talk to. I made sure I carried business cards with me all the time so that if one of these guys came up to me, I could give it to him to email me about it at an appropriate time for both of us—there is nothing worse than watching an All Blacks game at a bar while some stranger shouts in your ear about his sperm count.

My favourite was a guy who came up to me at a concert and said, 'I know you from somewhere . . . You're that guy on the TV, eh? Is your dick broken, bro?'

I laughed. Loudly.

What else can you do? No use getting offended or upset by it. He wasn't deliberately being an arsehole. And, even though his phrasing wasn't particularly eloquent, he was sort of right.

MY FAVOURITE WAS A GUY WHO CAME UP TO ME AT A CONCERT AND SAID, 'I KNOW YOU FROM SOMEWHERE . . . YOU'RE THAT GUY ON THE TV, EH? IS YOUR DICK BROKEN, BRO?'

Throughout our whole IVF journey, I ran. I ran in the mornings before I had to go in for operations. I ran in the mornings when Jay-Jay was being operated on. I ran in the mornings when we were waiting for a phone call to find out if the latest round had been successful or not. I ran—sometimes sobbing, with tears and sweat streaming down my face—on the days and weeks after we were hit with yet another negative result. I took the whole thing pretty hard. Being a dad was so important to me. I just never realised quite how important it was until it hit me that it may not be possible. There were some dark times. And, in hindsight, I'm sure they would have been way darker if I hadn't been able to go out and run. Running was my anti-depressant. The thing that kept me positive. The healing power of exercise is not something to be underestimated. Whenever I go for a run, I always feel better for it afterwards.

CHAPTER 6
FROM RUNNING ANARCHIST TO RUNNING NERD

I HAVE NEVER REALLY seen myself as a conventional sort of a runner. I have always liked to think of myself as being a guy who runs . . . but isn't like the rest of them. A running anarchist. This might partially stem from my motivation for getting back into running as an adult in the first place: I was fat. I'd spent the better part of my twenties eating, drinking and doing pretty much whatever I wanted. It was awesome. But then it reached a point where I couldn't deny it any longer: I needed to lose weight. I saw running as the best way to do this without having to quit eating and drinking the shit that put me on the fast track to obesity in the first place, so at the age of 28, after making numerous half-arsed attempts to get in shape by joining a gym, dabbling in weightlifting and even investing in some Lycra and having a crack at cycling, I got myself the first pair of running shoes I'd owned since I had retired from running back in secondary school, and I started running again.

I can tell you it is easier to stay fit than to get fit. I thought I might be able to slip back into running thanks to 'muscle memory' or something, but the truth is it *hurt* and it was *hard*. I had just moved to Hamilton to live with my then brand-new girlfriend, Jay-Jay, who evidently had a thing for fat blokes. The move coincided with me starting a brand-new job at The Edge radio station, hosting the breakfast show with Jay-Jay and another guy called Jason Reeves. I would be stepping up from doing a breakfast show for a local Palmerston North radio station to doing an almost nationwide one on The Edge. This was a big career opportunity, so I thought it would be a good time to try to get myself fit; I find the fitter I am, the better I am at work—and the better able I am to cope with those ghastly early mornings. Also, I repulsed myself when I stood naked in front of the full-length mirror, so I really wanted to do something about that.

Jay-Jay wasn't even concerned about me being a porker (or if she was she didn't say anything). But I thought I owed it to her, and to myself, to be the best I could be. In the initial days of my return to running, I would plod my way round the Hamilton lake, a loop that was around 4 or 5 kilometres long. Since this was before smartphones, I had to just guess the distance, so it was possibly even less than that. After every run, I would stand on the scales, drenched in sweat, and weigh myself, and every day I would be pissed off with my lack of weight loss. After years of treating my body like a toxic-waste-disposal site I suddenly had this unrealistic expectation that I should drop a kilo or two with each half-hour run.

Unfortunately, that's not how it goes. The sad reality is that weight is far easier to pile on than it is to strip off. It is also way more enjoyable to put it on, too.

Back then I would usually go out running in a pair of those Canterbury rugby shorts—the sort a farmer might wear when he is milking the cows. On top, I would wear a round-the-house sort of T-shirt. Proper-looking running nerds would pass me and I would shake my head and think, *I will never become one of those guys with their singlets and their almost offensively short-shorts with the little splits up the side.*

IF ONLY 28-YEAR-OLD ME could see the runner I have become today. Slowly, over time, I have morphed into a geeky runner just like the rest of them. I have flash shoes, moisture-wicking gear, GPS watches, and I talk about 'splits' and 'intervals' and 'marginal gains'.

I am a full-blown running nerd (with some lingering anarchist habits).

In social situations, though, I do try to keep the running chat to a minimum. I haven't yet reached the point where I've forgotten that most people don't actually care about my most recent marathon; they only ask to be polite.

The first step on the road to Nerdtown for me was when I was given some free gear by Adidas. It was a job perk. The radio station I work for was one of the sponsors of the then Adidas Auckland Marathon in 2003, and an email went around work asking if anyone wanted free entry to the event along with some free Adidas gear. By this stage. I had been back running for a couple of years and had lost a lot of weight. More importantly, I was feeling a lot better about myself and was less grossed out by what I saw in the mirror. I was still not very fast and I was yet to participate in any actual events but I could complete runs of 30 to 60 minutes without stopping, so I thought that with a bit of extra training I'd be able to run 21.1 kilometres.

IF I AM BEING HONEST, I DIDN'T EVEN WANT TO DO THE HALF MARATHON. I JUST WANTED THE FREE GEAR.

I was also no longer outright opposed to swapping my rugby shorts for actual running shorts . . . I was just reluctant to pay for the good gear myself. So I put my hand up. I received a bag of free gear containing everything I could want and more! I felt like an All Black on day one of the season. There was a pair of good shoes—Adidas Supernovas—along with numerous pairs of socks, shorts, shirts and singlets. Overnight I went from a guy who looked like he was out on a run to try to get fit for footy season to an actual runner. I was dressed just like one of those nerds I had scoffed at on so many occasions.

If I am being honest, I didn't even want to do the half marathon. I just wanted the free gear. If getting it meant running 21.1 kilometres, then so be it. As it transpired, participating in this event—my first as an adult—was what ultimately got me running marathons, so in a way that flippant decision ended up transforming my life. Had I not taken up that offer, who knows where I would be right now? Maybe I would still be running; maybe I wouldn't. But I doubt I would have run marathons all over the world, and I sure as shit would not be writing a book about running.

Up until this point, I had stubbornly refused to wear actual running clothes. I mean, I always made sure I had a half-decent pair of shoes, but when it came to clothes I still thought proper running gear was really pretentious and totally unnecessary unless you had a chance of making the Olympics or Commonwealth Games. But, as soon as I chucked on the free Adidas gear, my life changed. It felt *so* much better. It wasn't just psychological, either. It was so much lighter and less restrictive for starters, and it even managed to stay dry even though I was real sweaty. It was like magic. Suddenly I discovered what all those nerdy runners were on to with their flash gear. Whenever I see someone out running in the sort of clothing I *used to* wear, it makes me shudder. They honestly don't know what they are missing out on! I feel like letting them in on the secret, but I never do—I wonder if they are judging me the way I used to judge other runners dressed like me.

Now I have a full-blown set of criteria for all the running gear I own. They are always, without exception, proper running garments. No cotton; just that magic fabric that wicks sweat away from your body and to the fabric's surface, where it evaporates, so that even on a hot day you keep pretty much dry. Where possible, I try to buy shorts that have a little zip-up pocket at the back—handy for gels (which I will get to) and my EFTPOS card or cash. This fancy running gear can be a bit pricey, but if you shop around and go to outlet stores or sales you usually can find some good deals.

Then there's my shoes. I usually replace my shoes every four months. This one probably *is* psychological, but I feel like I am more likely to get injured if I am in an older pair of shoes. Also, your shoes are the most important tool of the trade. Each foot comes into contact with the ground around 80 times per minute when you're running, with the full force of your body weight behind each step, so it's not really something I'm too willing to be a tight-arse about. My mum thinks this is excessive. She shakes her head in disbelief and tells me I have more money than sense. She may have a point, but you just cannot beat the feeling or the smell of a fresh pair of running shoes—they are so springy and bouncy! I should point out that this high turnover of shoes is my personal preference, and my preference alone. I probably do change them before it is totally necessary. Just do what feels right for you—I have seen some old geezers at the start of marathons who look like they are running in shoes that were made from dinosaur skins 65 million years ago. According to the Asics website, you should change your shoes around every 750 to 850 kilometres. I'm sure they do care about keeping you injury-free . . . but it's also their business to sell shoes, so they obviously want customers to upgrade as frequently as possible as well.

If you are just starting out running, it's a good idea to do a bit of research to make sure you get the right running shoes for you. There are some great specialist running stores, like Shoe Science, Shoe Clinic or Smith's Sports Shoes, that will put you on a treadmill and film you running; this shows them what your feet do with each step, and helps them to advise you what shoes might be best suited to your running style. (Also, if you do go to one of these specialist stores and use the staff's time and knowledge, don't be a sad guy like my mate Neil. He went in and spent some time getting his running style analysed and was given a recommendation of what shoes would suit him best. Then the miserable bugger went home and ordered a pair online for a cheaper price!)

When you do find a brand or style of shoe that feels perfect and allows you to run without getting injured, you'll be reluctant to run in anything else. The irritating thing about this—and any other superstitious long-time runners will back me up on this—is that shoe manufacturers keep changing their bloody products! I'm not sure why they do this. My hunch is that they're probably spending millions on research and development, so they keep changing the shoes to make them 'better'. When I first started running again, I trained in an Adidas shoe called the Supernova, which I got for free in that epic bag of gear I mentioned earlier. I went through about three pairs of these before I was forced to change when the guy in Rebel Sport told me that Adidas were no longer putting that model out. I was gutted. I stuck with the Adidas brand, though, because I didn't want to jinx anything or increase my chances of getting injured. But, after talking to lots of other runners and experts, I realised I was just being silly. Since then, I have also run in New Balance shoes, and I currently run in Asics Kayano.

EACH TO THEIR OWN, I RECKON. GET SOME ADVICE, TALK TO OTHER PEOPLE, FIND OUT WHAT WORKS FOR YOU AND STICK WITH IT.

Whatever your running style, rest assured that every running-shoe manufacturer will have one that suits you—and looks good! There was even a phase a few years ago where people ditched shoes altogether and reverted to running in bare feet, or wore those ridiculous Vibram FiveFinger things, which are sort of like a glove except they go on your feet. I am not making this up. Google it! The barefoot movement was sparked by the bestselling book called *Born to Run* by Christopher McDougall. His theory was that, if you run in no shoes—or next-to-nothing shoes like those FiveFinger things—you will return to a more natural movement. When you read his book, it makes a lot of sense.

Each to their own, I reckon. Get some advice, talk to other people, find out what works for you and stick with it. I used to run in bare feet a lot as a youngster, and I never got injured (apart from the odd stubbed toe and blood blister). I wouldn't be keen to try it these days, though. I weigh 80-something kilos and the thought alone of my naked feet taking that sort of hammering, slapping down on the concrete footpath 600 times per kilometre, makes me shudder.

WHENEVER I GO AWAY on holiday, I take my running gear with me. A lot of people probably can't think of many things worse than going for a run while they are supposed to be on holiday, but I love it. I find I eat and drink more on holiday, so if I get out for the occasional run I don't feel so bad about the excessive calories. Also, as I've mentioned, it is a fantastic way to explore a new location.

The downside of these holiday runs is what to do with my sweaty gear once I'm back at the hotel. To be quite frank, the stench can be repulsive. In London, our hotel had no windows that could open, so I was forced to give my gear a rinse under the tap using the complimentary little hotel shampoo, then hang it up in the wardrobe and firmly shut the door. It worked . . . to a degree. The clothes dried as I had intended, but the smell was appalling the next day when I opened the door to retrieve them. Even after the gear had been taken out the smell still lingered. The poor hotel cleaners must have wondered where the rotting corpse of a rat was hiding.

When we went on a trip to Hawaii, though, we had a decent-sized balcony, so this was not an issue. After each run, I would just drape the offensive-smelling gear over the balcony—always careful to hang it more inwards than outwards so that if a gust of wind somehow got hold of my clothes, they would simply land on the tiles of our balcony instead of flying down into the street below. This method worked an absolute treat . . . until it didn't.

One morning, as I had done every other morning, I got up and went for a run. I hung up my gear, then we went out for the day. When we returned to our room on Level 17 of the Modern Hotel in Honolulu, I opened the ranch slider and went out to check if my clothes had dried. Before I even got to touch them, I knew something was out of place. At a glance, I could see my shoes and two socks on the tiles, just where I had placed them, and my shirt and shorts were hanging over the balcony, also where I had placed them.

The only thing missing?

My undies!

IF I RELIED SOLELY ON THOSE BUILT-IN UNDIES TO PROVIDE SUPPORT FOR MY GENITALS, IT'D LOOK LIKE I WAS RUNNING FROM THE POLICE WITH TWO GRAPES AND A PICKLE STUFFED DOWN MY PANTS AFTER ROBBING THE PRODUCE SECTION OF NEW WORLD.

My running shorts always have little built-in meshy underpants, but I have found these do not offer nearly enough support for the male runner. If you are a woman, imagine how awful it would feel (and also look) if you went out running with nothing but a tiny bit of thin, meshy fabric to keep your boobs in place. Well, for us men, it's the same deal below the waist. If I relied solely on those built-in undies to provide support for my genitals, it'd look like I was running from the police with two grapes and a pickle stuffed down my pants after robbing the produce section of New World.

I always back up these built-in undies with a pair of regular cotton briefs. Obviously, these cotton briefs end up getting very sweaty and unpleasant, so I have a technique that has served me well: when the nice Calvin Kleins that I wear as day-to-day undies start to look a bit the worse for wear, I'll transfer them into my running drawer where they start a new life as my running undies. Eventually, these things get so gross that I will make the call to throw them out—but it doesn't usually get to that point. More often, the undies just lose their will to live and walk themselves out to the wheelie bin.

I wasn't too upset about losing my undies in Hawaii. Out of all the gear that could have blown away, this was probably the best. My other stuff is expensive, but the undies are worthless. I peered out over the balcony to the street below, to see if I could spot them. I thought they might be sitting on top of a shrub in the garden or even on the footpath or the road.

Initially, there was no sign of them.

Then I spotted them . . . right on the balcony below us!

I was horrified. Those poor people!

This was not a cheap hotel. If you are spending hundreds of dollars a night for a room in a luxury hotel, there are a number of things that you do not want to find in your room. Ever. Things like a hair on your sheets, or an unflushed toilet. Or some bloke's sweat-drenched undies on your balcony.

I started freaking out.

Jay-Jay chose that moment to wander out and join me on the balcony. She leaned over the railing next to me.

'Oh, look!' she said. 'There's a pair of guy's undies on the balcony down there. Clearly someone had a good time last night!' She laughed.

Despite my panic, I forced myself to act calm, like I had

been out there admiring the splendid view of Waikiki beach and Diamond Head volcano all along. I laughed along with her.

She then craned her head forward another few inches, as if that would somehow give her a better view of the offending garment. After a short pause, she said, 'They're not your undies are they?'

Sheepishly, I confirmed the terrible truth.

Jay-Jay erupted into appalled laughter. 'You need to go down and get them back!' she said. 'Those things are expensive.'

I thought this was a bit hypocritical of her. This is the woman who owns seventeen handbags, despite only having the same number of hands as everybody else, and here she was, worried about a threadbare pair of $30 undies. We argued, and I won. There was no way I was going down to that room.

We went out for the afternoon, and when we got back the first thing we did was go and check if the undies were still in place. They were still there . . . but they had been moved! In a disturbing twist, they had somehow made their way from the floor of the balcony below to dangling over a chair.

Someone had fondled them!

WE NEVER WILL KNOW THE FATE OF THOSE CALVIN KLEIN MEN'S BRIEFS.

The next morning, a further check revealed the balcony below had been used for extensive entertaining. On the table was an empty pack of cigarettes and an ashtray full of butts, as well as three empty wine glasses. The undies, however, were nowhere to be seen.

We never will know the fate of those Calvin Klein men's briefs. But my worst-case scenario theory is that the female guest in that room found them and, assuming they were her husband's, took it upon herself to pack them up, take them home and wash them. Meaning it is possible that right now, somewhere in the world, some poor bloke is unwittingly wandering around in my starchy old running undies.

MY NERDY INFATUATION WITH fancy running gear doesn't stop at my shirts, shorts and shoes: there's also my GPS watch. I have a Garmin watch that cost me way more than I told my wife it cost. It is a Garmin 620, and coincidentally 620 is not too far off the price I paid for the damn thing. This watch is amazing though—it tells me everything I need to know about each run, plus a whole lot of stuff I don't need to know. It lets me know how far I ran, how fast, my cadence (how many steps I took per minute), my best pace, my average pace, my heart rate and how many calories I burned. It even lets me know what my average stride length was! Why I would ever need to know this, I have no idea, but it's cool. These days, runners of any ability can have access to data that was once reserved for the professionals and elites.

When I finish my run, I can sync the information from the watch on to an app on my phone and it gives me lots of pretty maps and graphs. I don't necessarily *need* this, but it is a great way to chart my progress and it's quite motivating to be able to watch yourself improving.

Happily, there are also plenty of cheaper watch options that will do the trick if you are just starting out. I used to run wearing a basic Nike watch, which cost under $200 and did the job just fine. If you don't want to invest much money, you could just get a cheap (or even free) app on your phone that will do the trick. I was put off taking my phone on runs a few years ago when my smartphone suffered the most gruesome of all deaths by drowning in my sweat. I'd had it securely tucked into a specially designed arm band that went snugly round my bicep, but it was a particularly hot day and my run was around two hours long. By the time I got home, the phone was damaged beyond repair. I still see tons of runners out with their phones strapped to their arms or in their hands, so I assume death-by-drowning is not a common occurrence. But, if you too are a 'sweaty beast' (as my wife refers to me when I attempt to spoon her on hot summer nights), it is definitely something to keep in mind.

If your aim is to just finish a marathon and never run again, I'd probably save the money. A running watch is definitely not a must-have. When I was a kid, Mum would go out for her long training runs on the weekend without even wearing a watch. She would just check the time on the stove in the kitchen when she left the house, then check it again as soon as she got home. Then, later that same day, we'd all go out for a family drive round the route she ran to calculate the distance she had covered on the car's odometer.

WHEN I FIRST STARTED running again, I really just wanted to find a solution that would enable me to continue to eat shitty food and drink wine without turning into one of those people you see on documentaries who need a team of firefighters to tear down a bedroom wall just to get them out of the house and into hospital. But, the more I ran, the better my diet became. Less and less often, I'd be tempted to sabotage myself with a two-piece quarter pack. Oh, don't worry. I still enjoy the

Colonel's secret recipe every now and then (what *are* those eleven secret herbs and spices?!), but the fitter I get the less I crave that sort of food—and the worse I feel afterwards. Fortunately (or unfortunately, depending on how you look at it), I also still love my red wine and consume way more than I should.

These days, I can still run with a hangover or if I have eaten a meal that ten out of ten nutritionists strongly discourage, but it makes everything so much more difficult. I have also noticed that it gets harder and harder every year. Now, when I'm training towards a specific event, I prioritise being well rested, well fed and not hungover. Some of my mates question my sanity when I explain I won't be going out because of a run the next day, but the way I see it is that it's only a small sacrifice in service of a bigger goal. Years from now, I know I'll remember the big race—the sights, the sounds, the other runners, how I felt. It would have to be a pretty extraordinary night out on the town with friends to beat that kind of memory.

Sometimes, though, it can get tricky, juggling life commitments with your running schedule and your diet. Last year, the night before a key long run in the lead-up to the Chicago Marathon, I fuelled up on a Big Mac Combo. It wasn't deliberate. Jay-Jay and I had been at a school concert that our son, Sev, was playing the drums at, and it had gone on way longer than we anticipated. So we just ended up going through the McDonald's drive-through on our way home— but I also know it would have only taken me an extra ten minutes to whip up some pasta when I'd got home.

I usually try to have pasta in the day or two leading up to a marathon, but I don't get too uptight or anal about it. If I can get it, sweet. If not, that's fine as well. I'll just find a suitable substitute. A few years ago, I took part in the Routeburn Classic, a 32-kilometre trail run over the breathtakingly beautiful Routeburn track, which overlaps both Mount Aspiring National Park and Fiordland National Park and is described as one of the world's great hikes. As a walk, it is generally done in three days. As a run, the winners will usually cover the distance in just under three hours, which is freakishly fast.

The night before the Routeburn Classic, I ended up tagging along to a restaurant in Te Anau called The Moose with a group of old blokes I'd met at the race registration who ran it every single year. I thought it would be a good opportunity to pick their brains about the course and what to expect. What I was not expecting was a lesson in pre-race nutrition. While I was busy sipping on my bottle of Powerade and eyeing up the Fettuccine Alfredo on the menu, these guys were knocking back pints of beer and ordering 300-gram prime rib-eye steaks and fish 'n' chips.

'MATE, THERE ARE PROBABLY MORE CARBS IN THIS DRINK THAN THERE WILL BE IN THAT LITTLE BOWL OF SPAGHETTI YOU'RE EATING!'

'Aren't you fellas worried about carb-loading?' I asked, with just a touch of food envy going on.

One of them raised his half-full handle and replied, 'Mate, there are probably more carbs in this drink than there will be in that little bowl of spaghetti you're eating!'

AS YOU CAN SEE, every runner is different when it comes to pre-race nutrition. I know of some real hard old bastards who have a cooked farmhouse breakfast of bacon, eggs, sausages and hash browns before doing a marathon! The thought of eating that pre-run makes me shudder, personally. But whatever works for ya! When you run that far and for that length of time, you rip through over 3000 calories, so a good breakfast is essential—but you also don't want to feel weighed down with food or lose valuable time by having to stop for a poo on the way.

Before a shorter run, I'll usually eat a banana and wash it down with a big glass of water. I can head straight out after a banana without any stomach problems. If I'm going out for a long run, though, I'll eat more than that and wait around half an hour for the food to settle. Usually I'll have honey on toast, or some porridge, a banana and maybe an electrolyte drink. For longer runs, I also take a couple of gel sachets. Those things taste like arse. They are truly horrible. Disgusting, sickly sweet things. I am yet to find one that I would describe as delicious. Before I die, I'd settle to find one that is bearable!

The most important thing with gels, if you're going to use them, is to try them out on a few training runs first. You may try one that *really* doesn't agree with you—and this is something you want to know well before you make it to the marathon start line! Actually, pretty much every running book will tell you not to try *anything* new on race day. I often go against this (cos I'm an anarchist!) and have some of the electrolyte sports drink they usually have at the water stops. It hasn't come back to bite me in the arse yet—touch wood.

My mum has run a total of 39 marathons and has never taken a gel in her life. She doesn't even drink water on her training runs. She has never been dehydrated or had to pull out of a run, either. It's really quite remarkable. I'd say over the decades she has spent running, her body must have just adapted and become more resourceful. She's sort of like a jerboa, one of those little rodents found in the Sahara Desert. Those little guys don't have to drink water, just like Mum. They like to run, just like Mum. But they have a top speed of around 25 kilometres per hour, which is a fair bit faster than Mum!

I tend to run without water, but that's because I have a few routes that I know like the back of my hand, so I also know where I can stop for a drink—the petrol station, the tap outside the fire station, the one in the carpark of the lawyers' office, the drinking fountain on the waterfront. For my really long training runs—the ones that can last up to three hours—I'll sometimes take my EFTPOS card or some cash in my pocket, along with a few energy gels and I will wash these down at the water stops I know along the way. Some people prefer to run with a belt that has a few water bottles on it, or even a backpack with a water bladder inside it, but I find the constant sloshing of water irritating after a while.

I REACH PEAK NERDINESS right before a race. That's when my pre-race ritual begins. I follow the same set pattern every time. First, I lay out on the floor everything I will need for the morning: shirt, shorts, undies, socks, shoes, watch, energy gels and race number. I then pick up my race shirt and put it on, then carefully attach the race number with four safety pins. I am very particular about the placement of my race number—sometimes it will take five attempts before I am happy with it. It needs to feel just right: tight enough and at the right height. The last thing I want is to be irritated during the run by my number flapping around or getting in my way when I use my shirt to wipe away sweat on my face. I'm aware it's a little OCD, and I have no idea why it's such a big thing for me. At the start line, I'll often see other runners attaching their number in the final few minutes before the gun goes off and it makes me shudder with anxiety—and just a touch of envy. How do they live so recklessly? Those runners are the real anarchists.

Once my gear is all sorted—and only once it is sorted—I can sleep peacefully. I know that all I'll have to do in the morning is wake up and chuck my gear on.

Then I get to kick back and relax. Sometimes, I put on some compression stockings and do some stretches on the floor while watching telly. I don't know if these stockings make any sort of difference, but I figure they can't do any harm. I'll eat some pasta for dinner, if I can, and I'll try not to go overboard with the food. There's lots of advice out there these days that suggests you shouldn't overdo the food the night before a run, which is in stark contrast to the advice runners were given 30 years ago. In the eighties and nineties, most marathons would organise a massive Pasta Party the night before the event to allow the runners to carb-load— which is to say fill their plate up and eat as much pasta as they could stomach. I am a runner, but even I think a Pasta Party sounds like one of the worst parties of all time. A room full of extremely fit people standing around in tracksuits and gorging themselves on mass-produced pasta while discussing their personal bests and goal times for the next day?

Ugh, somebody shoot me!

I haven't reached that point. Yet.

CHAPTER 7
COACH IAN

AS I'VE MENTIONED, DURING my fat years in my twenties, before I got back into running, I did make a couple of half-hearted attempts to get in shape. I gave cycling a crack. My older sister, Bridget, was seeing a guy named Harley who cycled competitively. Harl and I got on well, and he had an old bike he didn't ride anymore so I gave that a go. Initially I just wore normal clothes. The thought of wearing that Lycra cycling gear with the loud colours and logos all over it made me want to puke. But after only a couple of rides, I got sick of my loose clothes flapping around (not to mention the terrible thigh chafing) and I became one of the Lycra lads. I stuck with cycling for a couple of years, but never really enjoyed it. For starters, that little bone right in between my balls and my butthole always felt tender and bruised. *Always*. Then there was the issue of my spokes constantly snapping. At the time, my weight was over 100 kilos, which is quite a heavy load for one of those road bikes with its skinny little tyres. Because of this, whenever I went up a steep hill that required me to get off my seat and lean over the handlebars, a spoke or two would break. This may not sound like a big deal, given that there are so many spokes on each wheel, but as soon as a couple of spokes went the whole wheel would buckle, making a hard ride back home that much harder.

The final straw with cycling came when Harley convinced me to join him in Taupō for the incredible event, the Lake Taupō Cycle Challenge. This event started in 1977, and is held in November each year. It sees thousands of Lycra ladies and lads cycle the 160-kilometre circuit round Lake Taupō. I spent months and months training for it.

On the day of the event, I was only 3 kilometres into my ride when some dickhead just behind me clipped my wheel. This caused me to swerve; my handlebars nudged the handlebars of the cyclist beside me. The next thing I remember is someone just in front of us falling off, then I fell off, then a bunch of riders behind me joined the mountain of mess on the open road just out of Taupō. There were bikes and humans everywhere.

Within a few seconds, all of us fallen riders managed to get to our feet to assess the damage to our bodies and our bikes. I was in shock, a state of bewilderment, adrenaline flowing, trying to process what was going on. My bike was fine and I was too—or so I thought. I had a few grazes and a bit of blood, but nothing to worry about. So I got back on my bike, clipped my fancy cycling shoes back into the pedals, and started to ride.

I immediately felt a lightning bolt of pain shoot through my shoulder.

That was it. My ride was over.

I still had 157 kilometres to go and I had to pull out. Fucking hell.

Harley rode by a few seconds later and stopped to ask if I was OK. I told him my shoulder was rooted and I couldn't carry on. He was sad that my day had turned to shit, but, even in the depths of my misery, he spotted an opportunity for the day to get better.

HARLEY WAS CONCERNED ABOUT MY HEALTH— BUT MORE CONCERNED ABOUT GETTING HIS HANDS ON MY FOOD.

'Well . . .' he said, pointing to the pocket in the back of my Lycra pants. 'Since you won't be needing them, can I take your bananas and chocolate?'

As I reached around to grab them, I was hit with yet another sharp bolt of pain. I screamed.

Harley was concerned about my health—but more concerned about getting his hands on my food. 'Don't hurt yourself,' he said. 'I'll just get it myself.'

As soon as he'd got my goodies, he took off, leaving me broken and bloodied on the side of the road.

An ambulance came a short time later and ferried me to hospital, while a truck swung by to pick up my bike. In Taupō Hospital, I was told I had smashed my collarbone. The pain was unreal! To add insult to injury, the staff told me there was very little they could do for it. They gave me an ibuprofen tablet and a flimsy little sling and sent me on my way. I was mad as hell—I was in so much discomfort, I felt my injury was worthy of a big cast and a container of Tramadol! Before I left, many more cyclists would arrive, most of them in a far worse state than I was. When a cyclist hits the open road at speeds of 30 kilometres an hour or faster, the road wins. Every time.

IT WAS CLEAR THAT cycling was not the sport for me, so I signed up to a gym. I had never set foot inside a gym before, so I had no idea what I was doing. I would go on the stationary bike for a little bit (finally, I had discovered a form of cycling where it would be impossible to break a collarbone!), then I'd have a burst on the rowing machine for a few minutes, before moving on to the elliptical trainer—that's the thing that makes it look like you are power-walking on the spot. I stuck to these three exercise machines and never went anywhere near the weights room. Knowing how uncoordinated I was, I thought it was just too unwise for me to dabble in that area. If there was a way to harm myself, I would surely find it!

Also, it didn't help that one day during my first month at the gym, while I was busy fake-rowing, I heard a blood-curdling scream come from the weights room. I stopped what I was doing to go and be nosy. A man who was lifting weights had somehow dropped one of the big 20-kilogram plates on his foot. The end of his shoe turned red with blood in a matter of seconds. While around a dozen gym posers watched on in horror (myself included), a couple of gym assistants helped him to remove his shoe and saturated red sock to reveal the extent of his injury. His big toe had split open, right down the middle. Think of how a sausage looks when it is cooked too quickly on a high heat, then drench that sausage in tons of tomato sauce. That is exactly what this bloke's toe looked like.

He had his foot bandaged up and was whisked to hospital. I didn't really feel like doing any more pretend-rowing on the rowing machine after that. It was just the excuse I needed to suspend my workout. I went home and had some lunch instead. I can't remember what I ate . . . probably sausages drenched in sauce.

Eventually, I got over my fear or insecurity or whatever it was and went to the weights section. I had some friends who worked out with weights and they convinced me to join them. They would do their sets with the bar and the big weights on each side, then we would take all the big weights off and put some tiny saucer-sized plates on for my turn. The weights I was able to lift were so little you could drop them on your toe and remain happily uninjured.

One day, Graeme Sciascia, one of the personal trainers at the gym, suggested I should start doing weights with him. He told me that with proper training I could get really big and strong. I was in. He looked like he should know what he was talking about—he had the biggest chest I have ever seen on a human being. When he lay down to do bench presses, the bar only had to descend a couple of inches before it was touching his chest. Under Graeme's guidance I did indeed get really strong. I was lifting *huge* weights. The bummer was that after these workouts I would be so hungry that I would undo all the good work by eating ridiculously unhealthy stuff once I got home. I remained so chubby that none of the muscle I gained was visible. It was safely concealed from public view by a thick layer of wobbly fat. My torso never resembled Chris Hemsworth's; it was more like Chris Hemsworth wearing a puffer jacket.

Also, Graeme kept telling me that the more I weighed, the more I would be able to lift so he encouraged me to eat as much as possible. It makes sense, but I think he would have been shocked if he knew *exactly* what I was feasting on in order to put on weight. Most days for lunch I would go to the supermarket and grab a 1.5-litre bottle of Coke, a pack of cheese sizzlers and a loaf of cheese-and-bacon bread. I wouldn't eat *all* of it for lunch . . . but usually by the time dinner rolled around I would have got through most of it. I couldn't understand why I was getting fatter. I mean, I was working so bloody hard at the gym. It was only later on, when I read an article that said you would have to exercise for half an hour to burn off the calories in a small cup of Coke, that the penny dropped. With the food and soft drink I was consuming most afternoons, I would have needed to exercise for fifteen hours to burn it all off!

Occasionally, I would feel so bad about the state of my body that I would take drastic action, but since my knowledge about nutrition was so limited I even did the dieting thing horribly wrong. Some days I would simply not eat all day. No breakfast, no lunch, no snacks. But then by dinner I would be so ridiculously hungry that I would end up eating the equivalent of a couple of meals. Other days I would eat, but just eat salads. Nothing else. So fucking boring. (You already know my feelings about salad.) I felt like a man pretending to be a rabbit. I never made it past two or three days of these self-invented diets before I got frustrated with my lack of weight loss and gave up and went back to the stuff that tastes amazing.

I decided it was time for me to stop going to the gym with Graeme the day that I squatted 140 kilograms, which is a lot. As you probably know, when you do a squat you rest the bar across your shoulders, with the weights on either side, then bend your legs until your thighs are parallel with the floor, then you stand up again. There is a lot of potential for shit to go wrong, so correct form is absolutely crucial. Before I even gave it a crack, I had serious doubts about my ability to squat with 140 kilograms hanging across my shoulders. The Hurricanes rugby team trained at the same gym, and I had seen many of them doing squats with way less weight than that, so I knew that I—an overweight broadcaster and heart attack waiting to happen—had no business lifting that much. But Graeme believed in me, and I thought I could trust a man who had a chest the size and density of a mature kauri tree.

As bad luck would have it, my instincts were correct. Something did go terribly wrong. I didn't end up crushed into the floor under 140 kilograms of iron. Nope, it was way worse than that.

MY FACE WAS RED, VEINS WERE POPPING OUT ON MY NECK, I COULD FEEL MY EYES WATERING FROM THE STRAIN . . . AND THEN IT HAPPENED.

This particular day, I had come to the gym straight from work, and had to go back to work afterwards for another meeting. Because of this, I decided to train without my undies on underneath my gym shorts. That way, I could put them on again after my workout, and they wouldn't be all sweaty and gross. And, since my gym shorts were actually board shorts, which went down to just above my knees, I felt confident I could get the workout done without gracing anyone else in the gym with an eyeful of my junk. It was a flawless and well-considered plan—or so I thought.

I put the bar on my shoulders, psyched myself up with some deep breaths, then slowly lowered the weight until I was crouching not far above the floor. That was the easy bit done. Then I started to push to get the weight back up again. I pushed with everything I had. My face was red, veins were popping out on my neck, I could feel my eyes watering from the strain . . . and then it happened.

I sharted.

My bowels spontaneously expelled gas from the force, and along with a burst of flatulence a small, perfectly formed poo—slightly smaller than a scorched almond—fell from my shorts and rolled across the floor. It got a good roll on, too—it probably went the best part of 2 metres.

I was mortified.

I put the bar up and, without saying a word, walked over to the cleaning station and grabbed a paper towel. I then returned to gather the evidence and walked to the toilet to dispose of it.

When I got back to the squat area, Graeme just shook his head and said, 'I think that'll do us for today, mate.'

After the scorched-almond incident there was no way I could ever go back to that gym. As I drove away, I made a promise to myself: I would never do another squat ever again—or defecate on a gymnasium floor. Two promises that I have so far managed to keep.

But, after a decade of running for the pure and simple love of it, I found myself once again considering getting a trainer on board, this time to help me push my running to the next level. To help me see what I was really capable of. There is that old saying 'When the student is ready, the teacher will appear', and Coach Ian appeared in my life just when I was ready for him.

SOMETIME IN LATE 2014 I got myself a brand-new Garmin GPS watch that calculated something called my 'VO$_2$ max' and then gave me race predictions based on it. I had seen VO$_2$ max mentioned in running books and magazines, but I didn't really understand what it was. It all seemed a bit too science-y and serious for me. This was some next-level nerd shit!

After I'd been out for a few runs with this new watch, it used the data it had collected to give me predictions for my times across various distances. The prediction it gave me for a full marathon was 2 hours 57 minutes. I was intrigued and excited, but mainly confused. It didn't seem possible . . . but could it be? Here I was at 41 years old with around ten marathons under my belt and my personal best for a marathon was 3 hours 14 minutes, which I had run in Christchurch five years earlier. Since then, my marathon times had got slower and usually sat around 3 hours 20-something minutes. Did this watch know something I didn't? Was I capable of going faster than I had given myself credit for?

GOOGLE CONFIRMED WHAT I HAD SUSPECTED ALL ALONG: IT *WAS* VERY SCIENCE-Y AND SERIOUS.

I immediately went away and researched this VO_2-max thing. Google confirmed what I had suspected all along: it *was* very science-y and serious. Science and I are about as compatible as toothpaste and orange juice. My brain just lacks the ability to process and understand this shit. In my very last science exam ever at school I fluked my way to a result of 34 per cent. It was the lowest result of anyone in our class, but I was over the moon! My parents were gutted. I tried to frame it in a positive light for them.

'Guys!' I explained. 'You are missing the big picture here. Even though science is my worst subject, I still got over half the questions right!'

Dad told me I needed to pull my socks up and study my arse off or else my maths exam result would be even worse.

So negative. I'm not sure where he got the idea that I was no good at maths.

To be honest, I still struggle trying to explain what VO_2 max means in words that make sense to me. My coach, who you will meet in a moment, wrote this explanation for the purpose of this book. He even got his wife to edit it before he sent it to me because she has told him he has a habit of going into detail that most people don't understand.

> VO_2 max is the maximum amount of oxygen your body can use during intense physical activity, and determines how efficiently your cells use oxygen for energy. It is measured in millilitres per kilogram of body weight, per minute, on a treadmill in a graded exercise test in a clinical setting. While wearing a mask with a breathing tube connected to oxygen and carbon-dioxide analysers, you first start running slowly. As the treadmill speed increases every few minutes, the volume of oxygen used also increases. When faster speeds are reached, the consumption of oxygen eventually levels out, even though the speed keeps increasing. At this point, using test data gathered, your VO_2 max is calculated.

So that is the 'simplified' version of VO_2 max. I hope it makes sense to you because I'm still a little lost!

Anyway, after my new watch got me excited about my apparent potential according to this VO_2 thingy, I put a status update on Facebook, asking if any of my friends knew anything about it. I got a private message from a bloke called Ian Kostrzewa, who said he was an exercise physiologist and performance tester. Ian runs his own business called

Competitive Edge Sports Science, and he offered to test my VO_2 max for free doing the treadmill test described above and to design a training programme that I could follow in order to get faster.

All of a sudden, I had a coach! This was possibly the exact moment I officially went from being someone who happens to run to a full-blown runner. The day I went from being a running anarchist to a running nerd.

At this stage, I was training for the New York Marathon and it was only a matter of weeks until race day. I told Ian I would stick with what I was doing then get back in touch afterwards. I must admit, I was a little apprehensive. I knew getting a coach would mean I would have to work harder and push myself more than I currently was, but I also knew it was necessary if I wanted to get any faster. No pain; no gain.

Ian and I started working together at the beginning of 2015. My big goal for that year was the Chicago Marathon in October. The year was hard and the training was tough. There were many days when I fucking hated it. Instead of just lacing up my shoes and running according to how I felt, I was now running with a purpose. It was nice being told exactly what I had to do on each run; it just wasn't easy, and I kind of like easy! Every time I pushed myself to extreme levels of discomfort, I would find myself blaming this poor bloke. *FUCK. YOU. IAN!* I would think. What makes all of this even more bizarre is the fact that I pay this guy! I give him money every month so I can hurt myself.

Every couple of months, Coach Ian gets me on a treadmill to run some tests with these sensors stuck to various parts of my body to test that VO_2-max thing. These tests usually last about 45 minutes, and they always start and end the same way: they start with me walking happily on the treadmill, usually chatting to Ian about what shows we are each watching on Netflix, and end with me curled over in agony, wheezing and drenched in sweat. I begin at walking pace, then every three minutes I slightly increase my speed. The testing only stops when I can no longer run. By the time I hit the big red emergency stop button, I am usually sprinting at a pace that feels incredibly unsafe on a treadmill.

HONESTLY, ONE OF MY GREATEST RUNNING REGRETS IS NOT SEEKING OUT THE SERVICES OF A COACH SOONER.

These tests apparently tell Coach Ian exactly how fast I *should* be able to run and for how long—all according to my blood-lactate levels. To be honest, I *still* have a hard time trying to explain to other people what the whole VO_2-max thing means or what Coach Ian does in these testing sessions. He sends me long emails with charts and graphs attached, and he is even generous enough to explain it all to me in language as unscientific as possible, but even some of that stuff goes over my head. I trust Ian, though, and my times have got faster with him. So I will carry on doing as I'm told and leave the science to him.

Honestly, one of my greatest running regrets is not seeking out the services of a coach sooner. I always thought a coach was only for people who were already good and wanted to be better. That is wrong. Even if you are just starting out, a coach will be able to help you immensely. If you run and you want to go faster, get a coach! Ask someone you know who runs well—they may be able to point you in the right direction. Competitive runners are surprisingly helpful, or at least I have found them to be that way. That could be because they feel OK sharing their knowledge with me because the only time I will see them in a race is at the start line!

After spending the best part of the year following Ian's instructions, I ran a brand-new personal best at the Chicago Marathon in 2015: 3 hours 10 minutes 46 seconds. I was ecstatic! It would have been a real kick in the guts to have put in all that hard work—the hardest I had ever worked for a race—only to not have gone much quicker. But all that extra effort had paid off! I was pretty pleased with myself. Not only was it a new personal best by almost five minutes (which, trust me, is *a lot* over a marathon distance), but it was also twelve minutes faster than I had run the New York Marathon just a year before.

Back at the hotel after Chicago, before I showered or did anything else, I picked up my phone to text a few people. There was already a message waiting for me from Ian—he had been following my progress in real time on the official marathon website, even though it was the middle of the night back in New Zealand.

> Hey, Dom! Awesome work on the marathon. Was it just general fatigue that slowed you at the end or did you have an issue? I know it's slightly slower than we were aiming for but you still did an amazing job, and got a new PB! Well done, dude!

You still did an amazing job? What the fuck? I laughed out loud. It was both congratulations and commiserations all rolled into one. I pictured Ian sitting up in bed with his laptop back in New Zealand, trying to figure out what had gone wrong. According to all his testing and data from those punishing treadmill tests at the gym, I should have gone faster, apparently. But he was dead right: the last 7 kilometres had taken me way longer than they should have. I had started to cramp up and—to put it bluntly—I was simply rooted. I was reduced to a walk on a few occasions in those final stages. Even a brisk walk is slower than a jog and I knew precious time was slipping away, but I'm not honestly sure I could have changed the outcome because those brief walks felt necessary. If I had been able to keep running, I would have!

After I returned from Chicago, I told Coach Ian I wanted a break for the rest of the year and would get back into serious training in 2016. Not a break from running—just from following such a rigorous programme. I was physically and mentally exhausted, and I wanted a couple of months of running for the love of it again. Just running at whatever pace and whatever distance I felt like.

That break did me the world of good—and it gave me time to think. If Ian reckoned that some stuff had gone wrong with a marathon where I finished in 3 hours 10 minutes, then maybe it wouldn't be impossible for me to break three hours.

When I ran the idea past Ian, he replied, 'Yep, I'd say you could get on the cusp of three hours, definitely. There's no reason why you couldn't at least get close!'

With that, my mind was made up. I was going to give it the best shot I could. I was going to try to run the Berlin Marathon in under three hours.

CLIVE WOODWARD, THE COACH who led the English rugby team to victory at the 2003 Rugby World Cup, taught his players a theory called 'marginal gains'. Essentially, it is the idea that you do everything better by 1 per cent. One measly per cent. That's it! The logic was that if his team improved everything they did by that tiny amount, then those small gains would collectively add up to a remarkable improvement.

I like this idea a lot. Just imagine if you took a hundred little things that until now you haven't paid much attention to and made a point of doing each of them 1 per cent better. The cumulative difference would be huge. And it could be argued that, since I am just a reformed anarchist (and not someone who is trying to be the best in the world), my potential for gains is even greater. I mean, the English rugby team would already have things like nutrition and sports psychology sorted, so they would have had to try much harder to find areas where they could make small improvements.

I GOT EXCITED JUST THINKING ABOUT THE AREAS WHERE I COULD MAKE SOME OF THESE MARGINAL GAINS—IN MY TRAINING, MY NUTRITION AND MY SLEEP, FOR STARTERS.

Until I started training with Coach Ian, all I had ever done was run. I had never paid much attention to anything besides putting one foot in front of the other. I had never taken things more seriously than that. I began to imagine what might be possible if I changed that attitude *and* had some professional help from a coach. Maybe, just maybe, my goal of running a marathon under three hours could be possible after all.

I got excited just thinking about the areas where I could make some of these marginal gains—in my training, my nutrition and my sleep, for starters. Basically, I figured I could make training more of a priority in my life. The changes might only be minuscule, but as I ran through them in my head it occurred to me that they didn't actually sound that marginal at all. They sounded pretty bloody important. I tucked the idea of marginal gains away as just another tool to get me along that road towards my ultimate goal of being the best that I can be.

CHAPTER 8
RUNNERSPEAK

BEFORE I GOT COACH Ian on board, I wasn't really familiar with any sort of running terminology. I had come across words like 'intervals', 'lactate shuttle overload', 'repeats' and 'fartlek' in running magazines and books, but I saw all that stuff as being for serious runners and not for anarchists like me. However, I soon discovered that the only way I would ever be able to make myself run faster—fast enough to meet my Berlin goal—would be to embrace all these fancy running terms and train harder.

The first term I learned was fartlek. I know it sounds like a relative of the unpleasant shart, but thankfully it has nothing to do with anything gross. It's a training technique created by a Swedish running coach back in the 1930s and it translates as 'speed play'—*fart* is the Swedish word for 'speed' and *lek* means 'play'. (I have always wondered if this means that when you get pulled over by the police for driving too fast in Sweden you get a ticket for farting.)

While farts can sometimes be funny, I assure you there is nothing funny about fartlek.

It hurts.

It sucks.

WHILE FARTS CAN SOMETIMES BE FUNNY, I ASSURE YOU THERE IS NOTHING FUNNY ABOUT FARTLEK.

It basically means you run fast for bursts, then you slow down for bits, so a fartlek run is really just another kind of speed session (they all seem to have a different flashy name). As well as fartlek runs, Ian also got me doing what is known as 'lactate tolerance drills' as part of my training for Berlin. In order to get your head around these drills, you also need to have a bit of an idea about lactate and how it works in your body. (Hint: it has nothing to do with learning how to breastfeed . . .) But, as I've made clear, I'm not the expert here; Coach Ian is. So once again I asked him to give me a hand to offer a super-simplified explanation of what it all means, and why it is important for a runner if they wish to run faster.

Here goes . . .

First up, what even is lactate? According to Coach Ian, lactate is formed in your muscles when they create energy. Even when you're resting, lactate is constantly being formed and used as fuel by your muscles—including your brain. Contrary to popular belief, lactate is *not* lactic acid, and neither one causes soreness in your muscles during or after exercises. However, even though lactate doesn't cause soreness or muscle fatigue, it does correlate to these things. When we work hard, our muscles get sore and blood-lactate levels do increase—but this increase isn't the cause of the soreness. It just happens at the same time.

Now, to keep it simple, you have three types of muscle fibres:

1. slow-twitch
2. fast-twitch Type A, and
3. fast-twitch Type B.

All muscle fibres produce lactate to make energy. The basic principle to keep in mind is that slow-twitch muscle fibres fatigue slowly; fast-twitch Type A fibres fatigue more quickly; and Type B fibres fatigue even more quickly again. You use all of a muscle's slow-twitch fibres first, then as intensity increases you use fast-twitch Type A, then fast-twitch Type B for really intense exercise or movements.

To put this in context: during low-intensity running, most of the lactate produced is used by the same muscle as the intensity, speed or incline increases. As soon as there is too much lactate produced to be used in the same muscle, the body shuttles it to other working muscles to be used as fuel. The point at which this starts to happen is your lactate shuttle start (LSS) point or pace. You can find this out through bloodless lactate testing (the treadmill tests that Coach Ian makes me do). If you are relatively well trained—for example, you can run for 10 kilometres—you can exercise at your LSS pace for a long time (potentially hours), and your marathon pace will be around this pace, too.

As your running pace or intensity increases, so does the amount of lactate and other by-products produced. When it gets to the point where your other muscles cannot use as much lactate as you are producing, you have reached your lactate shuttle overload (LSO) point or pace. You can only run at this pace for a relatively short time (typically 45 to 70 minutes), so your LSO pace is usually around the same as your 10-kilometre race pace.

Now, the purpose of a lactate-tolerance drill (those things I mentioned that Coach Ian had me doing as part of my training) is to flood your body with lactate by initially running at a high intensity, or above your LSO pace. Then, without resting, you run between your LSO and LSS paces, where you are still working hard and forcing your body to use lactate as fuel, and still producing lactate. A good way to get an idea of this is to imagine filling a bath. The initial intensity of a lactate-tolerance drill is like you've got the tap turned all the way on, and there's more water going into the bath than the plughole can drain. For the next part of the drill—when you run between your LSO and LSS paces—you turn the tap down to a point where the water is going in at the same rate as it is draining out, so you've got a constant level of water.

Different lactate-tolerance drills use different paces, depending on what you are trying to achieve. An example of one of these lactate-tolerance drills that Coach Ian came up with for me is as follows:

- Stretch and warm up for 5 minutes.
- Run 1 kilometre as fast as I can.
- Run 5 kilometres at no slower than 4:30 per kilometre.*
- Run another 1 kilometre as fast as I can.
- Run another 5 kilometres at no slower than 4:30 pace.

---

* Pace in running is measured as the amount of time (in minutes and seconds) that it takes you to run 1 kilometre (or, if you're in North America, 1 mile). So a 4:30 pace means you are running 1 kilometre in 4 minutes and 30 seconds.

All up, excluding the warm-up, this is a 12-kilometre run—a distance I could easily manage if I just ran at a comfortable pace, which for me is usually around 5:00 per kilometre. But add the above time and pace targets and it becomes considerably harder and more exhausting. If your goal is simply to finish a marathon, you can avoid all of this, but, if you want to get faster, this sort of speed work is the only way to do it.

When I did the lactate-tolerance drill above, my watch reported that I'd done the two fast segments in 3:55 and 3:49, with the remaining 10 kilometres under 4:30 pace. I was totally drained afterwards, but I felt pretty good because I could see that I was already getting faster than I had been just a few weeks earlier. It's always motivating to get tangible proof that you're making progress, and it also helps make these kinds of hard sessions feel worthwhile. For me, seeing the struggle pay off quietens that negative little voice in my head that always seems to pipe up with something unhelpful like, *If I am rooted running at this pace—there is no way I'll ever break three hours in Berlin.*

ALONG WITH LACTATE-TOLERANCE DRILLS, Ian also had me doing sprint sessions every couple of weeks. I'd jog down to the park (usually with my legs still aching from the day before) and spend twenty minutes sprinting for ten seconds then walking for ten seconds, over and over, for a total of 60 sprints broken up with 60 walk breaks. It's harder than it sounds, but nowhere near as hard as a longer-distance speed run. Honestly, I was never 100 per cent sure why Ian got me to do these sprint sessions. It seemed a bit odd to me given that sprints and marathons have about as much in common as Charlie Sheen and Pope Francis, but when I questioned Ian about this his answer made me regret ever asking.

> Sprints are good because they cause changes in your muscles that increase your lactate shuttle start and lactate shuttle overload paces—specifically a protein called MCT1, which, among other things, shuttles lactate from working muscles to non-working ones, meaning you can create more energy and maintain your exercise intensity. To increase LSS and LSO (and your VO_2 max) you need to work at intensities either close to or above them. By forcing your muscles and body to work really hard, it makes it better when it's working less hard. (This is what people mean when they talk about improving your 'running economy'.)

Oooooookay. Glad I asked. That cleared everything up!

Ian has done a great job all along of explaining the science behind the training to me. Truthfully, I don't have a fucking clue what much of it means, but I figure as long as one of us knows what's going on that is good enough. I would make more of an effort to fully understand it all if I didn't trust Ian completely. But I do, so I am very happy to just do what he tells me.

RIGHT FROM THE MOMENT we started working together, Coach Ian got me doing regular 10-kilometre time trials. These are much more straightforward to explain than the lactate-things above: you go out and run a flat 10-kilometre course as fast as you possibly can. Don't be fooled by the simple explanation though. These things are horrible, even when you're already fit. And, if you haven't done any sort of speed training for five months, like me when I started training with Ian, they are on par with a kick in the balls. The pain is excruciating. When you run at a pace you can comfortably handle, the bottom half of your body hurts; when you run as fast as you can, everything hurts! Actually, when it comes to time trials, I find the top half of my body hurts even more than the bottom half. My lungs burn, my heart thumps so loud I can hear it inside my ears, my breathing becomes an intense pant much like a dog in the hot sun and I sweat to the point of being saturated.

On the day of my first time trial with Ian, I hadn't done any kind of speed training since the Chicago Marathon. I warned Ian that my time would be way slower than when I had last done one of these things.

'Your time doesn't really matter,' he said. 'I just want to get a gauge of where you are at in terms of fitness.'

He explained he'd use that information to make a start on a training programme for me, with a better idea of what sort of paces I could cope with. It all made a lot of sense . . . but that still didn't mean I was looking forward to it!

I drove out and parked my car on Auckland's Tamaki Drive. This is the waterfront road that the second half of the Auckland Marathon follows. It's the perfect place for a time trial, because it is flat with wide footpaths and no intersections, which means you don't have to stop or slow down for cars or people. Actually, make that the second most perfect place for a time trial; top of my list would be a steep downhill with a gale-force tail wind. That'd be a fair bit faster and easier . . . although not particularly helpful in getting a gauge of your actual fitness and speed.

The view of the ocean is spectacular all the way along

this road, and is only interrupted by Rangitoto, the volcanic island that pops out of the ocean. Oh, and the occasional cruise ship coming in to dock. These views are a nice treat for the dog walkers, rollerbladers and middle-agers out power-walking with their Nordic poles (what *are* those things for?), but when you are attempting to run 10 kilometres as fast as you can unfortunately even the most beautiful scenery goes unnoticed.

I FELT AMAZING . . . FOR THE FIRST KILOMETRE. SHORTLY AFTER THAT I REALISED I HAD GROSSLY OVERESTIMATED MY LEVEL OF FITNESS.

I felt amazing . . . for the first kilometre. Shortly after that I realised I had grossly overestimated my level of fitness. It's pretty fucking depressing when you start to feel horrible after only 3 or 4 kilometres on a 10-kilometre run. If you get your pacing right, the first half should be comfortably difficult; you don't really want to be feeling like you have to grit your teeth and dig deep until the last couple of kilometres. But, since I went out quicker than I was entitled to, I finished the first kilometre in four minutes, then got slower and slower as each kilometre ticked over. The final kilometre took 4 minutes 31 seconds, and my overall time was 43 minutes and a neat 4 seconds. Not bad I guess, but shit I had to work for it. Getting the pacing right is always the hardest part of a run of any distance that you are trying to do as fast as possible. Energy spent can never be given back.

That time trial proved a bit of a rude awakening. If I was to run the Berlin Marathon in under three hours, I would need to run faster than that *and* keep it up for an extra 32.2 kilometres. I'd felt like I was dragging a couple of cinder blocks behind me the whole way, and for the last few hundred metres it may as well have been a whole pallet of the bastards. In a marathon, you want to be still feeling fresh(ish) after 30 kilometres; if you feel rooted at the halfway point—or worse, earlier—you are in for a slow finish time and a second half that will be even more uncomfortable than finding your grandparents' sex tape.

After I'd finished, I sat on the grass berm to cool down for a minute or two, and finally got the chance to take in the scenery. This is when I feel most alive: immediately after a run. I tell people I love running, but I think the truth is that what I actually love is the feeling once I've stopped running. I peeled my sweat-soaked shirt off. It stuck to my torso like another layer of skin, and my shorts were in the same state. I'm not usually much of a sweater, but the heat of the sun combined with the faster pace had ensured no part of my body stayed dry. You could have wrung my clothing out and got a full glass of perspiration.

I untied my shoelace to remove the car key. When I drive to the starting point of a run (which is not all that often), I remove the one key I need from the bunch and tie it on to my shoe. That way it is safe and it also doesn't distract me while I'm running. I opened the car door.

'Awwwforfucksake!' I boomed—louder than I meant to. It was at such a volume that the father and son fishing on some rocks 50 metres away looked up. I gave them one of those apology waves—the sort you do when you know you've made a dick move while driving.

I had just realised that I had forgotten one very important thing: a towel to sit on.

I opened the boot in the hope there may be something in there—a plastic bag from the grocery store, an old windbreaker, a car-mat, anything really. Unfortunately, the car had been cleaned a few days earlier so there was nothing useful in it . . . apart from one of those sun-shade things that you put up in the windscreen on a hot day to keep the car's inside temperature down. There wasn't much for it. I lay this thing over the seat as best I could. It was not ideal, but it was a better option than an unpleasantly wet seat—not to mention the justified bollocking from my wife.

IT WOULD HAVE SEEMED MORE LIKE I WAS FLEEING AN ANGRY HUSBAND WHO HAD WALKED IN AND CAUGHT ME IN BED WITH HIS WIFE THAN A BLOKE TRAINING FOR A MARATHON.

In an effort to get myself as dry as possible, I stripped off my wet shorts and drove home in just the pair of tatty undies I had on underneath. The last time I drove as cautiously was probably when I was sitting my driver's licence. Nobody ever wants to be pulled over by the police, but if you do hear the phrase, 'Please step out of the vehicle', you kind of hope it won't be when you're soaking wet with sweat, sitting on a car sun shade, and wearing only a tatty old pair of Y-fronts. If I'd been forced to get out of the car now, it would have seemed more like I was fleeing an angry husband who had walked in and caught me in bed with his wife than a bloke training for a marathon.

PACING IS ONE OF the trickiest things to master across a run of any distance when you're trying to do it as fast as you can. The options for pacing yourself across a marathon are numerous. One way for me to break three hours would be by running every kilometre of the race at a consistent pace of 4:14 per kilometre. Another option would be to go faster for the first 20 or 30 kilometres, so that I build up a bit of a time buffer, then as my energy levels crumble and my speed deteriorates, hope like hell I can hold on and make it to the finish line in a good time.

Then there is the option of trying to run what is known as 'negative splits'. The term 'split' is used to describe when a race's total time is broken down into smaller parts, usually kilometres. So a negative-split marathon is where you run the second half of the marathon *faster* than the first half (as opposed to an 'even split', which is when you run the same pace the whole way). Doing this requires a remarkable amount of restraint and patience in the first 21.1 kilometres, because it means you have to force yourself to run at a pace that feels like you are jogging. Then, when you hit the second half, it is time to pick up the speed. This is way more difficult than it sounds, because even though you've been running at what feels like a jog you have still run a half bloody marathon! *And* you've got a whole other one left to go.

I have only ever run one marathon with a negative-split time, but that had more to do with luck than any sort of well-executed strategy. It was the 2011 Auckland Marathon, and even though it was nowhere near my fastest marathon time I would probably rate it as one of my best marathons simply because of how powerful and strong I felt at the finish.

My training for that marathon had been limited due to surgery I'd had to remove some torn cartilage from my knee three and a half months earlier. I'd battled on with a sore knee for over a year before getting it operated on. Even though running on it was uncomfortable, I'd gritted my teeth and tried to block out the pain—and in the process, gave myself a bunch of other injuries. So, on top of the fucked knee, I ended up with sore hips, shins, heels, and bruised and raw toes. I'd tried everything to fix the problem and avoid surgery: rest, aqua jogging, cycling, physio, acupuncture, herbal pills. The works. I was reluctant to go under the knife because once a piece of cartilage is removed that's it. It's gone forever, and it's not growing back. What if I couldn't run again afterwards? What would I do then? Invest in Lycra and find a cycling group to spend Saturday mornings with, riding seven abreast, before stopping at a café in clothes that should not be anywhere near food? No thanks.

Fortunately, the surgery was quick and easy, and three weeks later I was back out doing some light jogging again— but I was only running short distances because I was shit scared of buggering my knee. My only regret was not biting the bullet and getting it removed sooner.

At the time, my good friend Anna Hutchison had been training for the Auckland Marathon, and it was going to be her first-ever marathon. Three weeks before the marathon, I agreed to go out for a 30-kilometre jog with her. If I survived unscathed, I promised, I'd start the marathon with her. Even though it was less than three months after the operation, my knee was fine and I got though the long run sweet as. I even enjoyed it! It was liberating to be able to run again without any discomfort.

So I stood on the marathon start line with Anna as promised, and she and I set off at a comfortable pace. I planned to pull out halfway through if I was at all troubled by my knee. We got to the halfway mark in 1 hour 43 minutes. Since this was a little slower than my usual jogging pace, I still felt great. I wasn't a bit daunted by the prospect of running that distance all over again.

'You can run on ahead, if you want,' Anna urged me.

I *did* feel like it . . . but I hadn't been going to suggest it myself. We had one of those awkward exchanges where I said 'I couldn't possibly do that', but she insisted, so I asked if she was sure and she assured me she was sure she was sure. I was confident she would be fine for the second half of the race, so I lifted the pace a tiny bit and broke away—it wasn't a sprint, but more like a subtle gear change. I knew there was still a long distance to cover.

I made it to the finish line in 3 hours 18 minutes and I felt incredible. This meant I had run the second half of the race a full eight minutes quicker than the first. Without meaning to, I'd run negative splits, and I realised why it's a tactic that some runners swear by. It's incredible to finish still feeling good . . . or as good as you can feel after running that far! However, even if you plan to run negative splits, it is never a given that you will be able to do so; if it was, every single marathon runner would do it every time. The reality is that sometimes you go out at what you feel is a slow pace and *still* manage to run the second half even slower! That is the mystery of the marathon.

Anna, by the way, finished her first-ever marathon in an incredible 3 hours 39 minutes.

FINALLY, A CONCEPT THAT anyone who has trained for and run a marathon will be familiar with is that of 'tapering'. The taper period in your marathon training programme falls in the final few weeks before the marathon, and is when you slowly ease back on your training load so that any niggly injuries you may have will quieten down, and so that you arrive on the start line feeling fully relaxed, recharged and ready to blast through 42.2 kilometres.

As I approached the Berlin Marathon, my taper weeks looked something like this:

Monday: Sprints, 4-kilometre run at marathon race pace, more sprints.
Tuesday: 60-minute run at marathon race pace.
Wednesday: Leg workout at the gym.
Thursday: 40-minute run at marathon race pace.
Friday: Rest day.

To a non-runner, this probably still looks like a shit-load of running. But, when you have just logged almost four months of hard speed sessions and a few decent long runs, a week like this feels easy. (That leg workout on Wednesday did kick my arse a bit, though.)

The strange thing about the whole tapering-off period is all the extra time and energy you suddenly have on your hands. After months and months of constantly pushing yourself on hard and fast runs, it feels almost a bit lazy to suddenly be doing next to nothing (or what, by comparison to the rest of your training, seems like next to nothing). This is not to deny that it is still bloody nice to reach the point where you have all the hard shit out of the way—besides the marathon itself, of course.

CHAPTER 9
MARATHON FEVER

ANY STORY THAT STARTS with a middle-aged rubbish collector in his underwear and a fourteen-year-old boy is always going to sound a little dodgy. But, believe it or not, that is an accurate description of my very first full marathon—and, thankfully, it is all completely innocent and harmless.

The fourteen-year-old boy was me and the event was the Whanganui Marathon in 1987. The middle-aged bloke in his undies was Mike Stewart, a 35-year-old rubbish-truck driver from Naenae in Lower Hutt who became famous in New Zealand running circles as the guy who ran in his undies. Mike still runs. He is now in his sixties and has run over 500 marathons—a Southern Hemisphere record, no less. As a matter of fact, he did his five-hundredth marathon wearing pink Speedos.

The details of that day in '87 could not be replicated here in New Zealand today. Sure, a man can still run in his undies if he so chooses, but there is no way race organisers would let a kid as young as I was participate. Fourteen might sound alarmingly young for someone to cover the formidable distance of 42.2 kilometres, but it is nothing compared to the world's youngest marathon runner. That title goes to a young Indian boy, Budhia Singh, who was born in 2002. By the age of four he had run and completed over 50 marathons. That's not a typo—he was FOUR, and he had run 50 marathons.

IN SOME WAYS, I FEEL A LITTLE RIPPED OFF ABOUT MY FIRST MARATHON NOW, SIMPLY BECAUSE IT CAME A BIT TOO EASY.

In some ways, I feel a little ripped off about my first marathon now, simply because it came a bit too easy. These days, I will often see grown men and women crying tears of happiness when they finally cross the finish line, awash with endorphins and overwhelmed by the epiphany that if they can conquer a marathon then they can probably do anything they put their mind to. That's the power of the marathon: the glory of completing one—especially your first one—brings with it such a strong sense of personal satisfaction. But I never had that. It was probably partly because of my young age, and partly because it had never occurred to me that it was a big deal since I was raised in a running household. When you are a fourteen-year-old who thinks you know everything, and definitely more than your parents, you automatically believe that if they can do a marathon then you definitely can too.

I ran my first marathon in just under four hours. The course happened to be four laps of just over 10 kilometres each of what is one of New Zealand's more boring cities. Four laps! It was like a long-distance running version of the old Bill Murray movie *Groundhog Day*. Whanganui also happens to be the city where, in 1962, Peter Snell set a new world record for running the mile in 3 minutes 54.4 seconds. He must have been running to find the next town!

I don't recall following a training programme or doing anything too special to train for this marathon. This was when I was still in the Harriers team at high school, and we always went out for a long, hilly run of around 20 kilometres every Saturday, so I kind of coasted on that. I guess I just assumed I would be able to make it.

On that day I learned that a marathon requires two important things: fitness and mental toughness. What I lacked in these attributes was made up for by my unlikely running companion, Mike 'Undie Man' Stewart. I had seen him around before at other marathons that Mum was running in. Adults probably saw this wiry guy with his rickety teeth and longish hair running in nothing but a singlet and undies and thought he was a couple of cans short of a six pack. But, from a kid's perspective, he always seemed like a cool adult, a grown-up who never properly grew up.

Our paths crossed at one point during the run, and he took me under his wing, guiding me through the tough stages. Even though he was definitely capable of going faster, he ran with me, encouraged me, talked to me and told me stories to keep my mind off the pain. He also kept a constant eye on his watch to make sure that we would both finish under four hours. Mike Stewart has run 500 of the damn things and has probably helped hundreds of less experienced runners, so I doubt he would even remember me and the Whanganui Marathon of 1987—but I sure as hell do. It is not something I'll ever forget.

One of the stories that Mike told me was probably a little bleaker than it needed to be. But he told it with such detail that it helped to pass enough time for us to run maybe 2 kilometres in the later stages of the race. I'll try to recount it briefly, using just a tiny portion of the colour he put into it.

This is a story about boy called Dominic, who was in hospital with a broken leg. There was another boy in the same ward, who was there to have some tests because he had been suffering from severe migraines. This was a two-bed hospital ward, and the headache kid had the bed closest to the window.

(Why a kid with a fracture was being kept in for a long-term stay instead of just getting sent off with some crutches was not a plot point I questioned. I was fourteen and exhausted.)

Every day, headache boy would tell Dom what was going on outside the window.

(This is the part of the story where Undie Man really made it his own. His descriptions of what was going on outside the hospital window was the stuff fantasies are made of.)

There was a big park right outside this hospital window, and there was always something incredible going on. One day, there was a big skateboard ramp and a ring of fire that a stuntman was riding his board through. The next day, there were jetskis on the lake. One afternoon, John Kirwan was out there playing touch rugby with some kids. Another day, the Pet Shop Boys were playing a free concert in the park.

(This may not sound like such a drawcard now, but in 1987 those guys would have been quite the crowd-puller.)

Then, one night, Dominic was woken from his sleep. Something was wrong with the headache boy. The machines he was hooked up to were all beeping and making noises, but nobody from the nurses' station came to see what was going on. Dominic asked his mate if he was OK and didn't get a response. Just as he was about to get out of his bed and hop around the ward to try to find a doctor or nurse to help, he had a change of heart.

(And this is the part of the story where things get a little bit dark . . .)

Dominic rolled over and went back to sleep. In the morning, he woke up to find the bed next to the window empty and the nurses standing around him.

'We have some bad news,' they said. 'During the night, your friend tragically died. He had a brain aneurysm. That's what was causing his headaches. Unfortunately, it took his life before we were able to find it.'

(So I was effectively a murderer in this story? All of a sudden, my sore shins and knees were the least of my concerns!)

The nurses, assuming Dominic would be grieving the death of his young mate, asked him if there was anything at all they could do for him.

'Well, since that bed next to the window is now free . . .' Dominic said. 'Can I have it?'

SO I WAS EFFECTIVELY A MURDERER IN THIS STORY? ALL OF A SUDDEN, MY SORE SHINS AND KNEES WERE THE LEAST OF MY CONCERNS!

(Ahhh, so that was my motive in this hypothetical situation. I let another kid die just because I wanted the bed with the awesome view over the park? Wow. I was a piece of shit. I know Undie Man's intention was to try to pass the time and get me through a mentally difficult stage of the run, but surely a selection of knock-knock jokes or a game of I-spy would have done the job too.)

Immediately young Dominic was moved to the empty bed next to the window. He was feeling pretty pleased with himself. Now he could see what was going on down at the big park with his own two eyes. He asked the nurses for some extra pillows so he could prop himself up for a better view. And that's when he learned the truth.

(And here it is. I bet you can't guess . . .)

There was no park or lake.

All that could be seen out of the window was a dingy alleyway and a big brick wall.

It was certainly thought-provoking, even if I wasn't quite sure what relevance it had to our current situation. And I still can't understand why he had to call the story's villain Dominic. Something generic like Little Johnny would have sat far more comfortably with me.

Mike and I crossed the finish line together at 3 hours and 58 minutes—a time many marathon runners will spend their whole life chasing. As we ran into the finishers' area, the race MC announced over the loudspeaker that the youngest competitor had just finished.

And that was my first full marathon done. No epiphany. No tears of ecstasy. Easy come; easy go.

There was a little bit of applause from the small crowd that was gathered, mostly family and friends. We stayed for the prize-giving, then went home empty-handed, but we weren't too sad about that. It seemed like the only sponsors they were ever able to get on board at these regional runs during the 1980s were Kambrook and Sunbeam, and there are only so many cheese fondue sets a family needs. Occasionally there might have been a travel prize up for grabs, like an Ansett Mystery Weekend to somewhere mysterious like Rotorua or Blenheim. But usually it was just blenders, multi-cookers and cheese fondue sets.

The next morning, I got out of bed hobbling. This is to be

expected with any marathon, and the severity of the hobbling varies from race to race: you could find yourself walking slightly oddly, like you have a sharp piece of gravel in your shoe, or you could be in so much pain that the only way you can tackle a flight of stairs is to walk down them backwards. Seriously! Go to any hotel in New York the morning after the marathon and you will see a collection of ridiculously fit people all walking more awkwardly than the oldest residents at a rest home.

I asked Mum and Dad if they could give me a ride to school on account of my sore legs. Mum told me that riding my bike the 5 kilometres to school would be just what I needed to loosen up my legs.

'Plus,' she added, 'it isn't raining that hard anyway.'

So I got on my bike and gingerly started pedalling. A few minutes later, my parents gave me an encouraging toot as they drove past. I always thought I'd run another marathon after that. I just had no idea that there would be 21 years between finishing my first marathon and lining up for my second.

MUM TOLD ME THAT RIDING MY BIKE THE 5 KILOMETRES TO SCHOOL WOULD BE JUST WHAT I NEEDED TO LOOSEN UP MY LEGS.

MY 'COMEBACK' MARATHON OVER two decades later was on Australia's Gold Coast in 2005. Mum was living in Goldie at the time and was training for the marathon, so I thought I would join her. Deep down it was quite a profound moment for me, simply because of how far I had come personally. Three years earlier, Jay-Jay and I had celebrated our engagement. Mum had left our party early because she had been running the Auckland Marathon the following morning, but by the time I stumbled out of the nightclub and on to the street it was daylight, birds were chirping and my taxi home drove me past groups of marathon runners. A horrible feeling of guilt and fear had washed over me then—guilt because I'd stayed out the entire night and would now spend all of Sunday in bed, and fear because I knew the imminent hangover would be unpleasant . . . and potentially last until Tuesday.

Now here I was three years on from that, a 32-year-old reformed fatty feeling great about myself and my health, standing at the start line of a marathon with my mum. We both agreed we would run at our own pace. Mum was way fitter than I was and had done a lot more running, but part of me thought we would be a similar pace—she was a tiny 54-year-old woman, after all! I had prepared for the marathon by following my own fairly basic programme, which looked a lot like this:

Monday: 8–10-kilometre run.
Wednesday: 15-kilometre run.
Thursday: 8–10-kilometre run.
Saturday: Long run, typically around 20 kilometres but reaching 32 kilometres a couple of weeks before the event.

I was expecting the marathon to be a piece of piss. I mean, I'd run one when I was fourteen and I'd done even less training than that. How hard could it be?

Turns out the answer was pretty bloody hard.

I got to the halfway mark in 1 hour 45 minutes, which means I was averaging a pace of 5:00 minutes per kilometre. In theory, this meant I was on track for a 3 hour 30 minute marathon . . . but I already knew it was not going to be possible for me to maintain my pace for another 21 kilometres. I also knew I was not even going to be able to *run* for another 21 kilometres. I had gone out too fast and I was going to pay dearly for it.

I 'treated' myself to my first walk at the 25-kilometre sign. The remainder of the run was gruesome and humiliating. I was a contorted and crampy mess, reduced to a hobble in between short spells of running. For me, cramp always tends to creep in when my muscles have had enough for the day; it's their way of flipping me the bird and going on strike. At one point during the Gold Coast Marathon, I was in so much pain that I had a course marshal and two lovely spectators sitting on me on the grass berm, massaging and stretching out my muscles while I screamed in agony.

BY THIS TIME, I DIDN'T GIVE A RAT'S ARSE HOW RIDICULOUS I LOOKED. I WOULD HAVE DONE ANYTHING TO KEEP THAT CRAMP AT BAY.

If you have never experienced bad cramp, count yourself lucky. It is horrible! No part of my body was exempt: I would get it in the left side of my neck, so I would tilt my neck to the right and it would just transfer to my right side. I did what I could to keep it at bay—at one point in the final kilometres I was running with both arms outstretched so I looked like a human aeroplane. By this time, I didn't give a rat's arse how ridiculous I looked. I would have done anything to keep that cramp at bay.

I shuffled into the finish chute in a time of 3 hours 53 minutes, and my 54-year-old mum was already there to cheer me on. She had finished half an hour earlier, in 3 hours 24 minutes. Mum didn't gloat about kicking my arse, though.

Looking back, I reckon she deserved to—what she achieved was pretty damn impressive. Not only did she thrash her adult son, but she did it by running a super-impressive time in her mid-fifties.

I was in agony, but I was elated. I had finished! *And* I had beaten my fourteen-year-old self by five whole minutes. It had not been pretty, but it was still a new personal best. (What's more, I didn't know it at the time, but I was already running around with a fairly sizable tumour in my stomach region.)

The biggest lesson I learned from that comeback marathon was probably respect. Unfortunately, though, I am a bit of a slow learner, so it still would take me a few more marathons before I fully gave the marathon the respect it deserves.

WE TALK ABOUT A marathon being 42.2 kilometres, but in actual fact it is the strangely precise distance of 42.195 kilometres. Nothing shorter; nothing longer. Always 42 kilometres with an extra 195 metres tagged on for good measure. The story goes that for the 1908 Olympic Marathon in London the distance was going to be about 40 kilometres, but the organisers decided the course needed to start at Windsor Castle and finish on the track right in front of the Royal Box. So millions of marathon runners every year have the royal family to thank for having to run that bizarre and frustrating extra little bit of road.

I have to come out right now and make something clear: a half marathon is *not* a marathon. Nor is the 10-kilometre fun run held on the same day. Don't get me wrong: a half marathon and a 10-kilometre race are both admirable achievements, and huge milestones for lots of runners, but—I just have to say it one more time—they are not a marathon!

If you want to really piss a marathon runner off, referring to a half marathon as 'a marathon' is the way to do it. I can assure you that someone claiming they did a marathon when they actually only did the *half* marathon bugs marathon runners like you wouldn't believe. To us, it's like a cricket player getting out for 50 then going around telling everyone he scored a century. I know, I know—we runners are a bit of a precious bunch. But when you have spent months slogging your guts out, making sacrifices and putting whole chunks of your life on hold so that you can get out there and conquer the almighty distance of 42.195 kilometres, you deserve to be a little bit defensive. You earned it.

One of the aspects of a marathon that sets it apart from any of the shorter-distance events is this: a marathon is not a distance you can bluff your way through. If you're pretty healthy and have a basic level of fitness, you make your way through a 10-kilometre run without too much drama; and, with just a little bit of training, most people are able to make their way around a half-marathon course. But a full marathon? That is a different beast altogether. Training for a full marathon demands months of dedication and hard work. It requires training runs that reach distances of 30 kilometres and longer. You get out what you put in, when it comes to a marathon. The better you prepare, the more enjoyable it will be for you. If you shirk your training, you do it at your own peril because it could just end up being one of the most unpleasant and torturous days of your life. And, actually, even if you are really well prepared, a marathon can *still* be one of the worst days of your life! When I did the Auckland Marathon in 2010, I'd trained well but my ego got the better of me and I went out too fast at the start. I felt like such an idiot! I knew I was going faster than I should but I felt so good. By the halfway mark, though, I felt drained and like death—and I still had 21 kilometres ahead of me. I managed to finish the run in 3 hours 39 minutes, but I have never been in more pain. I was still hobbling around four days later.

That brings us back to the respect thing I mentioned earlier. You need to respect the marathon distance or it will punish you. I thought I had trained hard enough. I hadn't, and the Auckland roads let me know it that day.

But the truly magical thing about a marathon—the reason so many of us keep on coming back for more—is how you feel when you cross that finish line. It doesn't matter whether you are smiling or crying, in a state of euphoria or agony: finishing a marathon is an incredibly powerful feeling of accomplishment and self-satisfaction. You feel, in that moment, like the impossible is possible.

BUT THE TRULY MAGICAL THING ABOUT A MARATHON—THE REASON SO MANY OF US KEEP ON COMING BACK FOR MORE—IS HOW YOU FEEL WHEN YOU CROSS THAT FINISH LINE.

TWENTY-SOMETHING YEARS AFTER WE had left high school and drifted apart, my old Harriers mate Matt Cherri and I reconnected on Facebook. He was living in Sydney and, much like me, after taking an extended break from running he was back into it again. He too was tackling the marathon distance and, through sheer coincidence, the two of us had both signed up to run the 2015 Chicago Marathon. What's more, we were both hoping to run it at around the same pace: somewhere under 3 hours 15 minutes. I couldn't believe it!

Over Facebook Messenger, we made plans to catch up for a beer after the race, but I wondered if I might see Matt at the start line. Even though almost 40,000 runners were taking part that year, I figured we'd be in the same starting corral, since we were aiming for the same time. I kept an eye out for my old mate, and even though I didn't spot him, searching for him turned out to be a good way to keep my mind occupied for the 40 minutes I spent standing around in a pen with other runners, waiting for the gun to go off. It makes for some fascinating people-watching. Thousands of other runners as far as the eye can see, and so many different pre-race rituals: runners stretching or jogging on the spot, meditating, sucking back gels or eating bananas, people studying the splits written up their wrist in permanent marker, and even that lady squatting for a nervous wee in the gutter!

I messaged Matt later on that afternoon, and we caught up over a couple of well-earned drinks. It was quite surreal— two old best mates, both from fairly humble beginnings in a sleepy New Zealand town, catching up on two decades of life in a bar in Chicago. The last time we had seen each other, we had been kids, just setting off on our paths in the world. Now we were men. We were different, but still the same. And we were both in a great mood. We had both run personal best times that day, both well under the 3 hours 15 minutes we had been hoping for. Matt finished in 3 hours 8 minutes, and I came in at 3 hours 10 minutes. Matt finished in place 1497, and I was number 1732, a total of 235 places behind. That sounds like a lot of people . . . until you remind yourself that the total field consisted of 37,436 runners. That's half the entire population of Palmerston North, right there, running a marathon.

I got to meet Matt's girlfriend, Jo Telfer. When I mentioned I worked in radio, she said that I might know her dad, the veteran New Zealand sports broadcaster Brendon Telfer. In an incredible twist of fate, I had actually met Brendon just a couple of months prior. We had happened to be in a lift at the same time and had shared a bit of banter about running. He had mentioned he used to run marathons when he was younger and retired with a personal best marathon time of 2 hours 47 minutes. I mentioned this to Jo, and she and Matt both burst out laughing.

'I don't get it,' I said. 'What's the joke?'

'Dad's best marathon time seems to get faster every time he tells someone!' Jo replied.

After you have finished a marathon—regardless of how long it took you—you feel like a champion. As I mentioned, this feeling of euphoria wasn't something I experienced with my first marathon as a teenager, but with every marathon I have been fortunate enough to complete as an adult since, I have most definitely felt it. There is probably some scientific reason for this elated feeling, like an endorphin rush or something, but whatever it is, it's amazing. You just feel as though anything you put your mind to in life, you can achieve. That's how I felt after Chicago. It's a kind of pay-off for all that hard work you put in, for sure, and I reckon it's also a huge part of why these events get so many participants. The majority of us are not there to win or even to finish anywhere near the front. We are there chasing ourselves and our previous achievements, trying to be better than we were the day before. It's not about being the best; it's about being the best you can be . . . and getting that finisher's medal at the end!

THE BOSTON MARATHON IS the oldest and most prestigious marathon in the world. It was first run in April 1897, inspired by the revival of the marathon for the 1896 Summer Olympics in Athens. It also happens to be something of a Holy Grail for marathon runners, because not just any old weekend warrior can enter. Oh no, you have to *qualify* for the Boston Marathon, and that is just the first of a number of hoops that you have to jump through before you can take to the start line with the world's best in the tiny town of Hopkinton, Massachusetts.

Hoop number one: you need to run a full marathon under a certain time for your age bracket in an approved Boston-qualifier event the year before you want to run Boston— which is a really long-winded way of saying you need to be able to prove that you can run a marathon faster than most other punters your age. At the time of writing, there are only three marathons in New Zealand where you can qualify for Boston: Auckland, Rotorua and Christchurch. Following are the times you need to run for each age bracket.

BOSTON QUALIFYING STANDARDS

AGE	MEN	WOMEN
18–34	3 hours 05 minutes	3 hours 35 minutes
35–39	3 hours 10 minutes	3 hours 40 minutes
40–44	3 hours 15 minutes	3 hours 45 minutes
45–49	3 hours 25 minutes	3 hours 55 minutes
50–54	3 hours 30 minutes	4 hours 00 minutes
55–59	3 hours 40 minutes	4 hours 10 minutes
60–64	3 hours 55 minutes	4 hours 25 minutes
65–69	4 hours 10 minutes	4 hours 40 minutes
70–74	4 hours 25 minutes	4 hours 55 minutes
75–79	4 hours 40 minutes	5 hours 10 minutes
80 and over	4 hours 55 minutes	5 hours 25 minutes

Then, if you do manage to run your qualifier in the appropriate time, you still have to get online the moment registration for the Boston Marathon opens so that you can fight other mentally deranged runners from around the world to buy one of the limited places.

Why? you might well be wondering. *Why go to all that bother?*

Well, the answer to that probably depends on who you ask, but for me the attraction is the need to qualify and the effort required to get there. You have to *earn* your spot in the field, and that makes an ordinary runner like me feel special, like I have achieved something worthwhile.

I DID SOME RESEARCH ONLINE THAT EVENING AND BY THE TIME I WENT TO BED I HAD MY HEART SET ON BOSTON.

Like most people—runners and non-runners alike—I was aware of how special the New York and London marathons are, but Boston and the prestige of it wasn't even on my radar until after I completed the Auckland Marathon at the end of 2009 in 3 hours 19 minutes, which was a new personal best for me. As I was hobbling back to my car afterwards, I bumped into my mate Gaz Brown. When I told him my time, he seemed impressed and said it might be quick enough to qualify for Boston. Bear in mind that I still didn't really think of myself as your typical runner in this era; this was still years before I became the running nerd I am today. But the thought of maybe being good enough to actually qualify for an event sounded pretty good.

I did some research online that evening and by the time I went to bed I had my heart set on Boston. Sometimes after completing a marathon the last thing you want to think about is running another one, but here I was, limping around the house, already dreaming of my next one.

Sadly, Gaz was wrong about my time. I was 36 and the Boston qualifier time for 35- to 39-year-old men was 3 hours 15 minutes (and they have made it even faster since then!). I had run the race of my life and was still four minutes too slow for Boston. I was gutted. That was the moment that getting to Boston became an all-out obsession. I think it was the challenge that appealed to me. I signed up for the Christchurch Marathon in 2010 and I trained even harder than I had done for Auckland, using a free programme I had found online. And I did it! I ran a qualifying time for Boston and set a brand-new PB in the process: 3 hours 14 minutes 34 seconds. I had a whole 26 seconds to spare. I was elated.

With hoop number one successfully jumped through, I turned my attentions to registering. Entries opened at 9 am in Boston on 18 October 2010—which translated to a painfully early 2 am here in New Zealand. Reminding myself that nothing about the road to Boston is easy, I hauled myself out of bed and sat in front of the computer in the dimly lit office, wearing nothing more than my undies, and filled out the exhaustive entry information. Honestly, there was more paperwork to get into Boston than there is when you have to replace your passport! By 2.12 am I had finally typed in all the information the Boston Athletics Association apparently needed—the most important bits being my qualifying time and my credit card details.

I clicked ENTER.

That irritating little hourglass came up on the screen . . .

Then nothing.

I started again, re-typing all that information.

Once again, I clicked ENTER.

Once again that fucking annoying little hourglass popped up . . .

And, once again, nothing.

Assuming the page was just overloaded with other desperate runners, I kept trying. I gave myself until 3 am before I would drag myself back to bed; I had to get up again at 4.30 am for work, so I needed to be realisitc about it. When the clock reached 3 am, I still had no entry.

I went back to bed, but I was unable to sleep. I was too wired. I was furious, mad, sad—a whole range of emotions. It just all seemed so unfair. Often it's not until you can't have something that you find out just how much you really wanted it.

Later in the morning when I was at work, around eight, I decided to give it just one more try. This time it worked first pop. I was in! Moments later I got a confirmation email: I had been accepted to compete in the 2011 Boston Marathon.

The next day *The Boston Globe* ran a story about how the 30,000 available places had been filled in a record-breaking eight hours and three minutes. I was one of the lucky ones.

This may be difficult for non-runners to understand, but there are some runners out there who end up depressed, insane or divorced in their quest to qualify for Boston. When I got to Boston and had a chance to chat to some of the other runners from around the world at the race expo the day before the event, I realised just how much this run means to some people. I met one fella who had driven around the USA for the better part of 2008, taking part in qualifying races until he finally cracked the time he needed, only to then be unsuccessful in securing a spot in the field for the following year. So he did the same thing again in 2009, but didn't manage to meet his qualifying time—in one of his qualifier runs, he missed by eight stupid seconds. In 2010 he was finally successful: he ran a qualifying time in an approved marathon and at last managed to secure a spot in the 2011 Boston field. For many, like this guy, Boston becomes more than just a run; it becomes a beast that consumes them.

FOR MANY, LIKE THIS GUY, BOSTON BECOMES MORE THAN JUST A RUN; IT BECOMES A BEAST THAT CONSUMES THEM.

RUNNING THE BOSTON MARATHON was a feeling unlike any I had ever experienced in a run before. This is probably going to sound really lame, but I truly felt like a champion. From the moment we touched down in Boston, I felt like I was part of something special—there were signs at the baggage carousels in the airport welcoming runners to town for the marathon, and 500 banners hung up all around the city showcasing the event and some of the previous winners from the event's 114-year history, including New Zealand's own Allison Roe, who won it way back in 1981. Over three decades after her win, these banners still flap in the breeze and she remains ageless. In this part of the United States, she will always be that 25-year-old from little old New Zealand wearing white gloves and a Pan Am singlet with a silver fern on the front who won the world's greatest marathon. Of course, she went on to win New York later that same year, just to add an exclamation mark to her awesomeness. She is quite well known in New Zealand, but in Boston she has rock-star status. I wouldn't be surprised if she could go into any bar there and drink free Samuel Adams beers for the rest of her life!

Seeing the effort the whole city had gone to made me

realise exactly how important this event is, not just for the runners but for the people of Boston as well. If you are in the city during marathon week and have an accent, a runner's build or are wearing active wear, the locals will ask if you are there for the marathon and wish you luck if you are. The city wholeheartedly embraces this event, which is held on Patriots Day, a state holiday held on the third Monday in April in Massachusetts and Maine.

This was, of course, two years before the tragic bombing of 2013. Jay-Jay and I would later watch those ghastly events unfold on TV and feel our hearts break. These things seem to numb you so much more when you are familiar with the area. The two bombs went off in Boylston Street, the final straight before the finish line of the marathon. We had walked along there dozens of times. Three people lost their lives and the bombs injured 260 others. Most of the victims were spectators. Just awful.

BOSTON WAS THE FIRST OF THE WORLD MARATHON MAJORS I WAS LUCKY ENOUGH TO RUN, AND IT WAS A BLOODY STEEP LEARNING CURVE.

For an estimated one million Boston locals each year, the marathon is an occasion they get out and support whether they know someone running or not. They stand out there cheering on strangers for hours. Some make signs, some hand out sweets or fruit, and some blast motivational music from speakers.

When I ran Boston, I was humbled by the supporters. I'm sure I speak on behalf of anyone who has ever run a marathon when I say that the runners respect the supporters for coming out to cheer as much as the supporters respect them for running. The support really does make the day a bit easier.

Boston was the first of the World Marathon Majors I was lucky enough to run, and it was a bloody steep learning curve. I knew it would be cold and I knew there would be some downtime in the athletes' village in the grounds of Hopkinton High School before the starter's gun went off, but what totally blindsided me was just how fucking cold it was and how long the wait was before the run. I was wearing an old hoodie, a beanie and a pair of gloves, and I was *still* shivering. In the end, I found a black bin liner in a 44-gallon drum that was fairly clean . . . so I emptied it and used it as a makeshift sleeping bag for extra warmth. It stopped the shivering, but I was still uncomfortably cold for the two hours I had to wait before we were allowed to make our way to the starting area. I've since learned that this is the case with all of the World Marathon Majors: the long wait, often in the cold, means that patience is almost as important as being physically fit!

This is in stark contrast to some smaller runs I have done in New Zealand. In 2016, I ran the first-ever Hawke's Bay Marathon. The run starts in Napier and weaves its way through country roads, riverbanks and vineyards, before finishing in a winery. As luck would have it, my motel was right on the road next to the start line, which meant I didn't have to wait in line to use the Port-A-Loos. When the MC announced that it was five minutes until the start, I was still sitting on my balcony doing some stretches!

The highlight of Boston for me came just before the halfway point, at the 20-kilometre mark of the run, when you enter what is known as 'the scream tunnel'. You hear a high-pitched tone as you approach—a loud but distant squealing noise. It's a lot like the noise a jet engine makes. You soon realise that the source of this sound is the young women of Wellesley College, a posh female university with a roll of 2400 students. It has been a tradition for decades that Wellesley students line the roadside and scream for the runners, while offering up hugs and kisses! I saw signs proclaiming, among other things, 'Kiss me, I'm half Asian!', 'Kiss me, I'm single!', 'Kiss me, I'm from Lithuania!' and 'I majored in kissing!'

I did slow down to a jog to enjoy the atmosphere as I ran through the scream tunnel, but I didn't stop for any kisses. It would have been an act of cruelty to these poor young women. I had been running for just over an hour and a half by that stage. I was sweaty, there was a Gatorade stain on my singlet from an earlier drink station, I had my own saliva on my face from when I had spat and the wind caught it, and there was dry snot under my nose. It was very charitable of these young women to offer me their lip-service, but I could not be so mean.

Boston was also the first time I had run a marathon where I was never alone. Even in the big New Zealand marathons like Rotorua and Auckland, it is entirely possible that you will spend at least part of the race running on your own. There could even be occasions where you can't see any other runners in front of or behind you. In Boston, there were runners surrounding me every step of the way. It is quite hypnotic when, at the start of the race, the gun goes off and all the nervous chatter, laughing and breathing is suddenly replaced with the sound of a human stampede as thousands of pairs of rubber soles slap against the road. Before Boston, the biggest marathon field I had ever run in was the Gold Coast Marathon, which attracts around 5000 runners for the full marathon (and many thousands more for the shorter distances). To go from an event with 5000 runners to one the

1982

THE FEILDING TO PALMERSTON NORTH

FUN RUN

This is to certify that ....D. HARVEY........ 339TH. PLACE..

has completed the run between Feilding and Palmerston North

in the time of........1.30.47............

THE
GUARDIAN
NEWSPAPER

In association with the
Palmerston North Harriers club

signed

K· Palmer

MARCH 1985

3 SUNDAY — 2nd Sunday in Lent

completed the half marathon with sour legs'n 2.12 also. come 444 out of 160 we went to church today

4 MONDAY

ooch my legs were killing today I missed out on pe I also finished my project and watched my ride and it was grouse!

TOP: My finisher's certificate from the 18-kilometre Feilding to Palmerston North run that my parents *let* me do . . . in bare feet . . . when I was nine.

BOTTOM LEFT: The diary entry I wrote in 1985 when I was twelve and ran my first-ever half marathon.

BOTTOM RIGHT: Running my first half marathon at the age of twelve. My giant teeth finished a couple of minutes ahead of me.

TOP: The 1986 Palmerston North Boys' High School Harriers squad. I'm standing right next to the school's most feared P.E. teacher, Mr Wigglesworth. He's the one in the snug-fitting trackpants. Peter 'Sport' Jowett is the old bloke on the right, and my best mate, Matt Cherri, is on the chair right in front of him.

BOTTOM LEFT: With Mike 'Undie Man' Stewart after I finished my first full marathon in Whanganui at the age of fourteen. Mike ran most of the way with me. He still runs to this day, and has now done over 500 marathons—always in Speedos!

BOTTOM RIGHT: All dressed up in my Palmerston North Boys' High suit for the New Zealand Secondary Schools road race which, no doubt, I did terribly in. Must have been a proud moment for Mum to pull the camera out and take a picture, though!

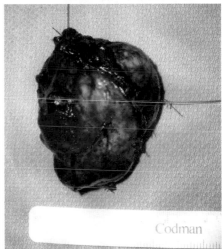

TOP LEFT: My comeback marathon! On the Gold Coast in 2005, eighteen years after my first marathon.

TOP RIGHT: Mum running in 1986 when she was 35. Fast forward three decades and she is still running . . . but her hair and stride have both got shorter.

BOTTOM LEFT: The fat years. It was around the time this photo was taken that I realised I had to do something about my weight. I was starting to look like a giant thumb.

BOTTOM RIGHT: The bad-ass tumour that just about killed me. It was only discovered thanks to running.

TOP: With Jay-Jay at the finish line of the 2007 Auckland Marathon. Jay-Jay ran the half marathon and I ran the full, and we were both equally stoked!

RIGHT: Helping pace my friend Anna Hutchison round her first-ever marathon in Auckland in 2011. She looks happy . . . but she is a very good actress!

TOP: Finishing the 2008 Auckland Marathon. Great photo, but what you can't see is my leg cramping up when I land. From cool to fool in under a second.

LEFT: Running over Tower Bridge during the London Marathon. Look closely and you can see a man dressed as a giant water bottle chasing me.

ABOVE: The New York Marathon—before, during and after.

TOP: My sweaty under-pants on someone else's hotel-room balcony in Hawaii. They were hanging out to dry when a gust of wind must have blown them down there. FML!

MIDDLE: Mum and me at the race expo before the Chicago Marathon.

BOTTOM LEFT: Mum walking around in the LA heat after the Chicago Marathon, proudly wearing the makeshift sweatband she fashioned from toilet paper.

BOTTOM RIGHT: My post-run ritual at home. I lie down while my little Sydney silky terrier, Kanye, helps himself to my perspiration. Yuck.

TOP: My pre-race ritual. This is what my hotel bed looks like the day before I do a marathon: I have everything laid out meticulously. Any little trick to help me sleep better the night before the run.

BOTTOM LEFT: Just through the Brandenburg Gate and seconds away from finishing the Berlin Marathon. I had barely enough energy left to give the photographer a thumbs-up.

BOTTOM RIGHT: Job done! Posing in front of the Brandenburg Gate a few hours later, while some pissed-off spectator walks by.

scale of Boston with around 30,000 was mind-blowing.

I finished Boston in 3 hours 22 minutes—seven minutes slower than my qualifying time. But I was too elated to be worried about my finish time. At that moment, I was no longer just a Boston qualifier or a Boston entrant; I was a Boston finisher.

Sometimes after a runner finishes a marathon they swear that they will never, ever do another one again, and if they're in pain or disappointed with their performance they might find themselves wondering if it was even worth it. Even though my time was nowhere close to being a personal best, I never had any of those negative feelings after Boston. It was such an incredible experience that I immediately decided I wanted that same feeling again. I was completely intoxicated by the camaraderie of the other runners, the cheers from the crowd and the respect that the Boston medal gets you when you walk around town with it round your neck.

I WAS COMPLETELY INTOXICATED BY THE CAMARADERIE OF THE OTHER RUNNERS, THE CHEERS FROM THE CROWD AND THE RESPECT THAT THE BOSTON MEDAL GETS YOU ...

It was from the official race programme that I learned about this series known as the World Marathon Majors—basically the world's 'big six' marathon events, of which Boston was one. So, the morning after finishing the Boston Marathon, I set my ridiculously expensive and time-consuming goal (you might even call it an obsession): I was going to run all of the World Marathon Majors. I wanted that feeling I'd had in Boston. I wanted it again. And again. And again . . .

CHAPTER 10
THE MAJOR BUZZ

THE WORLD MARATHON MAJORS are six of the largest and most renowned marathons in the world. Most people could probably guess that London and New York are in the mix; the other four are Boston, Chicago, Berlin and Tokyo. While most of these runs have been around for a long time, the World Marathon Majors themselves only started in 2006. They are known as the majors because they attract the world's absolute best marathon runners and offer huge cash rewards for the winners—but the prizes are of no concern to the 99.9 per cent of us who have no chance of winning. People like me are there for the finisher's medal and the satisfaction that comes from taking part in such incredible, huge events. Also, have I mentioned how much I like running when I'm overseas? Well, there is something very satisfying about running a marathon in a different country, then throwing in a holiday afterwards.

French fries, pizza and burgers taste so much better when you feel like you have earned them.

In 2016, a bonus was added for any runner who successfully completes all six of the majors: a Six Star Finisher medal and personalised certificate listing your finishing times. It might just be the most exclusive prize in marathon running. While I was in Berlin, I met Vanessa Oshima, who was on her way to becoming the first New Zealand woman to tick off all six of the majors, and at the time of writing this book only five New Zealand men have done it. The Six Star Finisher medal represents massive commitment, effort, sacrifice and cost on the part of the holder—but I don't think a price could be put on the memories anybody lucky enough to have earned one must have. I am already dreaming about the day I walk into my lounge and see my own Six Star Finisher medal framed and mounted on the wall . . .

As with any marathon, every runner's experience in the majors events will be completely different. It is such an individual thing. The winners finish these races in just over two hours, which I imagine means they are running too fast to take in the sights, sounds and smells from the course. Their focus is on breaking world records, winning races and earning large sums of prize money, rather than soaking up the experience. It's a reasonable trade-off, I guess. They may not notice the little kids holding their hands out to high-five sweaty strangers' palms as they run past; they may miss some of the hilarious signs people have gone to the trouble of making, the various DJs, bands, cheerleader squads, drummers, and the locals who stand at the sidelines with lollies or cut-up oranges for the runners; and they most definitely wouldn't be familiar with the sound of thousands of discarded plastic cups crunching underfoot at the drink stations.

At the opposite end of the spectrum, there are runners who do these events without a care or concern about how long it takes. They run with their phone or a GoPro camera in hand to take photos and videos, they stop to talk to spectators, and are there to soak up the atmosphere.

And me? I am somewhere in between. I have always tried to run my marathons in the best time I am capable of, but I also make sure I take some mental pictures along the way because I figure that later on in life these are the memories that will mean the most—not how fast or slow I ran, but what I experienced.

After the performance I had to go through in order to compete at Boston, I was prepared for more of the same when it came to registering for the remaining majors. But, as it turned out, it was easy! I discovered that there are travel agencies out there that specialise in marathon tours. (I'm not the only one who likes going on marathon holidays, apparently.) These agencies are genius! For certain events, they get a certain number of guaranteed registration spots for runners travelling in their groups. For the really popular runs like New York and London there can be a bit of a waitlist, but I have found that as long as you get in touch at least a year out from the event you'll get a spot. My mate Gaz Brown (as in my mate who first planted the idea of Boston in my head) has a business here in Auckland called GetRunning (getrunning.co.nz) that takes these marathon tours, as well as coaching and training runs. He will get you and the rest of the travellers marathon-ready for the event you are training for. Other places I have used and can highly recommend are Judy Wolff at Marathon World Travel (marathons.co.nz) and House of Travel in Hamilton.[*]

---

[*] For the record, I'm not getting any sort of kickback from this, and I have never been given mate's rates—this is just a tip from my experience, and I've found it truly useful.

These three places all specialise in international marathons. As well as securing your entry (which, as I learned from Boston, is the hard part), they also get you from your hotel to the start line (this can be way more of a logistical nightmare than you might imagine, so this is a big bonus) and they chuck on some events too, so that if you want to chat and mingle with other runners from New Zealand you can—but you are also just as welcome to do your own thing if the running chat gets too much.

IF BOSTON IS THE Holy Grail, then New York is the bucket-list marathon. It's the one that *every* marathon runner wants to do. Even if you are not a runner, chances are you have a friend or know of someone who has run it. The New York Marathon started in 1970, back when it was really just oddballs who ran marathons; it has now grown into the biggest marathon in the world. Around 50,000 people take part in it each year, and an estimated two million supporters line the streets. (Seriously, who's making these crowd estimates?!)

IF BOSTON IS THE HOLY GRAIL, THEN NEW YORK IS THE BUCKET-LIST MARATHON.

I first learned about the New York Marathon when I was just ten years old. The year was 1983, and a New Zealander called Rod Dixon turned up and won it. I'm not sure whether Rod's achievement really got a lot of attention or if it just felt that way to me because I lived in a running household. Both Mum and Dad were pretty excited about it. It was a thrilling finish too—with 10 kilometres still to go, some English bloke called Geoff Smith was in the lead and Rod was behind by over two minutes. Rod only caught Smith just past the 41-kilometre mark in Central Park, a few hundred metres from the finish line, and ended up winning by a margin of *nine* seconds. As Rod got down on his knees to kiss the road, Smith finished and collapsed in agony behind him.

Ten-year-old me was blown away and inspired, but I didn't think I would ever get to run in New York. This was a time when the USA felt as remote as the moon. International travel, even to somewhere nearby like Sydney, was something only the very rich did. Plus, marathon running was still very much a niche activity. I just couldn't have imagined running New York in my wildest dreams.

Thankfully, marathons steadily grew in popularity and airfares got more and more affordable. In 2012 I was lucky enough to secure a spot in the world's most famous marathon. Unfortunately, during the week of the marathon New York was nailed by Hurricane Sandy. The worst-hit area? Staten Island, where the marathon starts. It was announced that the marathon would proceed, business as usual. The then mayor of New York, Michael Bloomberg, said it would give the city 'something to cheer about'. But as the week progressed things got nasty. Protests began as many thought it would be in poor taste to hold the run. The growing calls to cancel the race escalated when *The New York Times* highlighted that the run would use enough generators at the finish area in Central Park to give electricity back to 400 homes without power.

Jay-Jay and I flew out of New Zealand on Friday afternoon. Twelve hours later, we landed in San Francisco and grabbed some food at a soulless airport restaurant while we waited for our next flight to New York. The TV was playing CNN and scrolling across the bottom of the screen was a breaking news announcement that the New York mayor would be holding a press conference about the marathon. This could only mean the run was being shit-canned. *Fuck!* We boarded our flight for New York assuming the run would be cancelled but not knowing for sure. There were a lot of runners on board the flight. You could spot them a mile away. Lots of tracksuits, compression stockings and clothing from previous marathons. There was even one tosser who got up from his seat at one point during the flight to do bloody lunges up and down the aisle! Stretches are crucial but come on, mate—take your hand off it! With so many runners on board there was a lot of chatter about what was going on. Then the pilot's voice came over the speakers.

THERE WAS EVEN ONE TOSSER WHO GOT UP FROM HIS SEAT AT ONE POINT DURING THE FLIGHT TO DO BLOODY LUNGES UP AND DOWN THE AISLE!

'I know there are quite a few runners on board who are heading to New York for Sunday's marathon,' he said. 'I'm sorry to bring you bad news, but Mayor Bloomberg has just announced that the run has been cancelled.'

There was a collective groan from everyone on board. It was the right call to make, but that didn't make it any less disappointing for everyone who had put months and months of hard slog in for this event.

The night before what should have been marathon day, Jay-Jay and I went out for dinner with some friends. Usually I would have been a bit anxious and highly strung, but that night I was just sad and frustrated. That mood was temporary though; after a few shots of tequila I was feeling pretty good.

The next morning, with a killer hangover, I got out of bed

and jogged from our hotel in Times Square down to Central Park. There was an unofficial run held for all the people who had made it to New York for the marathon and wanted to join up with other runners. Thousands of people turned up to experience the sense of community, and many even had their now-redundant race numbers pinned to their shirts. We were all gutted that the run had been cancelled, but this impromptu event allowed us to grieve together.

THE NEXT WORLD MARATHON Major event I scored an entry into was the London Marathon in 2014. Still without a coach and using another free training programme, I incorporated some speed work into my training—the programme I was using said that, in order to race faster, you have to train faster. Common sense, I know. But running 42.2 kilometres at an easy pace is hard enough; trying to run it as fast as you can is next level in terms of discomfort. The speed training worked though, and my body adapted to the point where I could run at a 4:30 pace in my training. At this point, my personal best was still the 3 hours 14 minutes I had run in Christchurch four years earlier. If I was able to run the entire London Marathon at 4:30 pace, I would finish in 3 hours 10 minutes, smashing my PB. Hell, even if I set off at that pace and faded towards the end, a new PB could still be on the cards.

I touched down at Heathrow a couple of days before the run. My good mate Andy Rowe, who lives in London, came to my hotel first and then together we went to the race expo. I needed Andy, because I am incompetent when it comes to figuring out public transport, especially in a new country. Andy ridiculed me for my uselessness as he helped me buy my Oyster card. (I still have no idea why it's called an Oyster card; surely 'travel pass' or something would have made more sense?) He then burst into laughter when I stood on the left-hand side of the escalator and got told off by an impatient Englishman. It was all quite a culture shock. I'm used to the escalators at a Westfield Mall, where if you get stuck behind a couple of standers you don't pass or say anything; you just wait.

I LOVE RACE EXPOS. I COULD SPEND HOURS JUST WANDERING AROUND THE HALLS LOOKING AT RUNNING PRODUCTS THAT I DON'T REALLY NEED.

Andy saved his biggest laugh for when we arrived at our stop and I got stuck on the train. The doors opened and before I had a chance to get off a sea of other passengers had pushed their way on. It was all very stressful. It wasn't all laughs at my expense, though. We did laugh together when the prerecorded announcement mentioned the stop 'Cockfosters'. It must be a Kiwi thing because no one else on our carriage even cracked a smile.

I love race expos. I could spend hours just wandering around the halls looking at running products that I don't really need. After presenting my ID and getting my race number, we wandered around and I bought some official merchandise. We had only been there about half an hour before Andy was bored shitless and begging me to leave. Since I needed him to figure out the bloody Underground, we left.

The day before the marathon was less than ideal from a preparation perspective because Andy took me out to do some sightseeing. To be fair, I was only in London for a total of five days, so it would have been a shame to spend the two days before the run sitting on my hotel bed watching telly, but standing in line for 90 minutes to go to the observation deck of The Shard then walking around the Tower of London and Churchill's bunker was not the greatest pre-race prep of all time. After our day out, Andy cooked me up some pasta carbonara and salmon—the perfect carb-rich pre-race meal in my opinion—then I went back to my hotel and managed my first proper sleep since I had arrived, probably because I was so shagged from all the walking we'd done.

I woke up nice and early on race day, and after porridge and bagels at the hotel restaurant, hopped on the prearranged bus that took me and the other runners staying at the same hotel out to a big field called Greenwich Park, where the marathon starts. This, I must say, was a lot more fun than Boston. For starters, it was a warm London day, but there was also a DJ playing music and a giant screen showing a commentator who was going around chatting to runners. As I've mentioned, the wait at these things is painfully long so the entertainment was a fantastic way to pass the time. I had also learned from Boston, and I took a few magazines with me that I could flick through while I stood there.

The race eventually got under way in perfect conditions, and after the first couple of kilometres I managed to settle into my target pace of 4:30. I can't remember much of the early stages of the run, partly because I was busy looking at my watch to make sure my pace was just right, but also because there were no real landmarks to speak of. It felt a lot like we were running through the opening credits of *Coronation Street*, minus the ginger cat on the roof. I do remember being blown away when I got to the first drink stop. Instead of water served in disposable cups like at every other run I had participated in, they were handing out small bottles. This was brilliant! I have never mastered the art of the drink station—it is quite an art form, running and drinking at the same time, and I usually end up with more fluid on my shirt than in my mouth. These small water bottles allowed the runners to take one and either throw it to the side of the road after a couple of swigs or run with it and sip away.

The first memorable sight on the course was about 10 kilometres in, when the run weaves past a big old sailing ship from the 1800s called *Cutty Sark*. Here, the crowd thickens and the noise increases with applause and music. The next memorable point in the run comes just before halfway, when you cross spectacular London Bridge. Andy was watching from one of the corners by the bridge and later told me I was looking real sharp. I was holding my goal time well at this point, and had managed to make up the time I had lost in the congested first couple of kilometres. My race plan was being executed perfectly! I was starting to hurt, of course, but you have to expect that in a marathon. Also, as far as I was aware, there were no novelty or fancy-dress duffers ahead of me—but there was a guy running a similar speed to me who was dressed as a giant water bottle. That pissed me right off. Here I was, having my best run ever, and this guy was making it look easy!

Once you get off London Bridge, you turn right. It was along this stretch that I got to witness the race leaders passing on the opposite side of the road: one of the most spectacular and awe-inspiring things I have ever seen. This was kilometre 22 for me; for these leaders it was kilometre 36. My hard work for the day was just starting, but theirs was almost over. And, while I was grinding out my 4:30 pace, these marathon legends were running each kilometre in just under 3:00 minutes. That's sprinting for most of us normal folk—and they were making it look effortless, with blank expressions on their faces.

Wilson Kipsang Kiprotich and Stanley Biwott were running

together at this stage, side by side, though Kiprotich ended up winning the race by sprinting off in the final kilometre. He set a new London Marathon course record as well of 2 hours 4 minutes 29 seconds. Shortly after these guys, I spotted Olympic legend Mo Farah, who was taking part in his first marathon. He crossed the line in eighth place in a time of 2 hours 8 minutes 21 seconds, and apparently later described it as a 'bad day at the office'.

Seeing these legends reminded me why I love these big runs so much. The Majors are some of only a few sporting events in the world where a nobody like me can take part in the same race as the world's best. Sharing the road with them, and getting my arse smoked by them, was a true privilege.

After the thrill of seeing the race leaders, I entered what is in my opinion the most boring and uninspiring part of the London Marathon course as it heads past Canary Wharf and the London Docklands. Unfortunately, this is also where the crowd thins out, leaving you with little more than your own internal strength to push you onward.

I reached the 30-kilometre mark in 2 hours 15 minutes, still managing my 4:30 pace. This was the precise moment where I started getting pangs of cramp. Shit! It was immediately clear to me that I would not be able to keep up my pace for the final kilometres, but I knew that if I could somehow keep to under 5:00 minutes per kilometre I would still run my way to a brand-new PB.

Unfortunately, the cramp just got worse and worse. My walk breaks got longer, and any hope of a new personal best slipped away. It really is heartbreaking to be reduced to a walk, looking at your watch and seeing precious time slowly slipping away.

The last few kilometres of the London Marathon are the

most breathtaking. Participants run past incredible landmarks including St Paul's Cathedral, the London Eye, Big Ben, the Houses of Parliament and finally Buckingham Palace right by the finish line. As I hit the red asphalt of the Mall and the final kilometre of the run I could hear Andy along with a few other Kiwi friends cheering for me, which was humbling. They had even gone to the trouble of making a big sign complete with a colour printout of my ugly mug and the New Zealand flag (along with a slogan that is not fit for print here).

IT REALLY IS HEARTBREAKING TO BE REDUCED TO A WALK, LOOKING AT YOUR WATCH AND SEEING PRECIOUS TIME SLOWLY SLIPPING AWAY.

Sadly, I was in such a bad way with cramp by this stage that I was walking-slash-running each kilometre in around six minutes. Setting a new PB was no longer a possibility. It was the first time I had ever had a cheer squad or a sign at a run, and I would have loved to have looked more like a runner and less like a corpse for my friends. Tim and Ang, who made the sign, later told me they had been waiting for ages because the marathon app had predicted that I would be there way earlier than I was. Those apps are very good, but they cannot foresee cramp or other possible malfunctions of the human body. (This same app also helpfully informed me later that in the final 7.2 kilometres of the run I had passed 41 people . . . but been passed by 686.)

I hobbled past Buckingham Palace in such discomfort that it could have been an abandoned abattoir for all I cared! I did give the Queen a friendly wave though, then it was a short jog to the finish in a total time of 3 hours 24 minutes. In the process, I got beaten convincingly by the guy dressed as a giant water bottle—and also by a lady who had run in a wedding dress. It looked like her day had been harder than mine, though; she had blood trails from chafing that ran from her armpits all the way down her torso.

I was slightly annoyed with my finish time. This was the time when I started to feel that, regardless of what training I did, 3 hours 20-something minutes was what I was destined to run.

The disappointment soon passed, though. I reminded myself that running a marathon badly is still better than not running one at all.

LATER IN 2014, I returned to New York for take two at the marathon. After the 2012 cancellation, the race organisers had done a superb job of taking care of all the affected runners: you could either get a refund or you could get guaranteed entry into any of the next three runs. What a dream—running London and New York in the same calendar year! Most people will never bother to run even one marathon in their life, but here I was running the world's two biggest ones in the same year.

With the pain from London still fresh in my mind, I came up with a different strategy for New York. By now, my expectations had dropped in terms of the time I wanted to run; I was no longer even thinking of beating my personal best of 3 hours 15 minutes. It seemed like that ship had sailed. I was a has-been. For the rest of my life, whenever another runner asked me, 'What's your PB?', I believed my answer would be, 'Three fifteen.'

I was OK with that. I was a guy who had only started running again as an adult because I had become a fat bastard;

I had never had any expectation of being anything more than just another bib in the sea of race numbers, so 3 hours 15 minutes seemed pretty tidy to me.

THEN I WOULD LIFT IT A COUPLE OF NOTCHES FOR THE FINAL 12 KILOMETRES AND GO INTO WHAT I CHOSE TO CALL 'BEAST MODE'.

My plan for New York was to start at a pace of just under 5:00 minutes per kilometre. If you hold that pace, your marathon time will be 3 hours 30 minutes. That was my natural training pace, which meant that I could run it without pushing myself very hard, and I was reasonably confident I could maintain that pace for the entire marathon. My plan was to get myself to the 30-kilometre mark in good shape, still feeling relaxed and comfortable, in somewhere under 2 hours 30 minutes, then I would lift it a couple of notches for the final 12 kilometres and go into what I chose to call 'beast mode'. If all went according to this grand master plan, it would be the opposite of London, where I'd gone out fast and stumbled through the final kilometres in absolute agony.

Most importantly, I wanted to enjoy New York more than I had London. I had been in such a bad way for the last 45 minutes of the London Marathon that I had missed out on soaking in the atmosphere and architecture of the best part of the race. Running New York was a 30-year dream and, even more than running it well, I wanted to relish the experience.

Like Boston three years earlier, New York was freezing, and the cold was made even worse by a strong wind. It really was brutal. Fortunately, I had learned from experience and turned up to the athletes' village at Fort Wadsworth on Staten Island with an almost comical number of garments on over my running gear: two pairs of fleecy track pants, a long-sleeve thermal top, a hoodie *and* a thick jacket. I also had two pairs of gloves on—a thick pair for while I was waiting to start that would have been suitable for a day up the mountain, and underneath a thin pair that I planned to run with for the first few kilometres until I warmed up.

Unbelievably, I was still cold when I got off the bus. I had forgotten to bring a beanie! Even with my hoodie on, my ears started to burn from the chill. As luck would have it, Dunkin' Donuts—a brand New Yorkers might associate more with cops than with runners—were there handing out promotional beanies. It was a stroke of marketing genius: in the aerial shots from the start line you could see thousands of pink-and-orange hats.

Getting into the starting area was similar to getting through an American airport. There were police and dogs everywhere, and all the runners had to pass through a metal detector. This was the year after the Boston Marathon bombings, so the race organisers were doing everything in their power to keep their runners safe.

The New York Marathon turned out to be worth the wait: it was one of the most spectacular runs I have ever taken part in. After the starter's cannon goes off, you hear Frank Sinatra crooning 'New York, New York' over the loudspeakers on repeat. The music fades as you hit the Verrazano–Narrows Bridge, and that's when you can see the fireboats spraying water in the air in salute to the runners. I will never forget the sound on that bridge: a stampede of feet and the flapping of race numbers in the wind. I had thrown away most of my layers of clothing a few minutes before the start, but decided to keep my thin gloves and my thermal top on underneath my singlet. I figured if I got too hot I could get changed and run at the same time without too much difficulty, but it was so cold that I ran the entire way in both.

I WILL NEVER FORGET THE SOUND ON THAT BRIDGE: A STAMPEDE OF FEET AND THE FLAPPING OF RACE NUMBERS IN THE WIND.

As you cross the bridge into Brooklyn, you're greeted by a band of drummers, their rhythmic pounding the perfect thing to time your foot strikes to. I remember running past them and then towards the first of the spectators thinking, *New York! Come at me!*

The crowd support was epic; there were people everywhere. A lot of runners had their names on their shirts and were rewarded for their efforts by strangers cheering them on personally. I am yet to do this in a race myself, as I prefer to run with a little bit of anonymity. For New York, I wore a singlet with the silver fern and New Zealand written on it. This got me hundreds of people offering encouragement by shouting out things like 'Go, Kiwi!' and 'All Blacks!'. That was enough encouragement for me.

When I was just 18 kilometres in, I had one of the most bizarre marathon experiences of my running life. When I reached Williamsburg, a strict Jewish area of the city, I suddenly found myself running in relative silence. There were a couple of spectators, but they seemed to be looking on in confusion rather than in support. I later learned that the majority of residents in Williamsburg belong to the Satmars, a Hasidic sect who came to New York from Romania and Hungary after World War II. They speak Yiddish, wear traditional Jewish clothes, turn their back on many aspects of modern life and generally keep to themselves—and, because of their modesty, they don't really appreciate 50,000 nearly nude men and women wearing skimpy shorts and tight T-shirts flaunting their bodies in their 'hood. I even saw one woman running in front of me almost get bowled over as two Jewish men walked across the road right in her path, as if they were blissfully unaware of anything or anyone else. Remarkable.

At 26 kilometres, you run over the spectacular 100-year-old Queensboro Bridge then turn on to First Avenue and 59th Street. This is one of those magic marathon moments I will never forget. They call this part of the run 'rock-star mile' because as you come off this bridge, which is a spectator-free zone, you are hit with a thick wall of sound as tens of thousands of spectators cheer you on. This roar is so motivating it carries you up First Avenue.

I DISCOVERED THAT 'BEAST MODE' DID NOT EXIST.

I made it to the 30-kilometre mark in 2 hours 22 minutes, which works out at an average pace of 4:44. I felt pretty relaxed. I had pushed myself comfortably hard without being a dick about it, but this was unfortunately where I found myself unable to execute the second stage of my race plan. I discovered that 'beast mode' did not exist. Unlike London, I was able to keep running the whole way and I avoided the dreaded cramp, but I wasn't able to make myself go any faster. My pace remained pretty steady.

I made it to the finish line in Central Park in a time of 3 hours 21 minutes. Sigh! My curse of the 3 hour 20-something marathons continued, but I was happy. It was faster than I had run in London, and faster than I had run Boston three years earlier. It was not my best . . . but it was my best in a long time.

NEXT ON MY MAJOR hitlist was the Chicago Marathon in 2015, which I ran with Mum. As you know, this was also the first marathon I'd done with the professional help of Coach Ian on my side, and I ended up defying my age and my own self-doubt by finally running a new personal best. Actually, that's a bit modest—I smashed my old PB! My curse of the 3 hour 20-something marathon was shattered, and I had managed to run almost five minutes faster than the PB I had set five years earlier.

After Chicago, a whole world of possibility opened up in front of me. I *had* got faster. Maybe I could get even faster still? Maybe—just maybe—I could crack the three-hour barrier?

I still had two majors left to tick off my list: Berlin and Tokyo.

I zeroed in on Berlin.

CHAPTER 11
BIG BAD BERLIN

THEY SAY THAT IF you are ever going to run your best time Berlin is the place you will do it. 'And who are "they" exactly?' I hear you ask. Well, pretty much anyone you speak to who knows a thing or two about marathon running. One man I include in 'they' is the current marathon world-record holder, Kenya's Dennis Kimetto. He set his world record in Berlin in 2014 when he won the race in 2 hours 2 minutes 57 seconds. Who needs to brag about a PB when you have set a world record?!

Berlin is said to be flat, on a nice, even asphalt surface, and with mild autumn temperatures and hardly any wind. In other words, perfect conditions for running a personal best, regardless of whether your aim is to break four hours, five hours or maybe even two hours (eh, Dennis?). Yep, Berlin is the place to give that PB a crack. Plus, the run starts and finishes right near the Brandenburg Gate, the most recognisable site in the city. If you paid even a tiny bit of attention in high-school history class, this should be ringing a bell. As far as gates go, the Brandenburg is pretty damn famous—possibly only second to the Pearly Gates.

The Brandenburg has stood in place since 1791, and has therefore witnessed a heap of history. In 1806, Napoleon took the sculpture of four horses and a chariot from the top of the gate as a war trophy and made off back to Paris with it. After the Battle of Waterloo, the sculpture was returned to Berlin as a symbol of victory. Then, in 1933, the Nazis marched through the gate to celebrate Hitler's rise to power. In 1987, US President Ronald Reagan made his famous speech at the gate, urging Mikhail Gorbachev, then leader of the Soviet Union, to 'Tear down this wall!' (And, of absolutely no historical significance at all but almost as jaw-dropping, the Brandenburg Gate also happens to be where hundreds of fans watched in disbelief as Michael Jackson stood on his balcony at the Hotel Adlon and dangled his baby out of the window.)

AS FAR AS GATES GO, THE BRANDENBURG IS PRETTY DAMN FAMOUS—POSSIBLY ONLY SECOND TO THE PEARLY GATES.

The Berlin Marathon has been run annually since 1974, but because the city was divided by the Berlin Wall until 1989 the marathon used to skip the Brandenburg Gate and the course was limited to West Berlin. In 1990, runners were at last able to run through the Brandenburg Gate for the first time, a moment that reduced many to tears. The Berlin Wall is all but gone now—small portions remain (and continue to be a drawcard for tourists), but for the most part the only evidence that a giant barrier once split this city in two is a line of pavers carved into the road.

'Hitting the wall' is one of the most-used expressions among marathon runners. I can't imagine a better city to tear down and smash through walls—both literal and metaphorical, personal and global. Overcoming barriers and pulling down walls is something every marathon runner strives to do.

AS A KID, YOU get told some pretty big whoppers by the adults around you. These are the kinds of lies that are supposed to be make you dream big. You know the sort I mean—you have possibly been told the same yourself once or twice. 'If you put your mind to it, you can do anything.' That kind of thing.

ANYWAY, MY POINT IS, WHEN IT COMES TO RUNNING A MARATHON, THERE IS ONLY SO FAST EACH RUNNER CAN GO.

It's all well-meaning stuff. And, while it's true that if you put your mind to it you can do *a lot* of brilliant things, sadly it's simply not true that you can do *anything*. Look at Richie McCaw, for example: the greatest All Black player and captain we have ever seen. As well as winning the Rugby World Cup *twice* he has also managed to get an Agricultural Science degree, and he flies gliders, planes and helicopters. If ever there was an example of someone who epitomises achieving whatever you put your mind to, it is Richie—but even with his level of drive and talent, he would have never been able to be a successful horse jockey. He just doesn't really have the body for it. Or the voice.

Anyway, my point is, when it comes to running a marathon, there is only so fast each runner can go. There are tricks you can use to make yourself go faster, but ultimately your individual make-up has a physical capability that no amount of training or willpower can change.

To my friend Jenny Hellen (the publisher of this book, actually), my goal of breaking three hours at Berlin seemed very achievable—even easy. In an email exchange, she wrote:

> From what I've read it's pretty damn likely that you'll meet your goal in Berlin. You're well on track. Or am I misunderstanding just what a challenge this is for you? I'm just not sure that it's such a hurdle . . .

Jenny is a smart woman and her enquiry was a perfectly rational one for a non-runner. My PB at that time was 3 hours 10 minutes, which I'd done at Chicago in 2015, and there was just under a year to go until Berlin. From Jenny's perspective, I had a whole year to get myself fit enough to shave just 10 minutes off my time. A walk in the park, right? (Or, more accurately, a very doable run through the streets of Berlin.) To a non-runner, 10 minutes over 42.2 kilometres sounds like nothing—some weekends it takes me longer than that to put the duvet back into the duvet cover!

But if you get into the nitty-gritty details of it and delve into some really boring runner's maths, you start to see just why this was a challenge that might be beyond what my body is capable of:

- My pace per kilometre in Chicago was 4:32. Across a total of thirteen marathons, this was by far the fastest I had ever managed to run.
- In order to run in Berlin in just under three hours, I would need to maintain a pace of 4:16 per kilometre. That's a difference of sixteen seconds per kilometre.

Going sixteen seconds faster over 1 kilometre is something most reasonably fit people could probably manage. But, when you have to take sixteen seconds off each kilometre and there are 42 of them all up it starts to become a lot tougher.

If you're not a runner, you might still be wondering if breaking three hours in a marathon is even a good time. Shit, yeah! It is for me, and for most runners. As a rule of thumb, only 2 per cent of people who line up on the start line of a marathon will run it in under three hours. In other words, breaking three hours is unlikely to win you any races but it will mean you finish ahead of 98 per cent of the other runners. To give you a little bit of perspective, consider the following.

- The current world record for the marathon distance, held by our pal Dennis Kimetto, is 2 hours 3 minutes 57 seconds.
- To qualify for the marathon at the Olympic Games, New Zealand men need to break 2 hours 15 minutes and women 2 hours 37 minutes.
- The average finishing time in any given marathon is around 4 hours 20 minutes.

When you take all this in, you can see that three hours is way better than average (in fact, it's something that fewer than 2 per cent of all marathon runners will achieve), but way worse than the professionals. To me, the best yardstick for what is considered a 'good' marathon time is the qualifying standards for the Boston Marathon.

Ultimately, though, my goal of breaking three hours had nothing to do with what anyone else thinks is fast. It wasn't about comparing myself to anyone else. My goal was to push myself to my absolute limits so that, whatever my finishing time ended up being, I'd know that I'd gone the absolute fastest my lanky old frame was capable of. That's all you can ask for in life, I think: to do your very best.

WE'RE THE ONES WHO START WATCHING THE CLOCK, WHO GET OUR OWN 'MAGIC NUMBER'.

There are lots of people out there who just do one marathon—a tick-it-off-the-bucket-list sort of thing. For many of these runners, time is irrelevant; the important thing is completing the distance. Then there are those of us who go back for a second, third, fourth or even hundredth marathon. We're the ones who start watching the clock, who get our own 'magic number'. And this is precisely the thing that made me really fall in love with the marathon event: it's a race against yourself. Always. Since the distance never changes, you always get a true measure of how fit and fast you are, and how well you have done in comparison to previous runs. It is a real buzz to run a personal best, and when I set my Berlin goal I actually had no idea if it was even going to be possible for me. But I think that those are the best kind of goals: the ones where you might still fail even if you give it your very best. After all, where's the fun or suspense in setting a goal that you know you'll easily be able to achieve?

For Berlin, I gave my goal three levels.

Goal one: Take part in and finish the Berlin Marathon.

Goal two: Finish the Berlin Marathon in a personal best time.

Goal three: Break three hours at the Berlin Marathon.

I thought of these levels as being a bit like Olympic medals: goal one was the bronze, goal two the silver, and goal three was gold.

Goal one was the easiest of the three goals, and in a lot of ways even seemed like a bit of a gimme. I already had my entry sorted, and I had already run a bunch of marathons, so I knew I could do it (awful unforeseen circumstances aside— touch wood).

FOR BERLIN, I DECIDED TO RESET MY ATTITUDE: I BECAME MORE FOCUSED ON GETTING THE JOB DONE BY ANY MEANS NECESSARY.

Goal two was a bit tougher. Every runner wants a PB. After Chicago, I did a bit of soul-searching and realised I had tried hard—I tried fucking hard—but I couldn't honestly say that I'd given it absolutely everything. On race day I gave it 100 per cent, but there was definitely more I knew I could have done in the months of training leading up to the event. For Berlin, I decided to reset my attitude: I became more focused on getting the job done by any means necessary. I promised myself that I'd implement the ideas that Coach Ian had suggested before Chicago, but which I'd shunned. I would embrace his dorky-looking warm-up and cool-down stretches, his 'mini peak' marathons, his weight training at the gym. I knew there was no guarantee that all this would pay off, but I wouldn't know if I didn't try.

Then came goal three. As I've mentioned, I was aware when I set it that goal three might not even be possible. But I knew I had to give it a shot.

IT MIGHT SOUND A little bit self-defeating to tell myself that a goal might not be achievable before I'd even given it a whack, as though I was shooting myself in the foot (so to speak) before

I'd even started running. But, like I said, it wouldn't have been any fun if I'd been dead certain I'd achieve it. Also, I'm a realist. I'm very aware that running a marathon in under three hours is an impressive feat at any age, and I'm not young anymore. I read somewhere that the best age to run a marathon in your life is when you're 28. Fuck! Where was that article when I needed it fifteen years ago?

Truthfully, though, I'm not really that bothered about my age. There's no point fretting about what you can't change. Plus, I had an amazing time in my twenties. When I was 28, I looked more like a rugby prop than a runner. I weighed over a hundred kilos and most days my lunch consisted of a big bottle of Coke, a loaf of cheese-and-bacon bread and three or four sausages. I was about as interested in running as I was in clean eating. Being unfit and overweight is not a lot of fun— but *getting* overweight is delicious! It wasn't until I'd reached the wise old age of 42 that I managed to run a personal best in the marathon, and I was encouraged by this. It showed I can still improve even if I am 780 weekends past my running prime.

Then there was also the minor issue of long-distance travel and jet-lag to take into account. As I've mentioned, due to the fact my work would be in a survey period during September, I was given only one week off in total. One week to fly to Berlin, get adjusted to the new time zone and climate, do the run, then turn around and fly back to New Zealand. When I booked my flights, my itinerary helpfully informed me that I was about to embark on a round trip lasting 155 hours in total from the time the plane left New Zealand late on a Wednesday night to the time it touched down back at home again the following Wednesday morning. Of that time, I would spend 71 hours either in the air or in transit at airports, meaning I would have just 84 hours—in other words, three and a half days—on the ground in Berlin. It was not ideal, but you have to work with what you've got. Plus, it's not lost on me that, if it wasn't for my job, I wouldn't even be able to pursue this bizarre and extremely expensive hobby of mine in the first place.

OOOH! THERE IT IS. THE F-WORD. HORRIBLE. JUST THE SOUND OF IT IS DEPRESSING.

Then there were the other usual aspects of a marathon that could conspire to slow me down—the size of the field of competitors, the ever-present possibility of injury, and the question of whether my own mental toughness was up to the task. And then there was the pure and simple fact that I just might not be good enough. If you get a donkey and train it really hard, you might end up with a fast donkey—but it is never going to be a racehorse. Perhaps my running ability would turn out to be similar to my metaphor-making ability? Perhaps I was already at the peak of the speed I was able to run the marathon distance in? Perhaps I'd put in all this effort, only to fail?

Oooh! There it is. The F-word. Horrible. Just the sound of it is depressing. The only time anyone would ever be stoked to hear it is after a drug test. The sucky thing is that, no matter how you coat it, failure is what it is. You can call it 'a bit below expectation', or 'not quite as good as I'd hoped', but nobody is fooled by the phrasing. It's a fail. And it's shit.

When I set my goal for Berlin, Jay-Jay and lots of other friends asked me how I would feel if I didn't break three hours. I gave them all the same sort of generic answer, something wishy-washy like, 'Even if I don't break three hours but I still manage to beat my personal best, I'll be stoked.' But the truth was, I had no idea how I'd feel. That was how I *hoped* I'd feel—that I'd done everything I possibly could, and therefore had done my best. But who honestly knows until it happens? I knew I might also feel fucking gutted, even if I did get a new PB. It was nerve-wracking.

On the flipside, I also had no idea how it would feel if I *did* manage to achieve my big, scary goal. I knew I'd be elated, but I also often find that, when you work towards big things, you make it to the summit and suddenly realise the view isn't as amazing as you had hoped. And that's OK. You just go back to the drawing board and find another mountain to climb.

There are plenty of hard-arse 'failure is not an option' people out there, but while that might be a very nice T-shirt slogan (or a tattoo you'll regret in five years' time) it's not truthful. Sometimes you don't get a say in whether or not you succeed or fail. All of the world's biggest legends have experienced failure; it comes with the territory of being a champion. It's part of the deal when you try to do something that you've never tried to do before.

CHAPTER 12
THE TRAINING BEGINS

I OFFICIALLY STARTED TRAINING for the Berlin Marathon on 11 January, 258 days out from race day. It was my first day back at work after a three-week Christmas break. I had kept running over the holiday—nothing too serious, just getting my shoes on and going out for long enough to get my heart rate up and make me sweat. Fun runs. Runs that remind me why I love running, why I do this. When I'm out for these casual runs, I'll stop and chat for five minutes if I see some friends outside a café. I'll pause to peek at the photos in the window of my local real estate firm as I go past. If I see a nice Ferrari at one of the car yards, I'll press my sweaty face and hand up to the windscreen to see if it is in my price range. It is never in my price range—but I quite like the idea of the snooty salespeople, with their judgemental stares that imply they already know I cannot afford their cars, having to get the Mr Muscle out to clean my smeared fluids from the glass.

On this warm summer's day, my first day of training, I set out for a 10-kilometre run and I gave it a bit of extra oomph. It wasn't particularly fast, but given my current state of fitness and my holiday bod it was as quick as I could go. I was stuffed by the time I got home. As I sat on the deck, catching my breath, I flicked off my shoes and checked the stats on my watch. I did some quick maths in my head to work out how I was running right now compared to the speeds I'd need to achieve in Berlin.

It was lucky there were still 258 days to go.

I would be needing every damn one of them.

THAT SEEMS LIKE A BULLSHIT, SUGAR-COATED DEFINITION TO ME. ISN'T THE MIDDLE SUPPOSED TO BE WHEN YOU'RE HALFWAY THROUGH?

A FEW WEEKS LATER, I turned 43. The weather could not have been better for my birthday. Mind you, my mood was already pretty good, so even if it had been an absolute shitter of a day I would have still been stoked. Some people might be gutted about turning 43. After all, I suspect I am by now well and truly into the second half of my life. I have somehow become a middle-aged man! According to the dictionary, 'middle age' is when you're between the ages of about 45 to 65—the period after 'early adulthood', but before 'old age'. That seems like a bullshit, sugar-coated definition to me. Isn't the middle supposed to be when you're halfway through? If a 60-year-old is describing themselves as middle-aged, they must think they are going to live to 120! If I get to enjoy another 43 birthdays, I'll be pretty happy with my lot. My bad habits (notably my fondness for wine and the occasional junk food) could possibly cost me a couple of years at the other end. While I'd rather be here for a good time *and* a long time, if having a good time means the long time will be shortened then I'll go for the good time, thanks. I couldn't think of anything more tedious and boring than living my whole life based on what is going to give me the best chances of being the oldest person in the retirement village.

Without a doubt, the thing I was most thankful for on my birthday was my health. When I got home from my run and had showered, I put a post on Facebook.

It's my birthday today. Forty-three. That's fucking old. The only time anyone ever refers to a 43-year-old as being young is if they die. I have face wrinkles that suggest I'm 43 (or even older) and I need to use a trimmer to control the hair in my nose and ears and eyebrows.

When I turned 40, I said to a mate of mine that we were all getting old, to which he replied, 'Not everyone is as lucky as we are.'

It's a pretty deep thought, but it's also a good reminder that we should embrace birthdays rather than dread them. I can honestly say that I have never felt fitter or sharper than I do right now. Physically, I can do more now than I ever could in my twenties ('the fat years'). I put this entirely down to running. And, because of my physical fitness, I feel mentally sharper. If you don't run, you should try. I reckon three fifteen-minute runs a week are all it would take to make you feel awesome. And if you're not into running, then find some other sort of exercise that floats your boat. If you have your health, your birthdays are cool.

COACH IAN PUT TOGETHER a rigorous training plan for me for Berlin. As you now know, it included all sorts of bells and whistles and nearly indecipherable science-y runnerspeak—things like threshold runs (where I had to perform at my 'anaerobic threshold', which is to say run so fast that my body would produce lactic acid slightly faster than it could be cleared from my bloodstream), 10-kilometre time trials (which I've already touched on, and which always suck) and these things called 'mini-peak marathons'.

DON'T LET THE 'MINI' PART ABOUT THESE MARATHONS FOOL YOU. THERE IS NOTHING 'MINI' OR 'CUTE' ABOUT THEM.

Don't let the 'mini' part about these marathons fool you. There is nothing 'mini' or 'cute' about them. They are still a full-blown marathon. Basically, a mini-peak marathon is one you run as part of your training for your target event. Yep, you read that right: you run a marathon to train for another marathon. Sometimes you even run two mini-peaks! Usually, marathon training programmes will have you run at most 32 kilometres or 36 kilometres in your training; the theory behind this is that you avoid unnecessarily fatiguing your body, and save yourself to give it your all on the day of the marathon. So, running a marathon or two (you know, just casually) as part of your training sounds bonkers—even to most marathon runners, who are already kind of bonkers. However, after I'd got over the initial shock, the more I thought about it, the more the mini-peaks started to make sense to me. The top guys and girls—the ones who will be trying to win at Berlin—would run the full marathon distance or even longer at their race pace many times a year. I realised that a mini-peak marathon is the sort of thing that is the difference between wanting to simply finish a marathon and wanting to do the absolute best you are capable of.

The mini-peak marathon that Coach Ian had me scheduled to do was the inaugural Hawke's Bay Marathon in May 2016. Fortunately, it looked like a really good marathon. The course goes off road and through vineyards, plus it would be the first marathon I'd run in New Zealand for a few years. I was actually looking forward to it.

Ian set a time goal for me that was all very scientific and based on the results of my most recent lactate-threshold tests from a couple of weeks earlier. According to Ian and his data, I would in theory be able to hold a pace of 4:40 minutes per kilometre across the entire marathon distance, and that would give me a finish time of 3 hours 16 minutes. There was just one problem with this: I wasn't sure myself if I'd be able to do it in this goal time.

AFTER THESE TOUGH RUNS, I WAS PLAGUED WITH INSECURITY AND SELF-DOUBT.

I'd been training hard and following Ian's programme pretty much to the letter for three months by this point—rest days were rare, and most days I either had a run with a specific purpose or a 90-minute workout session to strengthen my legs and core. I had definitely made improvements; I was running faster and the strength sessions at the gym had started to feel easier—at the beginning of the year, I had barely been able to move the morning after! But, even so, I still had training runs where I felt slow, where I battled physically and mentally, and where I worried that, even with all this progress and effort, I'd never even get close to the three-hour mark. After these tough runs, I was plagued with insecurity and self-doubt, and I'd had a tough run just the week before the Hawke's Bay Marathon. It didn't exactly boost my confidence.

The day before Hawke's Bay, Ian sent through instructions for the race. I read them several times over to make extra sure that I'd fully digested them.

Good luck for the marathon tomorrow! Just remember that you have trained well for this, and you're running at a pace we've worked out from your current ability, so we know you can do this. Remember to start your warm-up about fifteen or twenty minutes prior to the race start—walking to a light jog. This should take about five minutes and include a couple of light sprints. After this, do a series of lunges and squats. You should have this wrapped up ten minutes BEFORE the race starts.

For pacing during the race, we're working on a rough negative-split strategy. Run the first couple of kilometres at slightly slower than your target pace—around 4:50 minutes per kilometre. This only needs to be for 2 or 3 kilometres. After this, aim for a pace of between 4:40 and 4:45 for the first 30 kilometres. At this point, if you are still feeling fresh, you can increase the pace to 4:35. If you are up to it at 37 kilometres, you can increase your pace slightly more.

OK, got it. I was in bed by 9.30 pm, feeling relaxed . . . and a wee bit nervous.

AS IT TURNED OUT, I didn't need to worry about setting my alarm because I was woken up the next morning at 4.38 am by a fucking howling wind. I got out of bed and had a peek past the motel curtain and could see the branches on the giant Norfolk pines outside swaying ferociously. *Not ideal running conditions*, I thought as I walked back to bed. After that, getting back to sleep was impossible. I lay there going through everything in my head, focusing on what I had to do. I *hate* the wind. But, as luck would have it, this particular wind whipped right through Napier then disappeared. By the time I reached the start area of the marathon, it was pretty much dream conditions for a marathon: a nice, calm, still morning. No rain. Not too cold, not too hot. And not a breath of wind.

As per Ian's instructions, I did some jogging, sprints and some dorky-looking stretches up and down Marine Parade. Then when the message came over the public-address system to advise us that the run was about to start, I made my way to the start line along with around 1000 other runners. It was all so easy after the big international marathons that I'd most recently done: no long lines for the Port-A-Loos, no hassle getting to the start line, and then it was pleasantly uncrowded when the gun went off.

A couple of hundred metres into the run, I looked down at my watch to check my speed. Ian wanted me to take the first few kilometres *real* easy—at a pace around 4:50 minutes per kilometre. I had felt like I was jogging very slowly and comfortably, so I was surprised when my watch indicated I was going at a pace of 4:15. In other words, DANGEROUSLY FAST! This is the evil thing about a marathon: you feel so good at the start that you're inevitably tempted to run faster than you should. But this will always come back to bite you in the arse later on in the run, when you need every ounce of energy you've got. I slowed myself down and tried to settle into what felt like an unnaturally slow pace. Mentally and physically, I was feeling really good.

As I jogged along, a guy I had been chatting to at the start area ran past me. He'd told me it was his first marathon and that he'd be happy to run it in anything under four hours. I'd told him my goal time, and he'd seemed impressed.

'What are you doing back here?' he called out as he passed me. 'Shouldn't you be up the front somewhere?'

THIS IS THE EVIL THING ABOUT A MARATHON: YOU FEEL SO GOOD AT THE START THAT YOU'RE INEVITABLY TEMPTED TO RUN FASTER THAN YOU SHOULD.

I just smiled and waved, and made a note of his purple shirt as he receded into the distance ahead. I wondered if I'd come across him again later in the race.

The day turned out to be hotter than anticipated. It hit 25 degrees Celsius before I had finished. This made things a little more challenging than I'd anticipated, as did the variety of surfaces—roads, gravel paths alongside rivers, and grass fields through olive trees and grapevines. While this all made for a very scenic and interesting run, parts of it felt like a cross-country race.

I was still feeling good when I got to the 26-kilometre marker, though—well, as good as you can expect to feel when you've been running for a little bit over two hours! This was the point where I was supposed to try to push the pace a little bit. Unfortunately, it was also the precise point where I turned a corner and got slammed by a headwind that would taunt me and the rest of the runners most of the way to the finish line. *Shit!* This meant that, even though I was putting more effort in, my pace remained the same.

Just after I passed the 30-kilometre marker, I spied my mate in the purple shirt up ahead. Over the next kilometre, I got closer and closer to him, then I eventually caught him when he started walking.

'Keep going, bro!' I called as I went past. 'You've got this!'

He was not in great shape. 'I just want to finish! Am I gonna make it?'

I told him he would. I didn't see him after that. I really hope he did make it. I'm sure he would have, even if he had to walk the final 12 kilometres. I also hope the experience made him want to come back and give the marathon another shot.

I ran the final 5 kilometres at a pace of around 5:00. I was in a world of pain—but I was still running, and I was still passing others who had been reduced to a walk. I crossed the finish line in 3 hours 21 minutes 58 seconds. Yeah, I was a bit gutted that I hadn't been able to pick up the pace and finish strong as per Ian's plan, but mostly I was ecstatic! There were so many positives to take away from this mini-peak marathon.

- I finished in twenty-fifth place over all.
- I finished second in my age group (40–49).
- I didn't walk at all—something I had only ever managed in one other marathon.
- I managed to follow Ian's instructions and run at the set pace for most of the run.
- I didn't cramp up (a problem that has plagued me in many previous marathons).
- *And* I recovered faster than ever before—the day after the race, I was walking completely normally.

I sat on the grass at the gorgeous Sileni Estates winery, where the race finishes, and soaked up the post-run atmosphere.

I flicked off my shoes and texted my family and friends to let them know I hadn't dropped dead on the course. (Even though I had by now run ten marathons since my dramatic collapse in the Auckland Marathon, my family was still less concerned with my finish time than they were with making sure I actually survived!) Within half an hour, I also got a Facebook message from Coach Ian.

> Awesome work, mate. Well done! Can't wait to catch up properly and hear how it went! The fast finish was only if you could, and by the look of it the drop off was minimal and definitely a lot less than most. Second in your age group and it was only a 'practice' run—definitely a positive outcome!

I still had four months to go before Berlin. As I sat there in the sun, I started to think that maybe—just maybe—a sub-three-hour marathon could be within my reach.

SADLY, THAT LITTLE MOMENT of optimism I felt immediately after my mini-peak marathon didn't last. If only motivation was a constant thing—like, you could tell yourself, 'You can do this! Keep training! You'll be great!' and that was the end of self-doubt. I mean, in general, I was feeling pretty positive about things as my training progressed—but, as with anything in life, I had my good days and my bad days.

On the good days—the really good ones—I felt like I might even surprise myself and run something ridiculous in Berlin. *Shit, Dom,* I'd think, *You might really blow yourself away and do it in 2 hours 55 minutes!* Then there were the bad days—the days where I'd get home from a hard run or leg workout and just thinking about the goal I'd set for myself made me feel like throwing up.

This book was a huge part of that fear; I was worried that it would be a complete fizzer if I didn't reach my target at Berlin. I'd also told people about my goal, and that created a whole other level of expectation. In the past, I have always gone about my running with a reasonable level of privacy and never discussed my time goals with anyone, apart from occasionally with Mum.

THEN THERE WERE THE BAD DAYS—THE DAYS WHERE I'D GET HOME FROM A HARD RUN OR LEG WORKOUT AND JUST THINKING ABOUT THE GOAL I'D SET FOR MYSELF MADE ME FEEL LIKE THROWING UP.

In fact, by the time I was about three months out from Berlin, this was something that had begun to play on my mind a fair bit. If I hadn't told anyone that my goal was to break three hours, then any time *under* my PB of 3 hours 10 minutes would have seemed like a successful result. But I had to go ahead and verbalise my goal (and write a whole fucking book about it), didn't I? I feared that would mean that even if I beat my PB but it was still over three hours it would look like I had failed.

After one particularly gruelling 'speed' run around this time, I found myself limping about the next day. I put speed in quote marks there, because the run was considerably slower than it was meant to be, and that put me in a bit of a funky mood. I even said to Jay-Jay, who was sitting on the sofa while I lay on the ground stretching out my aching body later that night, 'I'm starting to think that I simply won't be able to break three hours in Berlin.'

'Stop that sort of talk,' she snapped back firmly. 'You need to keep thinking positively.'

I knew she was right, and I think I am quite a positive person—but, as I've said, I'm also a realistic one. I don't believe in spin, hype or bullshit. In that moment, I was convinced that I would have to accept the reality that, no matter how hard I tried, I might not be good enough. It brought back memories of when I was in the Harriers team at school and, even though I did all the same training as my teammates, I just never made the improvements they did. 'Maybe I'm meant to just run, but not quickly,' I wondered aloud.

All it took was a day for me to shrug this funk and realise the silver lining of these bad days: even if they didn't always go exactly to Ian's plan, I was still learning to run as fast as I could under extreme pain and duress—an attribute that I knew would definitely come in handy in the later stages of the Berlin Marathon. I was also learning resilience. I had to; there was no other option. After getting down in the dumps about these runs, I still had to get up the next day and lace my shoes up, put on my determination face, remind myself of my goal, and get out and do it all over again.

The other fear I'd had at the back of my mind when I set my goal was that I might start to lose interest mentally. Thankfully, with a few months of training left to go, I was still incredibly focused on doing whatever it would take to give myself the best chance possible of achieving my goal. No shortcuts; no excuses. The thing with goals, especially the tough ones, is that you really have to want it bad. If you don't have a deep, burning desire to make it happen, chances are you will lose interest and won't be able to stick to it. Plus, you need that deep, burning desire to help combat the self-doubt and the bad days—and to remind yourself why, exactly, you are putting yourself through the ringer for an idea you cooked up in your own head.

Despite my momentary worries, everything seemed to be on the right track as I approached the point in my training where, as they say, shit was about to get real. I was running well and had no injuries. (Although a lot of podiatrists might disagree with that—my right foot had a completely dead toenail, another dying toenail, and an area of peeling skin where a blister had recently popped. To a marathon runner, none of this counts as an injury though; it's just the small bit of collateral damage that comes with the territory!) I was also way faster by this stage than I had been when I started training back in January, so something was paying off. I just needed to stick at it.

DURING THIS TIME, NOT long after the Hawke's Bay Marathon was done and dusted, Jay-Jay and I went on holiday to Vietnam for ten days. I had to remind myself that my training had to be a priority while we were away. While I've never thought of running as something that doesn't belong on a holiday, it's different when you've got a demanding training programme to follow. Instead of being able to just lace up my shoes and head out for a casual, tourist-style run, I would have to spend more time keeping an eye on the data on my watch than doing any sort of quality sightseeing. I'd told Coach Ian that I wanted to stick to my programme as faithfully as possible.

My first training run in Vietnam was at Halong Bay, and was 18 kilometres at race-pace intervals—meaning I'd need to run certain sections at the pace I hoped to run in Berlin (my 'race pace'), which was 4:14 minutes per kilometre. I got up at 6 am in order to get it done nice and early before it got too hot. In the middle of the day, it can reach 37 degrees Celsius there, with a humidity of 90-something per cent. It was already ridiculously hot when I woke up; it was also raining torrentially with non-stop claps of thunder and lightning, so I decided to postpone my run until it cleared up a bit. I finally got out at 8 am, and within moments it was clear that I would not be able to keep up with the speeds Coach Ian wanted me to run.

THE CONDITIONS WERE UNLIKE ANYTHING I HAD EVER RUN IN BEFORE—THE HEAT, THE HUMIDITY, THE SURFACE FLOODING, THE TRAFFIC AND THE TOOTING.

The conditions were unlike anything I had ever run in before—the heat, the humidity, the surface flooding, the traffic and the tooting. It was a bloody hard run, and involved a lot of walking breaks; for the final few kilometres I'd say I walked as much as I ran. I just hit a wall and felt more exhausted than I have ever felt at the end of a marathon. Plain and simple, I was fucked. When I at last returned to the hotel, I felt some degree of satisfaction at having completed this challenging run while on holiday, but I also felt bummed out at my inability to keep up the pace. It was one of those runs that watered the seeds of doubt in my mind. I tried to remind myself that the weather would be nothing like this in Berlin, and that I could have probably done the same run at home with no trouble.

A few hours later, I still felt mentally and physically shattered, whereas I'd usually feel full of extra energy to get me through the day. That was when I realised that this might have been at least part of the reason that I hadn't seen one single other runner while I was out that morning. I laughed when I'd seen a family of four whizz past on one scooter and—as if that wasn't unsafe enough already—Mum, who was driving, was also texting. I hadn't been able to stop myself from staring. It was one of the more ludicrous things I had ever seen.

That was when I'd realised that the two older kids on the back of the scooter were staring right back at me—and they were pointing and laughing. Perhaps a foreigner out running was one of the more ludicrous things that they had ever seen!

CHAPTER 13
THE COUNTDOWN IS ON . . .

ON 30 JUNE, A total of 87 days out from the Berlin Marathon, I ran the fastest I had ever run in my life. As I glanced at my watch while I was out for my training run (a gut-busting series of intervals where I had to run a kilometre as fast as possible followed by a slower kilometre), I saw the magic number: 3:33. I'd covered 1 kilometre in 3 minutes and 33 seconds.

This was unbelievably encouraging because it showed that all my training, and my perseverance with Coach Ian's programme, was paying off. After the run was done, I was rooted, but I also felt like I could have possibly gone a wee bit quicker if I'd really pushed it . . .

By this stage of my training, it had become redundant to even say that I was feeling exhausted. I was tired and sore *all the time*. Not only was I out running almost every day, but

Ian also had me doing leg workouts at the gym. Often, I'd be doing both on the same day. A double session. On more than one occasion, I'd get home after a gym session and my legs would be having these random little muscle spasms. At first, I found it almost impossible to get a run done on the same day after one of these gym sessions, but as my training progressed I started to notice that my body had begun to adapt and to simply adjust to the extra work.

THE EXHAUSTION I FELT WAS DEEPLY SATISFYING: A GOOD FEELING OF TIREDNESS, THE SORT OF TIREDNESS THAT ONLY COMES FROM HARD, PHYSICAL WORK.

Also, the exhaustion I felt was deeply satisfying: a good feeling of tiredness, the sort of tiredness that only comes from hard, physical work. I was the fittest I had ever been in my life, and I made an effort to remind myself of that fact whenever I was bombarded with serious doubts about the goal I had set. Even in light of the progress I was making, I still worried frequently that breaking three hours in Berlin just might not be possible for me; I worried that I was simply setting myself up for failure. I had to remind myself that, at the end of the day, the three-hour goal really didn't matter as much as all the great progress I was making. I was fitter than I had ever been in my life, *and* I was going to get to run the Berlin Marathon. I was doing all right.

It helps to keep things in perspective.

Around this time, I was given the opportunity to visit a place called the Millennium Institute on Auckland's North Shore to do some speed testing. There's a sign up at the institute that proudly tells you as you walk in: 'Be the best you can be.' Well, OK then.

The test took place on what was the biggest treadmill I had ever seen in my life. Seriously, you could have chucked a racehorse on this thing! Some dudes in white coats and holding clipboards watched over me while I ran with an oxygen mask on my face, making myself go faster and faster until I eventually gave up. The purpose of all this was to give me a science-based report of where my fitness level was at and how close (or far away) I was from running a marathon in under three hours.

I felt like a total imposter. The Millennium Institute is where New Zealand's top-tier athletes come to be even more awesome than they already are, and here I was, just an ordinary guy who was doing what he could to improve his marathon time and go from 'not bad' to 'pretty good'. This was also during the time that a number of our athletes were gearing up for the Summer Olympics in Rio de Janeiro. One of the athletes training this particular day was then nineteen-year-old pole vaulter Eliza McCartney (who, of course, went on to win bronze and become the youngest Olympic medallist in the women's pole-vault event—but none of us knew that then). Eliza and I got chatting, and I wished her luck.

As I drove home, drenched in sweat and exhausted, I passed a billboard on the side of the road for Anchor milk that featured Eliza's face complete with a determined and focused gaze. It made me think a lot about perspective and pressure. Here I was, hoping to break three hours in a marathon—not bad, but something thousands of other runners do each year—while she was hoping to win an Olympic medal—something that only 103 other Kiwis had ever done before her. No big deal. The only pressure I faced was the stuff I put on myself; no one else, at the end of the day, really cared whether I achieved my goal or not. Eliza, on the other hand, had pressure not just from herself but also from sponsors, coaches, the Olympic selection committee, government funding agencies *and* the New Zealand public! It dawned on me that even though Eliza and I couldn't have been more different, and the scale of our goals more far apart, we still shared one massive thing in common: just like the cheesy slogan on the wall at the Millennium Institute had told us to, we were both trying to be the best we could be.

AS I HIT THE three-month mark on my countdown to Berlin, I was finding that my runs had become even more draining than usual—not just physically, but mentally too. A lot of the runs in my programme were so demanding that I was feeling anxiety and nerves in the lead-up to doing them. If you took a look at my training week exactly three months out from Berlin, you'd start to see why.

That Monday, I had a weights session for my legs at the gym, and that took about an hour. When I woke up on Tuesday, my legs were still a bit sore, and I had to head out and do a 13-kilometre run with most of the distance at a pace so quick it made my entire body ache—all my internal organs were working so hard it felt like I was burning up from the inside out! Then on Wednesday, my legs even stiffer, I was required to run 20 kilometres at race-pace intervals. These intervals were so precise and so numerous that I had to write them out on my hand in order to remember them (with a Sharpie, as ballpoint pen would have smudged off due to how much I ended up sweating). On any normal day, 20 kilometres is a challenging distance to run, but I had to run it *fast* and my legs were already in pain before I began.

Are you starting to see why these runs were causing me anxiety?

It had reached the point where I was needing to get an hour or two of sleep before even attempting these runs if I wanted to hit my target times. But, remarkably, I was getting faster, and I was hitting my targets. I was just really, really tired.

THE SENSE OF LIBERATION I'D GET FROM RUNNING IN THE FRESH AIR AND NOT HAVING TO TALK TO ANYBODY OR THINK ABOUT ANYTHING WAS AMAZING, LIKE A FORM OF MINDFULNESS.

As far as jobs go, doing a breakfast radio show is bloody easy. It would be hard to call it a real job with a straight face. For all intents and purposes, I am paid to have a good time and give the audience a laugh on their morning drive. That said, though, there is still a lot more to it than most people realise. The question I get more than any other is, 'So you finish at ten in the morning? Do you have another job?' It's a reasonable question, I suppose, but there's a lot more to it than those four hours on-air. By the time you add in all the behind-the-scenes admin—planning, show meetings, recording sessions, and other bits and pieces, it ends up being just as many hours as any other job. A four-hour day? I wish! What's more, it's also really mentally and physically demanding, and the 4 am alarm calls can drive you insane.

In fact, the mental demands of my work are part of the reason I fell back into running in the first place; I found it to be the perfect way to clear my head after a show. The sense of liberation I'd get from running in the fresh air and not having to talk to anybody or think about anything was amazing, like a form of mindfulness. Back then, it didn't matter how long

I ran for. I just did what I felt like doing. My programme for Berlin could not have been more removed from this free and relaxed approach, and I realised that I missed it. Pretty much every run in my Berlin programme was designed for a very specific purpose: to change my body so that I would be able to run a certain speed (4:14 minutes per kilometre) over a certain distance (42.2 kilometres) on a certain day (Sunday 25 September).

This was a positive realisation to have. If nothing else, Coach Ian's super-intense programme had given me some valuable perspective by forcing me to really think about what running meant to me and why I did it. While I was feeling psyched about making gains and seeing myself get faster, I had come to understand that these improvements were definitely *not* what I love so much about running.

This epiphany made me quite happy. It was heartening to have it reinforced that even if I get slower as I get older, that's not why I run. I run because I love running. Pure and simple.

AT THE START OF August, with just under two months left until the Berlin Marathon, Jay-Jay got sick. As is always the case with winter bugs, it only takes one person at home or the office to be struck down for it to get shared around everyone else—and it is possibly even worse at a radio station, where you talk closely into a microphone that numerous other people have also breathed their germs on to. Within a couple of days, I too began to feel like I was coming down with the stupid virus. Fuck!

The timing was brilliant, of course. It had already been a tough week, and I had a couple of really demanding runs waiting for me. I couldn't really afford to take any time off from my training at this point. I mean, I *could* have, but I was so focused and had already put so much work into getting prepared for Berlin that the thought alone of taking even one day off killed me. The thought of going backwards was simply not an option. After googling numerous articles about whether it was good or bad to exercise when you are sick, I thought, *What the fuck do doctors know, anyway?* and carried on with my training as usual.

THE THOUGHT ALONE OF TAKING EVEN ONE DAY OFF KILLED ME. THE THOUGHT OF GOING BACKWARDS WAS SIMPLY NOT AN OPTION.

I was feeling like a zombie a lot of the time by this stage, and my life had been reduced to little more than work, exercise and rest. The 'rest' part included occasional daytime naps to muster enough energy for my runs, and I was spending my evenings alternating between wandering around in those ridiculous-looking compression tights and lying on the floor doing stretches. (I like the stretching bit: it feels good and really does relieve any pain and soreness.) But the bug hovered around, and my runs were not any easier for it. I had a few confidence-depleting runs during this week, and the fantasy I'd had back at the start of the year of crossing the line in Berlin fast and strong and well under three hours began to seem highly unlikely. It was becoming clear that, even though I was getting faster, if I did manage to achieve my goal it'd still be by the skin of my teeth.

I knew that running a sub-three marathon would require pain and suffering, and lots of it. I would need to embrace this suffering, a notion that goes against every natural human instinct.

ON SATURDAY MORNING JUST one month out from Berlin I ran a full marathon before 9.30 am. I love running the marathon distance, but I'd be lying if I told you it was my idea of fun to get out of bed in total darkness on a Saturday morning and run one all by myself on the empty, moonlit streets of my neighbourhood. Coach Ian, however, thought it'd be awesome. According to him, it'd be a confidence-building exercise—a sort of dress rehearsal for the real deal in just 29 days' time. I could see his logic . . . but I wasn't necessarily thrilled about what it meant for me.

I put myself to bed by 9 pm the night before. This was officially the earliest Friday night I could recall having since I was a small boy! For dinner, I'd eaten a big plate of pasta to top off a whole day of carbo-loading. (I had lost count of how many bowls of porridge I'd eaten.) When you run a marathon, you burn something like 3000 calories, so you need to make sure you eat enough to survive the distance. It's a lot like putting petrol into your car.

I got up at 4.30 am and ate some more porridge (even Goldilocks would have had trouble keeping up) and some English muffins, then I went back to bed until 6 am to let the food settle. When I got back out of bed again, I threw on the gear I'd carefully laid out the night before, but I left my iPod shuffle at home. I always train with music, but I never take it with me for the actual event, and I'd decided I'd stick to the 'train like you race' adage. The main reason I don't take music when I run a marathon is because I feel like I'd be missing out on enjoying everything around me if my ears were plugged up—the sound of thousands of rubber soles slapping the ground, strangers cheering you on, the music that lines the route. Each to their own, but I feel lucky every time I get to run in an iconic marathon, and it's a few hours of my life when I want to feel like I am fully part of something special, rather than blocked off from what is happening around me.

Not long after I'd got dressed, I heard the loud downpour of rain on the roof. The wind was howling outside. I sat down and seriously questioned my life's choices. My brain was begging me to go back to bed, but I refused. In that moment, I realised I was mentally a lot tougher than I had been giving myself credit for: how could I be lacking in mental fortitude if I had the discipline to stick to a programme like this even in this sort of weather?

I SAT DOWN AND SERIOUSLY QUESTIONED MY LIFE'S CHOICES.

Thankfully, the rain came and went, leaving me with just a stiff wind as an opponent. I'd chosen to do three laps of a 14-kilometre loop around my neighbourhood. The first lap was quite enjoyable. It was still dark and quiet—apart from the sound of the wind, of course. There is a certain smug satisfaction that you get from being up and exercising while the rest of the city is still asleep. It makes you feel like you are somehow better than the sleepers.

By the time I began the second lap, the street lights were off and there was a bit more traffic on the roads. I was feeling OK, I guess, but the wind and hills were making it hard work. I ground on and the kilometres ticked over one by one.

Midway through my third and final lap, at 35 kilometres, I was supposed to speed up and start running at the pace I hoped to run in Berlin (or even quicker). This was not happening. I gave it a solid try, then my calf muscles cramped up in protest. Fucking cramp! Nightmare recollections from the London Marathon came rushing back. Self-doubt returned.

All I could think was, *If this happens to me in Berlin, any chance of a decent time is out the window!*

I took a quick break to stretch my muscles out, then continued to run while repeating a mantra in my head that one of my Facebook friends told me she uses: *Pain is temporary. Glory is forever.* Over and over, rhythmically, in time with my steps, I repeated it to myself. I especially like this mantra. When you're out running, you can be so sore, in a world of pain, but as soon as you stop the pain goes away. You just have to remind yourself to keep running through the pain, because your finish time is something you will have for life, while any pain will soon be forgotten.

In the end, I completed this marathon-distance training run in 3 hours 17 minutes. I'd failed to achieve exactly what Coach Ian had wanted from the run, but it was still a faster marathon than most I had done, so it was hard to feel too disappointed.

It did make me just a touch more nervous than I already was about Berlin, though. Even though Berlin is flat and not known to be windy, seventeen minutes was a big chunk of time to have to lose.

THREE WEEKS AFTER IT first showed up, that flu was still kicking around. I just wanted it to piss off already. It was making my training even more difficult than it already was.

The silver lining, I reasoned, was that my runs would feel way easier as soon as I was back to full health. Not only was I reluctant to take a day off training, but it was also virtually impossible for me to take a sick day from work. We were in a radio ratings period, and the pressure to perform was intense. I and the other on-air staff were encouraged to try to work through any illness during these surveys.

After I got home from presenting a croaky-sounding morning show, a text message was waiting for me from my mum. She told me I needed to take a couple of days off from training. It was probably good advice—and, as a marathon runner herself, Mum doesn't tend to be unnecessarily sympathetic with her advice when it comes to training! Getting a day off work is hard, but it is still way easier than it was to get a day off school under my mum's watch.

But, of course, I chose to ignore Mum . . . and two days later I was forced to take a day off.

GETTING A DAY OFF WORK IS HARD, BUT IT IS STILL WAY EASIER THAN IT WAS TO GET A DAY OFF SCHOOL UNDER MY MUM'S WATCH.

As far as I could remember, I had not missed a day of training since the start of the year, so this was not a decision I made lightly. I felt a bit guilty even considering it, like I was being lazy or weak or something. But I just felt like crap—totally drained and completely wrecked. I still had a croaky throat (not ideal when you are paid to talk for a living) and I was utterly exhausted. I felt like my body was trying to warn me that if I didn't watch it and get some rest, then it would force me into taking an extended break. I most definitely did not want that.

TWO WEEKS OUT FROM the Berlin Marathon, I hit the part of my programme that is known as 'tapering'. I was still running a fair bit, but my training load eased off. The idea by this stage was to just get used to running at the pace I hoped to run in

Berlin: 4:14 minutes per kilometre. It still felt like hard and fast running to me, but it was manageable, and my training up to this point had given me the self-belief that I *could* run that pace and I *could* keep it up for a while. Could I keep it up for 42.2 kilometres? Well, that was the big unknown. A question I wouldn't know the answer to until 25 September, on the other side of the world.

THEN, ONE WEEK LATER, what had seemed like a far-fetched and possibly even totally unrealistic goal at the start of the year was all of a sudden within my reach. After spending over 200 days preparing my body, it was time for me to prepare my mind. I had never really paid too much attention to the psychological side of things when I'd done previous marathons. It just didn't really seem necessary to me—until now. Earlier I mentioned the idea of improving everything by just 1 per cent, and it occurred to me that getting my head straight could be one of those tiny little things that could make a big difference.

I planned to write some key words on my hand for during the race. Just some reminders of different phrases and techniques to keep me on task when the shit started to hit the fan. Because, without a doubt, things *would* get tough. Guaranteed. Everyone who runs a marathon experiences highs and lows throughout the race. I hoped these notes would help me to stay focused during the dark patches.

One trick I'd read about and that I actually really liked came from Paula Radcliffe, a woman who knows a thing or two about running a decent marathon. She won the London and New York marathons not once, but *three* times each! And, at the time of writing, she still held the women's world record for the marathon of 2 hours 15 minutes 25 seconds.

She called her trick a 'disassociation technique', and it was basically to count from one to one hundred, three times over. For her, counting to a hundred three times would cover a mile of running, and by the time she'd finished she reckoned she had usually come right again. So I would definitely write the word 'count' on my hand.

IF I BREATHE ON AUTOPILOT, I GENERALLY END UP PANTING LIKE A DOG AND TAKING SHALLOW LITTLE GULPS OF AIR.

Another word would be 'breathe'. This may seem redundant, since it is something we all do without even thinking about it, but the word would serve as an important reminder. I find it helps if I focus on the pattern of my breath if I want to be running fast and be relaxed at the same time. If I breathe on autopilot, I generally end up panting like a dog and taking shallow little gulps of air. Seeing the word 'breathe' would remind me to take air in through my nose in long and deep breaths over three or four steps, then to exhale through my mouth over a few paces.

The last thing I would write on my hand would be the words 'courage wolf'. The courage wolf comes from an old Cherokee legend, and is a reminder to stay positive. It goes something like this: a Native American chief tells his grandson that everyone has two wolves in their mind—a courageous, brave wolf, and a bitter, negative wolf. These two wolves are always fighting each other. When the young boy asks his grandad which wolf will survive, the chief replies, 'The one that you feed.'

Yeah, it might be a bit cheesy. I have never been a huge fan of those wishy-washy motivational quotes that get shared online, but here I was, totally buying in to one.

Would it help having this stuff written on my hand? I had no idea. But what I did know is that it definitely couldn't hurt my chances.

ONE PROBLEM I HAVE had in almost every marathon I have run is a drop-off in speed somewhere between 30 kilometres and the finish line. This is perfectly understandable—your body is exhausted by that point, so of course you start to slow down. I had always just assumed this was unavoidable, my body's way of screaming at me to stop fucking running because it had had enough. *But,* I wondered as Berlin loomed large, *what if this slowdown in speed could be avoided or controlled? What if it happens because my brain is the part of the body that is calling the shots on behalf of my legs? What if I slow down because I am just not mentally prepared?*

I had so many what ifs, but only a week left until the big day.

I was nervous.

I was excited.

I'd experience waves of being anxious about the run, then have waves (albeit much smaller ones) of feeling quite confident and relaxed about things.

It was in this turbulent emotional state that I went out and did something that I had sworn I would never, ever, ever do: I went and got myself some proper running shorts. You know, the ones with the high split up the side of the thigh. The really nerdy ones. As I have mentioned, I had never been a fan of these shorts. They look seriously pornographic and always struck me as being unnecessary. I mean, how much time are runners *actually* saving by wearing these leg-revealing shorts as opposed to just a nice comfortable pair that goes down to the middle of the thigh? It's like swimmers who shave their legs—how much time are they *really* saving? Michael Phelps could wear a gorilla suit and still kick my arse over 50 metres of freestyle.

But, if I'm truly honest with myself, part of my resistance to the rude split-shorts probably stems from the idea that I've never thought of myself as good enough or fast enough to wear them. Silly, I know. It's probably also a bit of the lingering anarchist in me—I've never wanted to be one of those posers who have all the good gear but no actual substance.

AFTER ALL, THE SPLIT-SHORTS MIGHT JUST HAVE BEEN ANOTHER 1-PER-CENT CHANGE I COULD MAKE.

I decided that it was time for me to get over that. After all, the split-shorts might just have been another 1-per-cent change I could make.

When I took my porno shorts out for a test run I felt a little self-conscious . . . until a bunch of middle-aged men in Lycra (aka MAMILs) came riding past on their bicycles. I may have looked funny wearing these shorts with splits that offered a glimpse of the parts of my legs that are pale white because they never see the sun, but I still looked way less ridiculous than the cyclists!

DURING THIS WEEK, COACH Ian sent me a message on Facebook to ask how everything was going.

Ian: How is the packing and planning going for your trip? All set?

Me: Yeah, mate. All good. Got my running gear sorted and laid out today. Nervous, but excited. I know I'm in the best shape I've been in. Still lack a bit of self-belief—not entirely sure I'm capable of a sub-three—but got my game face on and ready to trust the training and give it everything! 👊

Ian: We always knew it was going to be touch-and-go for a sub-three, but everything is pointing towards it being more than possible! Best ever LSS and LSO pace, fastest 1 kilometre, 10 kilometre and half marathon. You have sub-three in your sights!

Me: Thanks for the positivity, mate! Who knows what's possible on the day? Gonna chuck everything at it . . . in a patient and controlled way. Haha.

Ian: Yeah, man, you have this sorted! That's based in science and not 'a feeling'!

I always find Coach Ian's messages encouraging, especially since he knows what he's talking about and is basing his predictions on detailed data. This exchange was no exception.

I needed it too, because as the clock ticked towards Berlin I was feeling *scared*. I think a huge reason for that was because I was so prepared. I know that might sound like a contradiction, but I hadn't put in anywhere near as much effort for my other marathons, so I'd always just been happy to turn up on the day and settle for whatever time the running gods saw fit to throw my way. This year, though, I'd worked harder than I'd ever worked before. I had stayed true to my promise: I had left no stone unturned. And, while this knowledge should have been filling me with confidence, I was also petrified. When you've invested so much in something, you've got a lot to lose if things don't turn out how you hope they will.

There was nothing left for me to do now except take my running shoes and my rude shorts to Berlin.

CHAPTER 14
HOLY SHITBALLS!

THE DAY BEFORE I flew out to Berlin, I worked on the radio
in the morning, then the rest of my day was stacked with
appointments and travel admin. I went to the osteopath so he
could have a tinker with my hip, which had been niggling me
for the past few weeks, then I went to see my doctor to try
to hustle some sleeping pills from her. My doctor is like the
opposite of Michael Jackson's doctor: getting any good drugs
out of her is nearly impossible! But I managed to succeed this
time. I wouldn't have left without them, though: I knew it was
imperative that I recover from the travel and get into a good
sleep rhythm in Berlin as quickly as possible, and sleeping
pills were the only thing that would help me do this in such
a short space of time. I wanted to be sure I'd eliminated all
possible hitches, including jet-lag.

After all my appointments and once I'd finished packing I
set out for one last run on Aotearoa soil. It was a 12-kilometre
jog all up, and I enjoyed it.

Jay-Jay dropped me at the airport around eight o'clock, a couple of hours before my flight was due to depart. I was travelling alone due to the fact we were in a radio ratings period; Jay-Jay had to stay at home for work. As you know, I was only allowed a week off, so it was pretty much a there-and-back affair. I'd spend almost as much time in the air as I would on the ground. In the departures area, I ran into a couple who were heading to LA and said they had heard our show on the radio that morning. After a couple of minutes of small talk, they said their goodbyes and wished me luck for breaking three hours. I was instantly flooded with a wave of nerves. *Fuck! Why did I tell anyone about my sub-three goal? Let alone broadcast it!*

I WAS FEELING WAY MORE ON EDGE ABOUT THIS MARATHON THAN I HAD EVER FELT ABOUT A RUN BEFORE.

I was feeling way more on edge about this marathon than I had ever felt about a run before. I'd expected to feel more relaxed about this one, due to the amount of training I'd done and my tangible improvements, but my pre-race nerves were out of control. I had discovered during the year that my level of self-belief wasn't that great. I wished I could be cocky about the run, with an 'I got this' swagger about me, but perhaps that is just something that some people are born with?

I started doing this little mind-game mantra thing I'd recently come up with—a technique, a strategy, call it whatever you want. Basically, whenever I became aware that I was getting nervous about Berlin, I'd repeat the following statement to myself a few times over: 'Trust the training. Enjoy the occasion. You've got this!'

It's not the sort of thing I'd usually have done, but it seemed to help. It stopped any negative thoughts right in their tracks and replaced them with a more positive frame of mind. I slowly started to feel calmer, and tried to focus on how cool it was that the time had come. I was finally going to Berlin, and I was finally going to get the chance to put my training to the test.

I GOT OFF THE plane in Berlin at 6 pm local time, three flights and 28 hours later . . . only to discover that my bag had been lost. Disaster!

I waited at the baggage carousel. And waited. And waited. Eventually, every last person from my flight had dispersed. I was tired and pissed off and I couldn't even shout at anybody because I couldn't speak any fucking German. I calmed myself down and took stock of the situation. On the bright side, I had (sensibly) packed all my running clothes and my shoes and watch in my carry-on luggage, just in case this happened. The only essentials in my missing bag were my gels, beetroot shots, energy-drink powders and porridge sachets for race day. Coach Ian had got me on to the beetroot shots, which are just a 70-ml bottle of beetroot and lemon juice and are apparently a wonder-drug for endurance athletes. I struggled to see how they could make a big difference, but I wasn't going to question it—it all came back to that rule of 1 per cent. (Athletic performance aside, one thing the beetroot shots definitely did do was freak me out whenever I took a pee. It is truly remarkable how one small shot of liquid can turn the entire contents of your bladder pink!)

You don't want to try anything new on race day, so all this stuff was pretty important to me.

Shit, why didn't I put that stuff in my carry-on as well? I berated myself.

After walking what felt like a similar distance to the marathon itself, I found a standalone building in the middle of the carpark, which is where you were meant to go to claim your baggage . . . if you were lucky. There were passengers in tears and lots of shouting and arm waving. After 30 minutes in line I got my turn—and that's when I found out the hard way that you should never throw away your baggage receipts. You know, those little barcoded stickers that go on the back of your boarding pass. Without these, I was told in broken English, the airport staff could not help me find my bag.

I was no longer angry. I was just sad. If there hadn't been so many people around, I might even have curled up on the lino in the foetal position and sobbed. In my defence, I had an obscene amount of paperwork going on. I'd had three boarding passes, so after each flight I had thrown out the pass I no longer needed. What an idiot.

And anyway, what were the chances that, of all the days, this would be the first time I'd lose my bags?

Defeated, I got into a taxi and headed to my hotel. There was nothing left for me to do but hope for the best and prepare for the worst. I checked into my room and showered, and immediately felt a bit better. Before going to bed, I called Jay-Jay and asked her if she could check if Air New Zealand had details of my baggage receipts, since they had issued them in Auckland. By this stage I was too exhausted to even think about dealing with this shit.

The next morning, I woke up to great news: the Air New Zealand team back in Auckland had located my bag. Thank fuck! After making the twelve-hour flight to Shanghai and another twelve-hour flight to Zurich, it had somehow got lost on the one-hour flight to Berlin. (Seriously, how is that even possible?) It was now waiting for me at the airport. I could have called and had it sent to the hotel, but I didn't want to take any more chances. Also, I had found that most of the local Berliners could speak only a little bit of English, so communication was much easier face-to-face than over a phone. I got in a taxi and headed back to the airport's most depressing little building to get my bag myself.

Disaster averted.

The taxi driver who picked me up was a Serbian man who spoke incredible English, but had very little knowledge about marathon running.

'You might win!' he exclaimed enthusiastically when I told him I was in town for the Berlin Marathon.

I laughed and assured him that I wouldn't.

'You just have to think positive,' he told me. 'You never know what can happen.'

'If I have a really good run, I'll break three hours,' I explained to him. 'But the person who wins will do the whole thing in just over two hours.'

He paused for a couple of seconds to absorb this. Then he shook his head. 'Maybe you will surprise yourself.'

'YOU JUST HAVE TO THINK POSITIVE,' HE TOLD ME. 'YOU NEVER KNOW WHAT CAN HAPPEN.'

WITH MY BAG IN hand at last, and less than 48 hours until the race, I could finally resume my normal build-up. I got out for my last run before the marathon—a 7-kilometre run at race pace. I managed it reasonably comfortably, but that annoying, nagging voice in my head popped up again. *But can you keep that pace up for another 35 kilometres?* it asked me. *That's* *around two and a half hours of running . . .*

I tried to block out this negative self-talk by reminding myself of all the training I had done, and picturing myself being spurred on by the crowds of supporters and the company of the other runners. *Stay positive and trust your training*, I told myself.

I headed out to the race expo. Some runners despise these things. They just want to get in, get their number, and get out again in the shortest time possible. Not me. As I've mentioned, I *love* the race expo. Imagine a mall of running shops full of things that you don't need and had no idea even existed. It's running-nerd heaven. There are toggles to make sure your shoelaces never come undone on a run, hats with pockets in the side to hold your running gels, straps and packs and pockets to hold every kind of running gadget—basically, if you can imagine something ludicrous to do with running, it has probably already been invented and will be for sale at the expo. I always seem to leave these things with a whole lot of commemorative gear that I hardly ever end up wearing. I have windbreaker jackets from Boston and New York, and hoodies from London and Chicago. It's overkill, but I don't care. On the rare occasion when I do wear any of these items, it takes me right back to the event and brings up all sorts of good memories.

One big difference about the Berlin expo from all the others I'd been to was this bracelet system: all the runners were given a lightweight material bracelet that was glued on tight, sort of like the wristbands you get at music festivals or waterparks. This bracelet indicated you were a registered runner. If you lost it or took it off, you would not be allowed to enter the starting area of the marathon the next morning.

I got in line and picked up my race pack, which included

my number. Then I made a tiny mistake that wouldn't present itself till later in the afternoon and would eventually morph into a rather big headache.

Once I'd got the formalities out of the way, I was free to wander around the halls and check out all the gear. This was probably the most disappointing expo I had been to. I ended up buying a couple of official Berlin Marathon tops and beanies, then I got out of there. The sheer mass of people made it claustrophobic and difficult to get around, and the big Adidas stall selling all the official race gear was shambolic. Imagine what K-Mart would be like on Boxing Day if everything was 50 per cent off. It was pretty intense.

Back at the hotel, I went through my race pack and got out my race number. I just stared at it for a few seconds: 19855. One thing I always do the day before a race is pin my number to my shirt. I am very particular about this, so it often takes me a few attempts before I get it just right.

THE SUPERMARKET AND TWO SMALL DAIRIES LATER, I WAS OFFICIALLY STARTING TO PANIC.

I like it to be straight.

I like it to be tight enough that it won't flap about or irritate me.

And I like it to be quite high up so that I can use the bottom of my top to wipe the sweat from my face when I need to.

It was at this precise moment that I realised the mistake I had made: I had left the race expo without picking up any of the safety pins provided.

'No need to panic,' I told myself. 'No big deal. I'll just wander along to that supermarket up the road and buy some.'

The supermarket and two small dairies later, I was officially starting to panic. Shit! I was running out of time. I still had no safety pins. My options were dwindling.

I could ask other runners in the hotel, I thought—but there was no guarantee they would have any spares.

I went to the hotel concierge desk.

'Do you have any safety pins?' I asked, a frantic note creeping into my voice.

The two men standing at the desk looked very confused. 'Safety . . . puns?' they asked. They clearly had no idea what I was talking about, so I googled a picture and showed them. After some brief discussion, one of them disappeared to the office out back and returned with a little hotel sewing kit. Brilliant. I tore it open hastily to find it contained one small gold safety pin. Not the ideal size for the job, but desperate times and all that. It would have to do.

'Can I have three more of these?' I asked, waving the sewing kit at the men at the desk.

They both looked at me quizzically, as if to say, 'Shit, mate. How much sewing are you doing?' But they provided the goods.

I was happy beyond belief.

The two men shot me one last weird glance when they saw just how much joy these four miniature sewing kits gave me.

THAT NIGHT I ATE a pasta dinner. I had found a restaurant a couple of buildings down from my hotel that did great pasta, so I ate most of my meals there. Since I was travelling alone, I also dined alone. I found the experience quite lonely. I usually like my own company, but when you realise you are alone on the other side of the world and surrounded by people who you can't have a conversation with even if you want to, you suddenly feel very isolated. All it did was give me more thinking time, when what I really needed were distractions—banter from friends, strangers, anyone—to keep my mind off the impending run.

That night, I slept terribly. The jet-lag, despite my best efforts, jumped up and bit me firmly on the arse. From 1 am, I tossed and turned, kept awake by my confused body clock and wracked with negative thoughts about the run. It was very unhelpful. Not even one of my doctor's sleeping pills knocked me out.

The next morning, with 24 hours to go before the run, I went downstairs for breakfast in the hotel and met some other English-speaking runners—a couple from London, half a dozen from Australia and two other Kiwis. It was so nice to hear a familiar accent. Actually, it was just nice to hear a familiar language! Even though the entire conversation was about running, at least it took me away from my own thoughts for a bit.

This Commonwealth crew were all catching the subway out to Olympiastadion Berlin, where the 1936 Olympics were held, for an event called 'the breakfast run': a 5-kilometre jog to loosen up the legs the day before the marathon. I didn't want to run, preferring to rest my legs as much as possible, but I tagged along to support. The distraction was more than welcome! And the stadium, where US sprinter Jesse Owens won four Olympic gold medals, was breathtaking and inspiring. Just what I needed.

Afterwards, I went out for lunch—more pasta at the restaurant along from the hotel. I took Coach Ian's race notes with me and read them over again. I wanted to have my race plan committed to memory.

Hi, Dom

I hope you're all set for your trip! Just remember that you have trained well for this, and you're running at a cross between a pace we've worked out from your current ability and your goal of a sub-three-hour marathon—so we know you can do this!

Start your warm up about fifteen or twenty minutes prior to the race start with walking to a light jog for about five minutes, and include a couple of light sprints. After this, do a couple of dynamic stretches, focusing on the lunge matrix: forward lunge, forward lunge and twist over front leg, side lunge, side and backwards lunge (45-degree), backwards lunge, and bodyweight squats. DO NOT do any low squats during this period. Once you're done, you should have ten or fifteen minutes left till the race start.

For pacing, we're working on a rough positive-split strategy, as this seems to work best for you. The first couple of kilometres will be run slightly slower than your target pace—around 4:20 minutes per kilometre. This only needs to be for 2 kilometres. After this, aim for a pace of between 4:10 and 4:14 for the first 30 kilometres. At this point, if you are still feeling fresh, you can keep to this pace or let it naturally slide down to 4:15. If you are still feeling good at 37 kilometres, keep this pace. Otherwise, a slow to 4:15 to 4:20 pace is OK—you'll have enough time in the bank to still get your 2:59:59!

Remember your beetroot shots, and your gels, and keep these the same as you've had—no experimenting on race day, even if they give you free stuff in your race pack!

4:15 is the magic average pace; 4:16 will give you a time of 3:00:01!

Don't forget that the fast-finish work you have done—along with the weight training and beetroot shots—means that you can up the intensity for the final 2–5 kilometres, even if this just means getting back to a 4:14 pace.

Don't get focused on negative splits or bummed out because you think they are the fastest way to run a marathon. Everyone is different, and stopping the slow down after 30 kilometres is your version of negative splits.

Cramp is not an issue for you, as the relative intensity of the marathon time trial where you got cramp is a lot higher than the pace you will be running at flat Berlin.

Does that all seem clear as mud?! Haha! Let me know if you have any questions . . .

You're going to smash it!

AT LONG LAST, THE day had finally arrived: 25 September 2016. The day that had consumed me for the whole year. The day that I had planned for, dreamed about, stressed about. The day that had kept me awake some nights. The day that I had thought about as I ran—often in extreme discomfort—up hills, down hills, in the rain, wind, dark, hot and cold. The day that had been my top priority since the year had started 269 days earlier.

I got up and showered. It seems like an odd thing to do when you are just going to go and get all sweaty, but it's something I have always done before a marathon. I shower and shave, then I put on my running clothes, which I always lay out the night before. I think I just enjoy getting to the start feeling as fresh and as sharp as I possibly can.

Once dressed, I went downstairs for breakfast. I used my own porridge from home and had a banana and a slice of toast with honey. I washed it down with a sachet of sports drink called S.O.S., which I had also brought from home.

After that I teamed up with the other runners staying at the hotel and we all took the subway to the start area, a long, straight road, more than long enough to accommodate 40,000 runners, that runs alongside a huge 520-acre park called the Tiergarten. As with all marathons, the lines for the Port-A-Loos were HUGE, so the bushes of this huge green space came in very handy!

It was a beautiful, sunny morning, a bit warmer than usual, which was not ideal for running but at least made the anxious pre-run wait more pleasant than it had been at Boston or New York. I methodically ran through all my warm-ups and stretches, swallowed one of my ghastly, sickly gels, then took my place in Start Block D when the 'twenty minutes to go' announcement was made. In all the World Marathon Majors I have run, I have found the starting corrals amazing. You will often notice people 20 or 30 kilometres into the run who were standing next to you before you started.

The wait went quickly and was actually quite enjoyable. There was a DJ playing dance music, the sun was shining and everyone was in a great mood. I knew that once I started running I was in for (hopefully) just under three hours of pain and discomfort, so I allowed myself to relax and enjoy this moment. I had done all I could; now all I had to do was run.

Then the gun went off. It was all on.

Thousands of white balloons floated up into the air above

us . . . and after 3 minutes 19 seconds of shuffling, I crossed the start line. 'Let's do this!' I said to myself as I started my watch.

From the start line, you run straight ahead for a couple of kilometres towards this huge monument called the Siegessaule (which means 'victory column') that sits in the middle of a roundabout. My goal was to run to this 60-metre-tall landmark at a pace of around 4:20, as Coach Ian had instructed but, as soon as I started to run, I began to worry that this may not be possible. The corral was a shambles and the road was crowded with slower runners. *Fuck!* I panicked a bit. Due to Berlin's reputation as the world's fastest marathon, I had assumed the starting corrals would have been excellent—much like those I'd experienced in the other majors—but I found myself dodging and weaving in and out of people, speeding up for sprint bursts, then being forced to slow down. I was running on footpaths then back on roads, running along raised median sections on the road. Hell, there were even a few occasions when I ended up running on the footpath behind the specators! It was crazy.

I'd run 5 kilometres before I was able to settle into a nice pattern and just focus on the act of running. Fortunately, I made it through the panic part and managed to keep to my planned pace: I'd done the first kilometre in 4:26, but had managed to make up the lost time and complete the second kilometre in 4:14.

Even though Berlin is famous for being flat and fast, a lot of the streets are quite narrow. That's not a problem for the runners up the front who are trying to break world records, but for the rest of us I learned that it can be a crammed nightmare. By the time I had battled my way through all the congestion and hit the 5-kilometre mark, it had taken me just over 21 minutes—thankfully still bang on target for a 2 hour 59 minute marathon.

I could at last relax, breathe, focus, and read the notes on my hand and listen to my body. So that is exactly what I did.

I don't remember noticing the amazing Reichstag building at 6 kilometres, or even the Fernsehturm Berlin TV tower that is so tall it can be seen from many parts of the course. I ran past so many incredible things. There was the beautiful hundred-year-old Rathaus Schöneberg city hall, where John F. Kennedy gave a famous speech in the sixties saying '*Ich bin ein Berliner*' ('I am a Berliner'), but I didn't even notice this head-turning building. Nor did I notice crossing the line of pavers on the road which are the scar left across the city from where the Berlin Wall once stood. All I noticed was the back of the person in front of me and my watch. I was too busy paying attention to how I was feeling to notice anything else. I could have been anywhere in the world—the sights and sounds were not something I could enjoy on this particular day.

I COULD AT LAST RELAX, BREATHE, FOCUS, AND READ THE NOTES ON MY HAND AND LISTEN TO MY BODY.

Everything was going well. I mean, it was hard and I never felt totally in control, but I was sticking to the necessary pace and executing my game plan to the letter. I made it to the halfway mark in 1 hour 28 minutes 14 seconds: my fastest half-marathon time ever! I even had some buffer, which meant I could run the second half in 1 hour 31 minutes and still be just under three hours.

Nonetheless, some doubts were starting to creep in. Yeah, I was still on track . . . but, with so much running left to go,

I should have been feeling way better than I was. I thought about Coach Ian's note that I could increase my speed a bit if I was feeling good at 30 kilometres, and I already knew that was going to be unlikely. A sub-three-hour run was still on the cards . . . but, if it was going to happen, it would be ugly and it would be tight.

Kilometre number 27 was when the real self-doubt started. That kilometre took me 4:18, which was only slightly off pace, but it felt like I was sprinting. The next kilometre took 4:20, then the next 4:28. When I got to the 30-kilometre sign I was still on pace, but that big goal time was slowly starting to slip away. I got angry. I thumped my left leg a few times with a closed fist. I'm not sure why; I wasn't really thinking straight by that stage. Maybe it was some sort of bizarre attempt to try to wake my legs up and make them work harder, like a jockey whips a horse? Who knows.

'You've worked all fucking year for this,' I told myself. 'You need to focus, breathe, count your steps, think of the courage wolf—do all that mental shit you had planned and just go for it.'

I ran that kilometre in 4:14—right on target pace. But it took everything out of me and from that point I was gone. Each kilometre got slower and slower. I should have been devastated, but I was too exhausted for that, both mentally and physically. I was honestly too fatigued to even care anymore. I was running as fast as I could and doing everything in my power to keep going, but it was nowhere near fast enough.

At the 35-kilometre sign, I glanced at my watch: 2 hours 32 minutes. A sub-three-hour marathon from here would require around a 4:00 pace. I had *no* chance.

I wasn't too far from the finish—somewhere in between the 41-kilometre and 42-kilometre signs—when I saw my watch tick over to three hours. I felt a moment of sadness. I had given it everything. *Everything*. And I had got *so* close. Nowhere near close enough, though.

I was still on track for a brand-new personal best, a time that would be way faster than I had run in Chicago a year earlier, but a time that was nonetheless a long way off the one I desperately wanted.

Dom, this is not the time for sulking, I reminded myself as I turned a corner and the Brandenburg Gate loomed up ahead of me. I was almost there. Gritting my teeth through the excruciating pain, I pushed myself forward, one painful step at a time. All the while, the wonderful German spectators shouted words of encouragement to spur me on (or, at least, I assume they were words of encouragement; it's not like I could understand any of it).

I might have missed out on taking in so much on the course due to my intense focus on myself, but I will never forget running towards the middle of the five columns of the gate, then under and through them. I had visualised this moment hundreds of times over the past year, so I made sure I savoured it. Yeah, it would have been way more enjoyable if I had run through the gate a few minutes earlier, but that was just not to be.

After the Brandenburg Gate, it is a straight run of around 300 metres to the finish line. Approaching that line was a feeling like no other. The finish sign grew bigger with every step. I could hear loud music pumping and the crowd in the grandstands cheering. Every part of me was in pain, but I knew it was just about over. With one last groan of adrenaline-fuelled pain, I pushed with everything I had, trying to muster my best version of a sprint in an attempt to shave every last second possible off my time.

I crossed the line in 3 hours 5 minutes 43 seconds.

After stumbling for a few paces, I stopped and leaned over, my head down and my hands resting on my knees. After a brief pause I felt a hand on my back; one of the race marshals was ushering me forward. I walked through the finishers' chute and had a medal placed round my neck by one of the thousands of volunteers.

'*Glückwünsche!*' she congratulated me (I think).

'Thanks,' I tried to reply, but it came out as a grunting noise instead of words.

I had absolutely nothing left to give. I had left it all out there on the roads of Berlin—every last drop of energy I had.

I was satisfied.

IT GOES WITHOUT SAYING that I was disappointed not to have broken three hours. Of course I was. But I was nowhere near as disappointed as I thought I would be. I had been worried that I would spend the entire 27 hours of my flight home sulking about the whole year being a complete waste of time, but as it turned out I actually felt really good about my run and about my finish time. I had shaved a full five minutes off my personal best. Even now, as I sit here writing this book, I look back over the run and wonder if I could have done anything different.

Sure, there are little bits and pieces that would have helped. The most obvious thing was that the zig-zagging, frenetic running I'd been forced to do in the first few kilometres in order to avoid the crowd had meant that I ended up running an extra 260 metres. That would have been over a minute of extra running. The marathon majors all have a blue line that marks the precise distance of 42.195 kilometres, and if you stick to this blue line as faithfully as possible you will avoid running further than you have to. That might be easy for the front runners; for the rest of us it's easier said than done!

But, even if I had got that minute back, it still wouldn't have put me under the three-hour mark. And that's a really cool feeling. I can say with absolute certainty that I gave it my absolute best shot. What more can any of us hope to do?

AS I WALKED (OR, more accurately, awkwardly hobbled) through the hotel lobby, I bumped into another runner who was heading in the opposite direction. We were both wearing our finishers' medals and covered in a film of dry sweat. We made eye contact and acknowledged each other in the silent way only marathon runners can, and I asked him how he'd got on.

'I ran in three hours seven,' he replied in accented-but-still-awesome English.

Two minutes slower than my time. 'Is that the fastest you've ever run a marathon?' I asked.

'No,' he replied. 'I have run five marathons, all of them under three hours. This one was just for the fun.'

Even though the three-hour mark had eluded me, I knew exactly what he was talking about. The work that goes into preparing the human body to run that fast is mind-blowing. Obviously, it varies from runner to runner, according to natural ability and other factors, but even the most gifted natural runner would have to make sacrifices and put in some serious work to be able to finish in that time.

Of course, the difference between the stranger I met in Berlin and me is that he can be at peace; he's already broken three hours, and can now run for the sheer love of it. What's more, he's broken three hours on several occasions, so it's no one-off fluke.

And that was the dilemma I faced in the immediate aftermath of the Berlin Marathon. I gave it a good, honest crack, I chucked everything at it . . . and I fell short.

When I got back to my room, I found a message waiting on my phone from Coach Ian. He'd sent it at 12.20 am New Zealand time.

> Fuck yeah! Well done, mate! A new PB!!! I know that was hard, and the sub-three was maybe a bit too far . . . but another PB is fucking awesome mate! And next year maybe that sub-three might be on the cards?

He had stayed awake through the whole race, watching it on telly and also following my progress in real time on the official race app. If there is one thing more painful than running a marathon, it would have to be staying awake on a Sunday night watching one on TV! Coach Ian later told me his wife, Fiona, who doesn't really care about running all that much, stayed up watching it with him. Ian explained to her that, since there were 40,000 people running, they probably wouldn't see me on the TV. But every time a new camera shot showed another group of the frontrunners, the world's fastest men over that distance, Fiona would lean forward and ask, 'Is Dom in that group?'

I wish!

Ian's message raised that nagging little internal voice. Should I put my goal to bed, knowing that I gave it my best shot . . . or should I try again? At what point does it go from being a tantalising challenge to being a sad obsession?

There was a part of me that felt that, as long as my times were still getting faster, it might still be possible. Another part of me wondered if it would really be worth the effort.

Ultimately, though, I knew for certain that I'd discovered that my love for running is not wrapped up in winning or in being fast—even though both of those things do feel fucking great. For me the joy comes from the simple act of just running. I was pleased with my result, and the endorphins had me riding a natural high . . . but I still felt restless.

That nagging voice kept haunting me with a variety of what ifs: *What if you just gave it one more go? What if you train even harder? What if you lose a bit more weight? Every kilo you lose is one you don't have to run with.*

What if . . .

CHAPTER 15
THE BERLIN COMEDOWN

IN THE HOURS AND days immediately following the Berlin Marathon, my mind was all over the place. I'd have periods of calm satisfaction during which I felt assured I'd done everything in my control to put together the fastest marathon I was capable of. Then I'd have moments of unrest, when I'd have flashbacks to all the work that I'd put into my sub-three goal and the shitton of sacrifices I had made—the runs when I was sick, the long runs in the searing heat of Vietnam, the excruciating, gutbusting speed sessions, the treadmill tests, the weights sessions at the gym, the vomit-inducing 10-kilometre time trials and the two full marathons as training runs. And then there were the numerous personal and social sacrifices I had made, like leaving my best mate's fiftieth birthday right after making my speech because I had to put my training first.

It was a wonderful result to have shaved five minutes off

my personal best—but a crazy amount of work had gone into doing it.

Part of me still wondered if I had overthought things. Maybe my worst enemy was my own mind? Perhaps I had failed at my goal of breaking three hours in my own head, long before I even got to the start line in Berlin? I was fit enough and fast enough, and all of Coach Ian's scientific results suggested it should be possible, yet somehow I had managed to fuck up science! How is that even possible?

PART OF ME STILL WONDERED IF I HAD OVERTHOUGHT THINGS. MAYBE MY WORST ENEMY WAS MY OWN MIND?

Running is a simple sport. It is literally just a matter of putting one foot in front of the other as quickly as you can. I wondered if I had overcomplicated it with my anxiety, or my perfectionism, or whatever the hell else. For months, almost every waking moment (and many of the moments when I should have been sleeping) had been consumed by this one run—whether I was reading about it, thinking about it, writing about it or talking about it. It had become an obsession. Even when I got to Berlin, the 60 hours I had on the ground before the run were completely focused on my goal. But I had done all the hard work; I had got myself in peak physical condition. Perhaps the only message I needed was 'just run'?

The day before I had flown out to Berlin, Mum had popped round to say goodbye and wish me luck. 'Even if you don't break three hours, I'll still love you,' she told me.

I'd burst out laughing. It seemed a strange thing to say, but with a bit of hindsight I realised that Mum had probably been able to see just how highly strung I had become. Mums are pretty good at spotting that kind of thing.

THE NIGHT AFTER THE Berlin Marathon, I went out for a drink with Paul Martelletti and his wife, Karen. Paul might just be the fastest New Zealand runner you have never heard of. He currently holds the world record for being the fastest person dressed as a superhero to run a marathon, which he earned running the London Marathon in 2 hours 29 minutes 57 seconds. Like me, both Paul and Karen are from Palmerston North, but they now live in London. Paul had also run the Berlin Marathon the day before.

We'd had Paul on our radio show just prior to the start of the Summer Olympics in Rio. Paul had run a marathon under the Olympic qualifying time, but Athletics New Zealand decided not to nominate him for the Olympics because he didn't meet the New Zealand Olympic Committee's independent standards, which are even quicker than the times set by the Olympic bosses. Basically, it's a roundabout way of saying that if you don't have a chance of finishing up the front they don't want to know about you; they don't want to send someone who is just going to be making up numbers. After an on-air campaign, some prime-time TV coverage and tens of thousands of dollars in legal fees to lodge an appeal, Paul's Olympic dream was denied.

Paul finished in twentieth place in the Berlin Marathon, with an eye-watering time of 2 hours 16 minutes 58 seconds. He and I got talking about 'magic numbers'.

'I'm still trying to crack two hours fifteen!' he confessed. 'I'm sure you can and will break three hours if you keep the training up, Dom.'

We then got talking about training and what we had both done that year. I was running an average of 70 kilometres most weeks, and the biggest week I had was just over 100 kilometres. Meanwhile, Paul was running over 200 kilometres some weeks, and never less than 100 kilometres. Yeah, I had given it everything, but evidently there was room to give it even more.

Paul's words were encouraging and inspiring, and made me think that if I trained even harder I could run even faster, but this conversation also made me wonder whether breaking three hours would bring me any sort of peace or if I would simply start chasing a new magic number.

ON THE WAY HOME from Berlin, I had a seven-hour stopover at Shanghai airport. There was a massage spa in the airport—it was like a proper day spa, rather than one of those weird little mall set-ups—so, with time to kill and legs that were killing me, I went in for a treatment. Once I'd been shown to the massage table, I stripped down to my undies and got up on to it.

My masseuse came in. She was a delightful Chinese woman. 'You have very, very nice body,' she told me. 'Good muscle.'

I'm not sharing this to skite. (Well, maybe just a little bit.) I'm sharing it because the shape I was in was simply a by-product of running.

Then she got to work on me. When she got down to my feet, she let out a little gasp of shock.

She didn't say anything. She didn't need to. I knew what she had seen.

Running might put you in great shape. It will improve your physical and mental health, and your quality of life—but it will also give you feet that look like they could be one of the warning photos on a packet of cigarettes.

WHEN I GOT BACK to Auckland, I found a card waiting at home for me from Jay-Jay.

> Welcome home! I was brought to tears by my pride for you during that run. All that hard work, passion and determination paid off. You are amazing. I am so happy for you! I love you so much.

I can't describe what that meant to me. Jay-Jay hasn't ever really cared for running. She knew I'd spent the past year working harder and coming home more exhausted than ever before, but she had zero interest in hearing about what I was doing during each run—and who can blame her? But, when you do something that impresses people who really matter to you, that's a pretty special feeling.

WHEN YOU DO SOMETHING THAT IMPRESSES PEOPLE WHO REALLY MATTER TO YOU, THAT'S A PRETTY SPECIAL FEELING.

BERLIN WAS DONE AND dusted, but I still had one of the World Marathon Majors left to conquer: Tokyo. There was no question that I was going to do it. I was as determined as ever to get my hands on that Six Star Finisher medal! The only thing I wasn't sure of yet was exactly what I wanted to achieve when I set out to cover 42.2 kilometres in the Japanese capital. In the wake of the Berlin Marathon, it was time to do some soul-searching.

Was breaking three hours still something I wanted to do? Was there any point?

Or, bearing in mind how hard I had worked in preparation for Berlin, was I simply trying to push shit uphill by going after something that was still a long way off what I was even capable of?

I knew I'd get that finisher medal no matter what time I ran at Tokyo, so perhaps I would be better off just running for pleasure and enjoying the whole experience. If I set my heart on that sub-three once again, I knew I'd get all stressed about my finishing time and, in the process, miss out on soaking up the atmosphere and having fun.

As it turned out, I didn't have to rush into a decision. I ended up having a whole year to make up my mind about what I wanted to achieve at Tokyo, and it was all thanks to The Boss.

THE TOKYO MARATHON IS held in late February each year, and the 2017 date ended up clashing with a Bruce Springsteen concert in Auckland. If there is one thing I love more than marathon running, it is probably The Boss and his marathon-length live shows.

It was a no-brainer for me. Tokyo would have to wait for another year. Running is pretty important to me, but Bruce is *very* important. My mates and I have shared many good times with his music as the backdrop, sort of like a real-life version of a movie soundtrack. There was no way I was missing this concert.

It was totally worth it. Bruce was amazing, playing to a sell-out crowd at Mount Smart Stadium on a warm summer's night. However, when he played his hit song 'Born to Run', I admit that the Tokyo Marathon did cross my mind. For the briefest moment, I even felt a little bit guilty for having fun at a concert instead of running in Tokyo. I realised then that I think of a concert by an artist I love as a treat, whereas a running event (which I often pay just as much, if not more, to be part of) is more like a chore. I guess it's because a concert doesn't involve any preparation; you just turn up and party. With a big run, however, the enjoyment for me comes afterwards: after the event, after months of hard training, and after god knows how many hours of worry, anxiety and sleepless nights.

Fortunately, this moment of introspection was short-lived, and didn't ruin my evening. Almost as soon as the thought popped into my mind, it had evaporated, drowned out by the singing of my mates as we did our best to match Bruce's vocals with our own. I'd worked so hard towards the Berlin Marathon, and the self-inflicted stress of it all had even sucked a bit of the joy out of running for me. This night was an opportunity to just be present and enjoy the moment. Tokyo—and what I wanted to achieve there—was a decision for another day.

CHAPTER 16
TAKING A BREAK

BERLIN HAD MESSED WITH my head. Actually, no. That's not right. The truth is I messed with my own head. The whole trying to crack three hours thing had really caused me some anxiety. It was a goal that had completely and utterly taken over my life. It was time to take a break . . . sort of. I decided to run a bit less in order to enjoy it a bit more.

My training continued, and it was going well, but I'd scaled things back to train for a half marathon. When you've been thrashing your body in an attempt to run a marathon as fast as you can, dropping back in distance and training for a half marathon is fun. By comparison, it feels like a holiday.

Together, Coach Ian and I came up with a plan of attack for the 2017 year. I'd ease off on the amount of training I was doing and focus on trying to improve my half marathon time. Then, towards the end of the year, I could decide on what my goal in Tokyo would be: to finish enjoyably, or to finish fast. The idea was that, by (hopefully) building a good speed base with my half marathon training, I'd then be able to increase my training and gun for a bad-ass finishing time at the Tokyo Marathon in a year's time.

I liked the sound of this.

THE HALF MARATHON EVENT I set my sights on was at the World Masters Games, which were being held in Auckland in April 2017. I'd been recruited by the games' organisers as an ambassador for the games. Other ambassadors included retired New Zealand sporting legends such as Sir Bryan Williams, who was an All Black before I was born, so it was a huge honour for me. And probably a huge let-down for Sir Bryan.

The last time I had trained for a half marathon distance was when I'd done the Huntly Half Marathon back in 2013. That was before I had teamed up with a coach, and I'd just used a training programme I had found on the internet. I'd trained pretty hard, I thought, and I ended up crossing the finish line in 1 hour 31 minutes 59 seconds. (Yeah, I know, I should just write it as 1 hour 32 minutes, but not many runners will ever round up their finishing time.)

I was 40 at the time, and it was by far the fastest that I had ever run a half marathon. I was pretty pleased with my effort, but I also remember thinking, *How the fuck does anyone run a full marathon in under three hours?* Back then, my marathon time sat firmly around 3 hours 20 minutes. Running a sub-three wasn't even on my radar. It was an impossible goal, something I didn't think I would ever be physically able to achieve. Come to think of it, if someone had told me that day that I'd eventually run a marathon in 3 hours 5 minutes, I would have found that hard to imagine.

I enjoyed my training for the Masters half marathon. The speed work was still gruelling—that stuff never gets any easier—but the longest training runs were only a couple of hours. There were none of those long weekend runs that marathon runners have to do. You know, the ones that suck up your entire Saturday or Sunday morning!

When I turned up on the day, I really had no idea how I was going to get on. So you can imagine how stoked I was when I managed to pull off a sharp personal best of 1 hour 27 minutes 22 seconds. It was an incredible reminder of how far I'd come with my running since that Huntly run just four years earlier. As well as earning a new PB, I also finished twenty-fourth out of a total field of 502 runners and garnered fourth place in my age bracket. The other Masters runners were all quite serious sportspeople—definitely nobody dressed up in a novelty tutu here—and I had managed to finish at the top end of the field. I was ecstatic.

I HAD RUN A GREAT TIME, AND THE GLOWING VOM PATCH AT MY FEET WAS EVIDENCE I HAD GIVEN IT EVERYTHING I HAD.

I was also totally fucked. I had given it everything. Absolutely everything. Just across the finish line, exhausted, dizzy and drenched in sweat, I stumbled to take a seat alongside an advertising hoarding . . . and threw up. An unidentifiable substance splattered the ground at my feet. I'm not sure what the hell it was, but it was fluorescent yellow and I can tell you it tasted terrible as it travelled up my throat and out of my mouth. Maybe I should have been embarrassed, but honestly I was over the moon. I had run a great time, and the glowing vom patch at my feet was evidence I had given it everything

I had. The post-race endorphins were obviously running hot.

A couple of days later, though, I came crashing back down to earth with a gutting realisation. There was no way in hell I could have kept up that pace for even one more kilometre, let alone another 21, but that is exactly what I would need to do if I wanted to break three hours in a marathon.

And just like that, the negative thoughts started creeping back in. My training continued to go well, I was definitely getting quicker and, what's more, I was enjoying myself and remaining happily injury free . . . but I just couldn't shake that doubting little voice in my own head. Whenever I'd start thinking about Tokyo and my dreams of running a sub-three marathon, the voice would unhelpfully pipe up. *You'll never do it. You might be running fast, but you need to run faster—and keep it up for longer. You're dreaming, mate.*

The ridiculous thing is that I could have shut up this negative voice in seconds by just putting the whole stupidly ambitious sub-three goal to bed. If I'd done that, I wouldn't have had to worry anymore about how fast I was running, and could have just enjoyed myself. But I'm obviously a sucker for self-punishment, so I carried on this ridiculous dance inside my own head. Glass-half-empty me would give voice to all the dread and self-doubt I had, and glass-half-full me would have to come along and clean up the mess.

You'll never do it, the downer part of me would say. *You should just stop trying. What's the point?*

Then the eternally hopeful part would chip in. *Keep trying! Be the best you can be. Better to try and fail than to not try at all.*

Don't get me wrong, I'm not a negative person. As I've said, I'm just a realist. So, while I prefer to take the optimistic route, I also can't help but see the facts for the facts. And, as they stood, the facts said that I was running faster than I'd ever run before, but it still wasn't fast enough. Talk about daunting.

AROUND THIS TIME, JAY-JAY and I separated after thirteen years of marriage, and eighteen in total together. People talk about a relationship break-up being one of the most stressful life events a person can go through, and I've seen it ranked even higher than the death of a close family member or imprisonment. Well, I'm not sure if our split has been that *stressful*, but it has definitely been painful.

Jay-Jay and I shared so much in our time together. As well as working alongside each other as radio-show hosts for fifteen years, we also went through a stressful family adoption, numerous failed rounds of IVF, and all the other trials that life throws at you. And, over time and right under our noses, we somehow devolved into just mates. We had become almost like siblings. The spark had gone. At the risk of sounding horribly cliche, we reached the point where, even though we still loved each other, we weren't *in* love with each other. I always used to think that line was a bit of a cop-out, but now I sort of understand what it means.

It was so fucking hard. Honestly, it still is. There are some days when, for no good reason, I will think about it all and just feel so sad. When you spend almost two decades of your life with someone, you reach the point where you know them almost as well as you know yourself, so to suddenly not have that person in your life every day is very weird.

Having my running training to focus on during such a difficult time was a lifesaver. Aside from the obvious physical and mental health benefits, it kept me sane. As well as serving as a much-needed source of healthy distraction, it helped me to sleep better at night—literally.

Even though we're not together anymore and I've started dating again, I'm still not able to take down all the photos of Jay-Jay and me from around home. Jay-Jay is such a phenomenal person, and I will always wonder if I did everything I could to make things work. Whenever other couples used to say things to us like, 'We've had our ups and downs,' we'd smile at each other, because we never did. We always got on great—and we still do.

And, even though her interest in running remains about as high as Madonna's interest in growing old gracefully, Jay-Jay still messages me before or after big running events to wish me luck or to congratulate me. I truly believe and hope that we will be in each other's lives forever. Of course, it's impossible to know what the future holds, but I'd like to think that, no matter what, Jay-Jay and I will always be there for each other.

WITH THE MASTERS HALF marathon behind me—and a new half marathon PB under my belt—Coach Ian and I turned our attention to my training for Tokyo. He decided that, just like in my training for Berlin, it'd be a *great* idea for me to run a mini-peak marathon. His theory was that a mini-peak would give me something to work towards, and it would also build a solid fitness base for me to begin the training countdown to Tokyo.

This all made perfect sense . . . but, when Ian emailed his proposal to me, just reading it made me feel exhausted, knowing all the hours and miles of training it would involve!

I started writing a reply that was way longer than Ian's message. I talked about how busy I was with work, and how

I was scared of injuring myself by overtraining before Tokyo. Then, before hitting send, I re-read the email, and realised how whiney and afraid I sounded. Running a marathon requires bravery and courage. I deleted my brittle message and instead sent him a two-word reply: 'Sounds good.'

For the mini-peak, I entered the Tauranga Marathon, which was in early October, nearly five months before the Tokyo Marathon. In my training for Tauranga, Coach Ian scheduled a full marathon-distance training run just a few weeks before the actual event. To clarify: I would have to complete a 42.2-kilometre training run in order to run a 42.2-kilometre event which was itself a mini-peak for another 42.2-kilometre race. It was like mini-peak inception.

THE THOUGHT OF DOING A FULL MARATHON ALL ON MY OWN FREAKED ME OUT. RUNNING THAT DISTANCE CAN BE NOT ONLY TEDIOUS, BUT ALSO BOTH PHYSICALLY AND MENTALLY CHALLENGING.

Honestly, the whole mini-peak thing stressed me out. Before teaming up with Coach Ian, I had never seen a marathon training programme that included a full marathon distance as a training run. Most go no further than 37 kilometres. But who was I to argue? Through trial and error, Coach Ian had figured out how to make me go faster, and if that involved running full marathons in training then so be it. And, to be fair, I always got through these runs OK. It was just that the thought of doing a full marathon all on my own freaked me out. Running that distance can be not only tedious, but also both physically and mentally challenging.

Anyway, three weekends before the Tauranga Marathon, I got into my car and drove down to Tauranga to run the course. I figured that if I was going to put myself through a whole marathon as a training run, I might as well use it as an opportunity to familiarise myself with the course. I was also getting a bit sick of plodding the same old routes around home, and thought a change might spice things up a bit.

Unfortunately, my timing was immaculately bad. Turns out I chose what was the wettest day of the year in Tauranga. No shit. Ordinarily, I don't mind running in the rain. In fact, I actually kind of enjoy it. It gives me a sort of smug sense of satisfaction, as though I'm somehow a little bit better than all the people sitting in their cars staring at rain-runners like they're weirdos for being outside in the wet. However, there's a difference between a gentle drizzle and an all-out deluge. As soon as I got out of the car, it was like someone had tipped a bottomless bucket of water on my head . . . and just kept on tipping. Before I'd even clocked up the first kilometre of my run, my shoes and socks were so soaked that, with every step, my feet made a thick, wet sloshing noise. That was when I knew it was going to be a long and punishing day out.

I still had 41 kilometres to go, so I gave myself a pep talk. *Suck it up, Dom*, said the voice in my head. *If the weather's like this on the day of the actual event, you'll still have to do it.*

I ran a few more kilometres. It continued to pour. The rain was so thick I couldn't blink fast enough to keep the water out of my eyes. It was unpleasant. And cold. The sort of day when you want to throw in the towel and reschedule.

Surely it can't be this shit on the day, the voice in my head said, trying to see the bright side. *So this run's probably going to be waaayyy worse than the event itself!*

Silver linings and all that, eh.

That was when I stuck my hand in my pocket to check the map I'd printed off and brought with me. I don't know

Tauranga all that well, so I thought it'd be a good idea to bring the course map with me to make sure I didn't get lost. There was just one problem: it wasn't a map anymore. It wasn't even a piece of paper. Black printer ink dripped from the grey, wet ball in my hands and ran down my wrist. I tried to unfold it, but that was a mistake. It disintegrated in my hands.

This was going to be a character-building day. One of those days that the saying 'what doesn't kill you will make you stronger' was designed for.

There wasn't much I could do besides keep on running, so that's what I did. It was a brutal day out. But, eventually, my aching legs, shivering torso and reliable GPS watch told me I'd been out in the rain for 42.2 kilometres.

Job done.

It sucked.

It was hard.

But I did it. And it was fine . . . once I finished it!

Later on in the day, the weather cleared (of course it did) and I decided to treat myself and go to the Mount Hot Pools. By then, I was feeling much happier about everything. I mean, I was bloody tired and my legs were thrashed, but the endorphins had kicked in and I was in a brilliant mood. There's nothing quite like the feeling you get after a tough run in horrible conditions. It's super satisfying to finish something that sucks so badly while you're doing it. It's also a massive relief to have it behind you.

I relaxed in the hot water for the best part of an hour. I would have stayed longer, but I was exposed to dangerous levels of PDA (public displays of affection). Right in front of me, a pair of pimply young lovers were engaging in petting so heavy it might have been illegal. Seriously, it was too much.

Nauseated, I removed myself from the pool.

As I hobbled to the changing rooms, a thought crossed my mind that made me smile. Who'd have thought that running a marathon in cold torrential rain wouldn't make me ill, but a pashing couple with braces and back acne would do the trick?

A FEW WEEKS LATER, Mum came to Tauranga to run the marathon with me. She had been inspired by the improvement in my times since I'd teamed up with Coach Ian, so I'd told her I'd get Ian to train her as well. Initially, she'd rejected the offer. She thought she was too old to worry about speed work or trying to go faster. I think she was also probably a little bit nervous after seeing the work I was doing in order to go faster! Eventually, though, she caved, and she entered to do the Tokyo Marathon too, excited by the possibility of running faster than she had done in many years.

The Tokyo Marathon was still almost five months away, but Coach Ian had been crunching the numbers from the horrific treadmill tests he loved getting me to do. Just before I headed off to Tauranga, he'd delivered his findings: according to his very scientific data, he told me, I should be able to finally crack three hours.

'And,' he added, 'even if you don't, a brand-new PB is on the cards for you, Dom!'

It sounded too easy . . . which made me think it was too good to be true. I had, after all, proved Coach Ian's science wrong in the past. I wasn't holding my breath about the sub-three, but a new PB? Yeah, maybe. Better not to get too cocky.

Mum was cocky enough for the both of us. She was a hundred and ten per cent certain that I was going to smash it.

'I've brought a bottle of wine with me,' she told me in the car. 'It cost a small fortune. You can have it when you cross that finish line in under three hours.' She was pretty chuffed with herself.

An expensive bottle of wine might have motivated other people, but it had the opposite effect on me. Instead of serving as some sort of carrot at the end of a stick, all it did was increase my already rampant nerves. I know Mum was trying to help, but that bottle of pinot noir just added to the feeling that if I failed to achieve my sub-three goal I'd be letting her—and everyone else who believed in me—down. I know it's a bit fucked up, but other people's belief in me sometimes feels like an expectation that's weighing me down. It's what makes me wonder if I'd be better to keep my lofty goals to myself, because then I'd only let myself down if I didn't succeed.

'Thanks, Mum,' I said. 'We'll see. But don't get too excited about opening that bottle just yet . . .'

She smiled at me.

We stayed at her brother Luke's house that night. Luke was running the Tauranga Marathon too, and it would be his very first marathon. He was 51, and to be honest I wasn't quite sure why he hadn't already run a full marathon. He'd done heaps of half marathons plus a tonne of triathlons, and is one of those fit bastards who only gets faster the greyer he goes. His hair is the only thing that gives his age away. His torso, which is chiselled to perfection thanks to 1000 ab crunches every morning (yes, a thousand!), makes David Beckham look like a slob. Like me, Luke was hoping to race in under three hours—but I was way more confident of his chances than my own. His half marathon time sits comfortably under 1 hour 25 minutes, which is fast for any age group but especially quick in the over fifties bracket.

However, the full marathon can be an unpredictable beast. All sorts of things can go wrong in those final kilometres. One of the most notable examples of an epic last-kilometre meltdown is Scottish runner Callum Hawkins. In 2018, he was only a couple of kilometres away from winning gold in the marathon at the Commonwealth Games on the Gold Coast when he collapsed in a desperate heap mid-stride due to heat exhaustion. He had a two-minute lead on the next runner, but he was so wrecked he ended up being carried off the course by ambulance staff. Tragic.

HOWEVER, THE FULL MARATHON CAN BE AN UNPREDICTABLE BEAST. ALL SORTS OF THINGS CAN GO WRONG IN THOSE FINAL KILOMETRES.

AT THE MARATHON START line the next morning, I bumped into my pal Gene Rand. He was walking around with a balloon attached to the back of his singlet with the words 'three hours' written on it. He was running as a pacer, and would cross the finish line bang on three hours (no big deal), so his balloon was going to be my best friend for the race.

I met Gene through another running friend. Running can be a bit of a loner sport, or it can be a social community. That's one of the reasons why I love it: it can be pretty much whatever you want it to be. To begin with, I got into running because of how easy it was—anywhere, any place, any time, you just lace up your shoes and away you go. But, thanks to social media and the app Strava, I'm now part of a running community. That's how I met Gene—sort of.

After the Berlin Marathon, I got a random Facebook message from a runner called Brad Luiten. We met up to train together at a 400-metre Lovelock track in the Auckland suburb of Mount Roskill. This track is free for public use, and is where the famous Arthur Lydiard used to train Peter Snell, Murray Halberg and others. I had no idea this hidden gem of a track even existed until Brad told me about it. It seems not many other people know about it either, as more often than not I have it all to myself when I train there. If it's a really busy day, I'll share it with a couple of the elderly locals who use it to walk laps.

Brad is a far better runner than I could ever hope to be. He's also an all-round good bastard. We continued messaging each other, and he was really supportive and generous with advice and encouragement, especially when I was feeling bad about a run that hadn't gone to plan. At the time we met, Brad was having a crack at setting a new world record for speed-golf. Yes, it is an actual thing. The basic idea is that you get twelve hours to play as many holes of golf as you can. Being both a very fast runner and a pretty decent golfer, Brad thought he'd give it a crack—and ended up setting the record by playing 221 holes of golf and running over 100 kilometres. Mad!

In pursuit of his record attempt, he needed 'ball spotters' on the course to spot stray balls for him, so he didn't lose time wandering around the rough grass looking for them. These ball spotters needed to be fit enough to run ahead, and I agreed to help Brad for a couple of rounds. *This* is where I met Gene.

While we chased rogue golf balls, Gene told me he had been drinking too much and it was killing his marriage, so he'd replaced the booze with running and never looked back. Now he's a running beast! So fast that he can confidently pace other runners through a sub-three marathon.

'Hey, Gene,' I said, walking up to him in the starting area. 'What's with the bananas?'

Gene lifted both hands, proudly displaying a banana in each one. 'Better than those disgusting gels, mate.' He was beaming. 'I'll eat one at the halfway point while I'm running, then nibble away at the other one for the second half of the race. Can't beat it.'

'Whatever works for you, mate.'

Gene, like all runners, had found what worked for him. And that's the great thing about the individuality of running: through trial and error, you find what works for you and stick with it.

The air-horn went off, and Gene and I ran together for the first few minutes.

'So what's your plan?' I asked him.

'I'm running even splits,' he told me.

That meant he was going to run every kilometre at around 4 minutes 15 seconds. I could try to do the same, but I had some serious self-doubt about my ability to crack three hours in this race. In the second half, the course heads off road and along undulating trails for a few kilometres round the base of Mount Maunganui. While I don't mind hills, I am the running version of a dirty old truck—you know, the sort you get stuck behind as it crawls up a hill with a big cloud of diesel smoke spewing from the exhaust. Since I was expecting this to cost me some precious time later on, I decided to race ahead of Gene and the three-hour pack. I figured that if I was just a few seconds faster each kilometre, I'd hopefully have a minute or two up my sleeve for the last stretch.

I hit the halfway mark in 1 hour 29 minutes, still ahead of Gene and his sub-three pack. I was running smoothly. My pace was good. It was hard, but manageably hard. If I wanted to hit the magic three-hour mark, I needed to run the second half of the race in 1 hour 32 minutes. However, as my watch ticked over the twenty-fifth kilometre of the race, I reached the Mount and Gene and his crew flew past me. The slight hill and my tiredness conspired together, and I slowed down massively. Just like that, almost all the time I had banked in the early kilometres evaporated.

Mentally, this fucked me up. By the time I got back on to the road a few kilometres later, I was on the home straight—a very boring 15 kilometres of straight flat road—but the physical and mental damage had been done.

It was an ugly finish. Physically, I could feel my body starting to cramp up. Mentally, I was heartbroken. I was in so much pain that I didn't even try to reason with myself. I didn't give a shit about letting myself down. I just wanted to finish. I had tried my best, and what else could I do?

IT WAS AN UGLY FINISH. PHYSICALLY, I COULD FEEL MY BODY STARTING TO CRAMP UP. MENTALLY, I WAS HEARTBROKEN.

As I battled through those last kilometres, my thoughts were filled with Coach Ian and his science and how I had somehow managed to flip the middle finger to it yet again. I thought of all my new running buddies on Strava who had been following my training and progress and were confident I would run well based on my form. I thought of Mum and that bloody bottle of pricey wine. Fuck my life!

The end couldn't come soon enough.

At long last, I crossed the finish line in 3 hours 12 minutes and 44 seconds. A whole eight minutes slower than Berlin a year earlier.

THE LAST HALF MIGHT have been a struggle, but I was rewarded for my efforts with a massive endorphin rush. Even the feeling of completing a marathon badly or in a disappointing time is still a magical one.

Uncle Luke was waiting for me at the finish line. He had already put his tracksuit on over the top of his running clothes and was sipping on a coffee and eating a bagel. He'd finished his first full marathon in a sweet 2 hours 56 minutes—just two seconds ahead of Gene, who had picked up the pace at the end and smashed that three-hour pace goal.

Within a couple of minutes, I got a message from Coach Ian. Always the optimist, he had managed to bullet-point a total of four silver linings on this one big grey cloud.

I had finished seventeenth out of 280 runners.

I had come third in my age group.

I had just run my third-fastest marathon ever.

And, two years earlier, I would have been over the moon with a 3 hour 12 minute marathon.

A bit later on, Luke and I cheered Mum across the finish line. She completed her run in 4 hours 44 minutes. It was way slower than what she had hoped for, but even so she managed to win her age group. For her trouble, she was awarded a three-pack of socks.

BOTH A BIT BUMMED out by our finishing times, Mum and I decided to drive straight back home to Auckland instead of spending another night in Tauranga. When I pulled up outside Mum's apartment, she couldn't get out fast enough—a couple of hours stuck in the car listening to my favourite rap songs had only made her bad day worse.

'You should probably take that bottle of wine back to the

shop for a refund,' I joked, as she opened the car door.

She just laughed. 'No way. I'm holding on to it. You'll do it next time. Then you can drink it.'

Next time would be the Tokyo Marathon, which was almost five months away.

'Well, they say a good wine gets better with age,' I replied. 'At this rate, it'll be the most amazing-tasting bottle of red on the fucking planet by the time the cork finally comes out!'

CHAPTER 17
TRUST THE
TRAINING

I ALWAYS ENJOY THE week after a marathon. Often, I'll go the full week without running at all. Sometimes this is because my legs are so damn sore that I couldn't run even if I wanted to. Other times I simply want to give myself time to recover, both physically and mentally, so that I'm ready and motivated to get back into some hard training.

One thing I get a bit nervous about is that every failed attempt at achieving a goal will push me closer to giving up on the goal altogether. In a weird way, the closer that I got to my sub-three marathon the further I actually felt from being able to do it. With every near miss, a voice would pop up in my head that said, *Fuck it! Let's scrap that idea and just go back to running for love rather than a time!*

This voice only gets louder after what I'd call 'a shocker of a run'. Even though in Berlin I was still six minutes off my goal time, I set a sharp new PB and that made me feel like I was improving so my sub-three goal was still worth chasing. Tauranga, on the other hand, felt like a step backwards since it was slower. It made me start to wonder what the hell I was doing with my life.

I had, however, already signed up for Tokyo. It was happening—and I realised it was now or never for my sub-three goal. If I couldn't do it on the flat streets of the Japanese capital and with another four and a half months of targeted training under my belt, I would never do it.

I committed.

I was going to gun for a sub-three marathon at Tokyo. I would throw everything at it, but this would definitely be my last crack. If I didn't do it this time, I would have to be at peace with the fact I would never do it.

THREE WEEKS AFTER TAURANGA, I lined up at the start line of the Auckland Half Marathon. I hadn't planned to run, but had recovered so well from Tauranga that I thought I might as well. Also, if I am being completely honest, I was still fucked off about the time I ran in Tauranga and I wanted to have a good run. I hoped it'd boost my confidence a bit.

I ended up finishing in 1 hour 27 minutes and 56 seconds. After my Tauranga disappointment, I was stoked with this time. It was only 30 seconds slower than the time I'd run in the Masters, and that race had been on a flat course. The Auckland half, on the other hand, contains a few hills plus the decent climb over the Harbour Bridge, so my faith in my progress was restored. Sort of.

It was hard to get too excited about things, though. I was totally rooted at the end. I wasn't even able to speak for a good ten minutes afterwards! In order to run a sub-three marathon, I couldn't help reminding myself, I'd have to do that same speed and distance *twice*. Not possible!

I tried to remain positive. I *was* improving. And Tokyo was still four months away.

EINSTEIN APPARENTLY ONCE SAID, 'The definition of insanity is doing the same thing over and over again and expecting a different result.' This is evidently a credo Coach Ian also holds close, as he loves nothing more than tweaking my training programmes after each event I finish. What this meant when it came to my training for Tokyo was that it was going to be even more intense than it had been for Berlin. It *had* to be.

I had thought I'd trained my arse off for Berlin, but Ian soon made it clear that I still had even more arse that could be trained off. I had gone around telling people I had given it 100 per cent in Berlin, and I had meant it. But, while this is a nice sentiment and an easy percentage to quote, it is rarely truthful.

Recently, I was watching *Married at First Sight* and one of the married couples was explaining to the show's three relationship experts why they were no longer compatible. When the experts accused them of not trying hard enough, the couple assured the panel that they had given their relationship 'a thousand per cent'. One *thousand* per cent? Really? They'd only been *ahem* married for three weeks. Call me a cynic, but I was doubtful of the truth of their claim.

I was pretty sure I'd shown a bit more commitment in my Berlin training than these two had in their made-for-TV marriage, but Coach Ian—much like those relationship experts—obviously thought there was some room for me to try a little harder in my attempt to run a sub-three marathon.

One thing was certain: if there was room for improvement, the gruelling training programme Coach Ian set me for Tokyo was going to find it. I was ready for the hard work, though. The way I looked at it, all my training up until this point— for Berlin, and for Chicago earlier—had been stepping stones towards Tokyo. I was fitter, stronger and leaner than ever, and therefore knew I was better able to cope with the demands I was about to place on my body.

ON SOME OF THE PARTICULARLY HARD RUNS, I FELT MYSELF NEARING BREAKING POINT. SELF-DOUBT WOULD SEEP IN, AND I'D START TO QUESTION JUST WHY I WAS DOING ALL OF THIS.

It's lucky I was ready to work, because the build-up to Tokyo was bloody hard. The really hard stuff kicked in at the same time as summer did. I was having to run further and faster than ever before, and the weather definitely made sure I would not get a free ride. Every run was cloaked in hot, sticky humidity, and some days I would get home so saturated that my socks and shoes would be sloshing with sweat.

On some of the particularly hard runs, I felt myself nearing breaking point. Self-doubt would seep in, and I'd start to question just why I was doing all of this. Of course, I already know what you're thinking. I'm a paying customer in my relationship with Coach Ian, so I could have told him at any time that it was too hard, right? I could have said it was time to chill out, that I wanted to do shorter or slower runs.

But there was no way in hell I was going to do that. Not yet. I could do that after Tokyo. Whatever the result in Japan, I would be at peace knowing I had given it as close to an honest 100 per cent as I could. And the hard work was paying off. With every run, I was getting better, faster, stronger. And, don't forget that before I started working with Ian my marathon time sat around 3 hours 20 minutes. Thanks to Ian's professional advice, I'd shaved fifteen minutes off that time. I might have lacked self-belief, but I had full faith in what Ian was instructing me to do. I absolutely believed that, so long as I did exactly what Ian told me to, my finishing time in Tokyo—sub-three or not—would be the fastest I was physically capable of.

IT MIGHT BE STARTING to sound like my life in the lead-up to Tokyo was fucking horrible, consumed with running and little else. Let me assure you that this wasn't the case. Yeah, my thoughts were dominated by running, especially on days when I had a hard training run to do. By the way, when I say a 'hard' run, it's the speed that poses the difficulty. I've now reached the point where it's not the running that I find hard, but the pace—running as fast as you can is incredibly uncomfortable for anyone. The bonus of these hard runs is that there are no words to describe the immense satisfaction and relief I feel after each one. The harder the run, the greater the feeling afterwards. It was 100 per cent worth it (see what I did there?).

Anyway, even though I spent a lot of time thinking about running, I really wasn't spending all that long actually running in the scheme of things. Most weeks, I was only running between seven and nine hours in total. Since there are 168 hours in a week, that meant I was only running for about 5 per cent of each week. Easy!

I did definitely have to prioritise my running in order to get it done, though, and I admit that did require some sacrifices. I spent Christmas with my family at my sister Bridget's house in Perth. On Christmas Eve, I got up early in the morning to knock off a 20-kilometre run before everyone else woke up, then that same evening I went out before dinner to run up and down a steep hill for another 5 kilometres. Honestly, though, that sounds worse than it was. The hill run only took me away from my family for about half an hour, and, even though the morning run took just over an hour and a half, Bridget and the kids were still in bed when I got back.

A few days later, I headed to the Bay of Islands to go camping with my girlfriend and some friends, and while I was there I had to remove myself for a couple of hours to do one of my long runs. Rather than an inconvenience, this run actually ended up being one of the highlights of the trip. I ran from the campsite at a place called Houhora on one side of the North Island to Ninety Mile Beach on the other side, then back again. I got to brag on social media that I'd run the width of the North Island—twice! It was a fact . . . but it seems way less impressive as soon as you take a look at a map and see that it's the skinniest little bit of New Zealand there is!

It was while I was out on this run that I met a man by the name of Marty van Barneveld. As I was running towards Ninety Mile Beach, minding my own business, a car drove past me. I watched it carry on down the road a couple of metres, then the tail lights lit up as the brakes were slammed. A moment later, it was reversing down the road back to me. The driver's window came down, and a man poked his head out.

'Are you Dom?' he said.

I stopped, and paused my watch. 'Yeah, I am.'

'Cool!' He jumped out of the car. 'I'm Marty. Can we get a selfie?'

He seemed excited to see me. So did his dog. The other two humans in the car—a woman and a baby—didn't seem to know or care who the hell I was.

I was sweaty and hot—not exactly prime selfie material—but he also offered me water, so I could hardly refuse. As soon as he'd taken a picture, he handed me his drink bottle and I guzzled an impolite amount of his water—but still nowhere near as much as I felt like drinking. I wasn't carrying any water, as I'd assumed I'd pass a service station or something along the way where I could grab a drink. It was a foolish assumption. The road to Ninety Mile Beach is unsealed, and there's nothing but forestry on either side.

After thanking Marty profusely, I carried on running. He carried on driving, no doubt doing his best to explain who the hell I was.

A little while later, as I was on my way back towards Houhora, Marty's car appeared on the horizon and headed towards me in a cloud of gravel dust. I felt my dry mouth tingle with excitement at the prospect of getting another couple of gulps of water.

This time, the woman was driving. Marty leaned over and gave her a kiss before he leaped out of the passenger side. He was now wearing running gear.

He must have caught me looking into his car and trying to spot the water bottle in the cup holders, because he leaned back into the car then handed the bottle to me without saying anything.

'I thought you could do with some company to help pass a few kilometres!' he said. He was half offering, half telling me.

The truth is that I prefer to run on my own. I don't want to be so slow that I hold other people up, but nor do I really want to be held up by other people. I also like being able to stop or walk whenever I want to. I wasn't going to say any of this to the bloke who had possibly saved me from becoming a desiccated skeleton on the side of the road, though.

'Fuck yeah!' I said instead, smiling like a goon. 'That would be amazing!'

As we ran, we chatted, and I learned that Marty was a real estate agent but, before that, he'd been a professional triathlete. So, for the next 14 kilometres, I got to run at my own pace, which is to say fast enough that my talking was restricted to grunts and the occasional short sentence. Meanwhile, this ex-athlete who was 'out of shape and unfit' (his words, not mine) jogged along comfortably beside me and kept the conversation alive. He quizzed me about Berlin and we talked about my training.

Back on the main road, we passed a sorbet caravan. I was still thirsty and had a few kilometres left to go, so I stopped for a drink. They didn't have a tap, only bottles of water for sale, but I hadn't brought any money with me.

'Is it OK if I come back after my run to fix you up?' I asked, and the young woman behind the counter shook her head.

'Here.' Marty stepped up beside me, offering his flash-as Garmin GPS watch. 'Take this until we come back. That watch is worth 800 bucks, so I promise you we'll be back to pay for the water.'

The woman took the watch and eyed it suspiciously, then stared at Marty and me for way longer than was needed to weigh up this ridiculously unbalanced exchange. 'OK,' she said eventually. 'But you *better* be back!'

I have never seen anyone so protective of a 750 ml bottle of h2go in all my life.

By the time we made it back to Houhora, I'd changed my mind about running by myself. Just an hour or so earlier,

I'd been lying when I told this guy I didn't know that it'd be amazing for him to join me. Now, Marty wasn't a stranger any longer, and running with him had been exactly that: amazing.

JANUARY 2018 WAS GOING to be the key month in my training for the Tokyo Marathon. As of New Year's Day, the event would be exactly 56 days away. Eight weeks. Two months. It was going to be bloody hard. I was a little bit daunted by that prospect, but mostly I was excited, because I knew it was what I had to do in order to be at peace with my result in Tokyo.

UNFORTUNATELY, ONE THING I HAVE BEGUN TO DISCOVER AS I TRANSITION FROM 'PRETTY OLD' TO 'BLOODY OLD' IS HOW IMPORTANT PROPER NUTRITION AND HYDRATION IS. SLEEP, TOO.

I had a very big New Year's Eve. I got my last run for 2017 out of the way early by getting up at 8 am to tuck away an easy 10 kilometres. Then I caught up with my friends and got drunk and stayed out until four in the morning. It might not have been the smartest thing to do, but it was awesome. In my quest to run faster I'd made many sacrifices, but missing out on the most famous party night of the year was not going to be one of them! Plus, it would be my last blowout for a long time so I figured I might as well go hard or go home.

Unfortunately, one thing I have begun to discover as I transition from 'pretty old' to 'bloody old' is how important proper nutrition and hydration is. Sleep, too. It's ironic that I got into this crazy sport so that I could eat and drink whatever

I please, but now find myself making an effort to get to bed at a sensible time and avoid eating too much shit so that I can get up and run the next day. If I eat crappy food and drink too much wine the night before a 30-kilometre run, the run is always so much harder. I reached this fairly obvious realisation years later than most people do, and even so I still sometimes ignore it! And, whenever I do, I suffer dearly. Sigh.

Honestly, though, I'm OK with it. It's a necessity if I want to get the most out of my training and my running.

I took a rest (mostly to nurse my hangover) on New Year's Day, before getting straight back on the horse the day after with a half-marathon training run done at three-hour marathon pace. That's when shit got real. January was going to be the biggest running month of my entire life. It was time to get my game face on. I was fully expecting that run on the second of January to be a shocker. Given how I'd partied just over 48 hours earlier, I deserved for it to be an absolute horror show. However, I was pleasantly surprised: I finished it right on time in 1 hour 30 minutes. It was a great way to kick off the year, and a good confidence boost.

The hangover was officially over. With eight weeks to go until Tokyo, I felt like I might just be in with a fighting chance.

BY THE TIME JANUARY came to an end, I had clocked up a total of 486 kilometres. In an average month of training, I usually do around 300 kilometres, so for me this was massive. It represented an average of 15 kilometres a day, and 121 kilometres a week. Remarkably, my body felt OK. I was exhausted and constantly tired—which was to be expected, I guess—but, apart from a slight niggle in one of my knees, I felt good and was injury free.

I still worried that I was slower than I would need to be. The runs that I was required to do at my marathon goal pace still felt like a struggle. When I expressed my concerns about my speed, friends on Facebook and Strava told me to 'trust the training'. It's a mantra that's popular with a lot of runners, and basically means you will get the result you deserve based on the work you put in. My problem was I had trust issues with my training. I felt like I had been let down in the past by results that did *not* reflect the work that had gone into them.

In terms of my mindset, I was still experiencing a lot of self-doubt, so I'd been working hard on getting myself into a more Zen-ish place. Whenever I started doubting my ability, I tried to remind myself that I was starting the year fitter, stronger and faster than ever before. I also came up with a selection of bullshit lines to feed people whenever I was talking about my training.

IN TERMS OF MY MINDSET, I WAS STILL EXPERIENCING A LOT OF SELF-DOUBT, SO I'D BEEN WORKING HARD ON GETTING MYSELF INTO A MORE ZEN-ISH PLACE.

'What will be will be.'

'Training's going well, so I'll just have to do my best and see what happens.'

'Going sub-three would be amazing, but I'd be stoked with a new PB, so anything under three hours five minutes would be ace.'

'I'm going to run my arse off, but my main goal is to enjoy the atmosphere and the occasion.'

I'm not quite sure why I'd say these things. I guess I was subconsciously trying to downplay my sub-three goal because

I felt a bit gun-shy after being so public about my desire to break three hours in Berlin. It was probably also some kind of defence mechanism so that I wouldn't be too pissed off if I fell short again.

One thing I did know for sure was that I still had very little confidence in my ability to actually crack three hours. The way my training had been going, I was certain I could run the pace required for 25 or 30 kilometres. But as for those final 12 kilometres? I had no clue.

There was something else that had been nagging at the back of my mind, too. I'd done a number of training runs at my goal marathon pace, and was starting to manage them comfortably, but they were never fully honest runs. What I mean is that I would often stop and pause my watch. Sometimes this was unavoidable, like when I was waiting for traffic lights to change, but other times it would be a break to swallow an energy gel or take a drink from a water fountain. When you run an actual event, the clock starts ticking when you cross the transponder mat at the start line and it does not stop until you reach the finish line. In between those two points, if you decide to walk, use the loo or stop for water, you absolutely can—but the clock keeps ticking. There is no pause button.

In order to break three hours, I'd need to run at a bloody quick pace *and* maintain it non-stop for the entire duration of the race. The quickest runners would be able to do that with whole minutes to spare. Eliud Kipchoge, currently the world's fastest marathon runner, would break three hours even if he stopped running at the 30-kilometre mark and slowly walked the remainder of the race! For me, though, every last second would be crucial. I couldn't afford to waste a moment.

Friends tried to assure me that, come race day, it wouldn't

be a problem, because I would be in the zone and be way more focused. I wasn't convinced. I worried that my propensity to push the pause button might be just another chink in my armour. When things got too hard, I'd have to stop and catch my breath for a second. A second that could cost me my sub-three goal.

AS THE CALENDAR FLIPPED over to the first weekend in February, I reached the three-week mark from the Tokyo Marathon. Before I got to taper off and recover for the final event, though, my training programme featured many more runs at marathon goal pace, as well as a full-marathon training run. Fun times. Not! But, as I kept being reminded, I had to 'trust the training'.

The 42.2-kilometre training run was set down for Saturday 10 February, fifteen days out from the Tokyo Marathon. The night before, I interviewed North American pop star Macklemore backstage before his concert for work. I was offered tickets to stay and watch the show, but reluctantly declined. I knew that if I stayed out late and had a few drinks it would mess me up for my run the next day. Plus, I would have found it really hard to enjoy myself anyway, knowing I had to get up the next morning and smash out a marathon.

My alarm went off at 4.30 am. I got up, put my running gear on, and ate some breakfast. Then I went back to bed, and set my alarm for 5 am. This would give me an extra half hour of sleep at the same time as letting my food digest. The reason I put my running gear on before going back to bed was to make sure I got up again! Sleepy me doesn't always make the best decisions.

By ten past five, while the rest of the city still slept, I was outside running under the street lights. Even though I had my trusty iPod in my pocket, I didn't put my headphones on right away. For the first few kilometres, I just enjoyed the sound of my breath and my footsteps. There is something quite special about being up and running that early in the morning.

By the time the sun rose and the street lights flickered off, I was already 8 kilometres in, and I made it back home well before nine o'clock. All up, the run—my last big one before Tokyo—had taken me 3 hours 23 minutes. Even though this time didn't include a couple of stops for water and traffic lights (of course), it had gone really well. I felt fantastic. I even reckoned I could have run a few extra kilometres.

Maybe my hard-ass training in January really was paying off. Maybe all I did need to do was trust the training. It was a real confidence boost, and I realised that was probably why Coach Ian had insisted on getting me to run a pre-marathon marathon. A full-distance dress rehearsal that goes well is hugely motivating.

I took a rest day the next day, but was right back into it on Monday with a 20-kilometre run that included speed work. Remarkably, even though I'd run a full marathon two days earlier, I managed it. I was, finally, starting to trust the training. Despite my lingering doubts about keeping my pace up for a full marathon, I was beginning to see results. I was coping with the runs and the speeds that Coach Ian was tasking me with. Even if I was tired or sore—or both—I was still managing the times we were aiming for.

I KNOW SOME RUNNERS hate the taper in training in the couple of weeks before a run. They feel restless and don't know what to do with the extra time and energy they suddenly find themselves with. Not me. I bloody love it. However, even though Coach Ian cut back my distances, he was keeping me at my three-hour marathon pace. I had shorter runs, but they were still uncomfortably fast. I momentarily wondered if he was getting me to do the right thing, as it seemed to go against a lot of what I have ever read. But by now I had well and truly learned not to question my coach. I pushed my concerns to the back of my mind, and I trusted the training.

My last run in New Zealand before flying out to Japan was just four days before the event itself. I ran 15 kilometres at race pace, and it happily went better than a run of the same distance but slower speed that I'd done just a few days earlier. I'm not sure why I found the harder run easier, but I guess that's just running sometimes!

By this stage, I'd run hundreds and hundreds of kilometres at the three-hour marathon pace. I should have been able to do it by feel alone, but that was not the case. I still found myself totally reliant on glancing at my Garmin watch to check my pace. Some days the three-hour pace felt relatively easy. Most days it felt like a bit of a struggle. The key thing, though, was this: I was managing to maintain it every time. Even on the days when I felt stuffed after only a couple of kilometres, my body was holding on for the distances.

Something had worked.

The real test for my training, though, would be the Tokyo Marathon in just four days' time. That was when I would find out if all the hard work I'd put in was enough to get me to hit—finally, once and for all—that sub-three marathon.

Now, there was little more left for me to do besides cross my fingers, pray to the running gods, and trust my training.

CHAPTER 18
TOKYO TIME

AS I BEGAN PACKING for freezing-cold Tokyo, the ghosts of the Berlin Marathon lurked in the corner of my room, watching me. A year and a half ago, I'd been doing the exact same thing: meticulously packing my running gear and preparing to traverse the globe in order to pit myself against the marathon. Back then, I'd been wracked with self-doubt. I'd put in all that work for Berlin, and I'd honestly thought I'd given it 100 per cent to try to break three hours—and, ultimately, it hadn't been enough.

But, if my preparation for Tokyo had taught me anything, it was that even when you think you've given it your all there's definitely more in the tank. Now, I still carried the self-doubt with me—those ghosts made sure of that—but, weirdly, I realised I actually believed in myself more than I had pre-Berlin.

Where was that snippet of self-belief coming from? I knew I'd run many more kilometres and trained even harder this time, but could I really trust the training? Would it be enough to help me hit my goal?

As I ticked the last items off my checklist and zipped up my suitcase, I took the opportunity to have a brutally honest look at where I was at. I believed that I could maybe—just maybe—run the Tokyo Marathon in under three hours, so long as everything went as well as possible. But, even then, I'd be cutting it fine. *Real* fine. The realist in me couldn't help but point out that the odds weren't exactly in my favour there.

Mum, like only someone's mum could, believed I was going to own it. 'You might even surprise yourself,' she said to me when I expressed my reservations. 'You might run it in way under three!'

That would be nice . . . but that was not going to happen. As far as I was concerned, if I *was* going to run under three, it would be by the seat of my pants. The time on my certificate would be something like 2 hours 59 minutes and a good number of seconds.

I did believe, however—and quite strongly—that I could run faster than the 3 hours 5 minutes I'd done in Berlin. That'd give me a new PB, which would be amazing.

And, since it never hurts to consider the worst-case scenario: even if things really turned to shit (barring a Callum Hawkins-style tragedy), I reckoned I could probably still finish in around 3 hours 15 minutes. Just three years earlier, a run of that time would have been a PB. Now, it was a bad day at the office, which was a pretty cool reminder of just how far I had come.

Also, so long as I finished, I was going to get presented with my Six Star Finisher medal. I'd been working away at getting that medal for seven years and I wanted to make sure that I enjoyed the moment of finally receiving it. It'd be a real bummer to finally get this thing that represented a whole lot of work, only to walk around sulking because I hadn't hit my goal time.

This might all sound a bit defeatist, but I was actually just trying to be realistic. Prepare for the worst and hope for the best, as they say.

MUM AND I MADE our way to the airport together on Thursday morning, and met up with Gaz Brown and the rest of the runners heading to Tokyo through GetRunning. When a group of marathon runners get together before an event, the conversation steers towards goal times faster than you can say 'iliotibial band syndrome'. I hovered in the background, trying to avoid talking about my goal, until one of the other runners realised I was being very quiet.

'What about you, Dom? You must have a goal time!'

A bunch of annoyingly healthy-looking marathoners gazed expectantly at me.

'Oh, yeah, totally!' I half-arsed an answer. 'I did three hours five at Berlin, so I'd be stoked with anything faster than that.'

Mum was busy taking part in another conversation, but she obviously had one ear on what I was saying. She stopped mid-sentence to turn round suddenly and yell, 'Dom's going to break three hours!'

Cheers, Mum! Just what I needed.

As we walked to the departure gate, I sarcastically thanked Mum for putting me in it. She just laughed.

I got the last laugh, though. When we boarded the plane, I turned left for my business-class seat, while she turned right. When I was little, she used to put me in time out. Now, she was about to get nine hours in the middle seat of an economy-class row—the aviation version of time out.

IT WAS LATE ON Thursday night by the time we finally arrived at our hotel in Tokyo. Mum and I checked in, headed straight for our rooms and immediately crashed out. The long day of travel turned out to be the best thing we could have done. We were both so exhausted that we slept right through the night, then woke up on Friday morning feeling well rested.

Before breakfast, we met the rest of the GetRunning crew for a run to a park a couple of kilometres away. Coach Ian had given me clear instructions: 8 kilometres at marathon pace. I jogged to the park at a nice, cruisy pace with the others, then went off to do my own thing. All up, it was a 12-kilometre run. Some of the other runners expressed surprise that I was doing a run of that distance and intensity only 48 hours before the event, but I'd done so many runs like it by this point that I wasn't worried. I knew I'd recover and be good to go for the marathon on Sunday. Trust the training and all that!

This run was a good introduction to the Tokyo climate. It was fucking freezing. I wore a beanie and gloves the whole time, and still felt cold. At one point, I removed my gloves so I could take a couple of photos on my phone and my fingertips went white.

Running those 8 kilometres at marathon pace was what I would call 'comfortably hard'. Even though I managed to do most of the run quite a bit quicker than I would need to on Sunday, I still had very little confidence that I could keep it up for 42.2 kilometres. I was, however, totally confident that I was fitter than ever and faster than ever. I was also determined to have fun. The hard work had been done. What would happen come Sunday was in the lap of the running gods.

LATER THAT DAY, MUM and I tagged along with the other GetRunning runners to pick up our numbers and race packs from the race expo. We took the train, and I honestly don't think we would have made it if Gaz hadn't been there. He's been to Tokyo several times, so knows his way around. Without him, Mum and I would probably still be wandering around some random corner of the Japanese capital, all dazed and confused.

The main problem for me and Mum was that everything was in Japanese. Obviously. Neither of us speak a word of Japanese, and very few of the locals spoke any English. Mum and I had no bloody clue how to navigate the train system on our own, so we soon decided we were better off taking taxis. The taxis were way more expensive than public transport, but ultimately preferable to the amount of time we would have wasted otherwise trying to get around when we couldn't understand anyone and hardly anyone could understand us.

We even struggled with the taxis, though. At the start of every taxi ride, the exchange would go something like the following.

Me: 'Any English?'

Taxi driver: 'No.'

Me: 'Emperor gardens?'

Taxi driver: confused shrug.

I unlock my phone and type the destination into Google Translate, then play the taxi driver the Japanese translation, holding the phone out encouragingly.

Taxi driver: another confused shrug, followed by some words in Japanese.

I find an image on the internet of the location, and show it to the taxi driver.

Taxi driver: 'Ahhhhh!'

Me (giving the thumbs up): 'DO YOU KNOW THE

PLACE?' (My voice has become obnoxiously loud and I'm speaking really slowly.)

Taxi driver (also giving the thumbs up): 'YES YES YES.' (The taxi driver's voice has become obnoxiously loud and he's speaking really slowly.)

In this fashion, we always managed to get where we needed to go, but it was more difficult than I'd anticipated. Thankfully there are smartphones for stupid people.

Also, as an interesting side note, the taxis in Tokyo were mostly these hilariously old-looking Toyota Crowns, just like the car my grandad in Levin got himself as a retirement present back in the eighties. Something these taxis in Japan had that Grandad's car didn't were car-seat covers that looked like they'd been crocheted by someone's nana. We learned that these vehicles were actually designed for taxicab use in Japan, and continue to be manufactured because they are so popular with taxi drivers. Meanwhile, all the shitty Priuses get exported to New Zealand!

ON SATURDAY MORNING—THE DAY before the Tokyo Marathon— Mum and I went for a gentle jog before breakfast with some of the other runners in our group. Some people don't like to exercise the day before an event, but that just feels strange to me. I'd prefer to do a few slow kilometres to shake my legs out, because I worry that they'll feel heavy or tired if I don't.

It felt good to get out in the cold, fresh air. As we ran back towards the hotel, we passed the marathon start line and I felt a jolt of something—fear, panic, adrenaline?— surge through my body. It had come and gone in the space of a moment, but for that fleeting instant I was overcome with what I hoped to do, how much work I'd put into it, and how hard it was going to be. I calmed down by reminding myself, *What will be will be. Trust the training.*

Mum and I were only in Tokyo for six days, and we decided we didn't want to waste a whole day doing nothing, so after breakfast we walked to a shopping area a few blocks away (no taxi interaction required). Lots of runners spend the day before an event watching movies or reading in a deliberate attempt to expend as little energy as they can, but I think Mum and I subconsciously wanted our day to be as normal as possible in order to keep the anxiety and nerves at bay. If we kept ourselves busy, we wouldn't have time to overthink the run.

Mum doesn't usually get stressed about marathons. She's done so many that she could knock one out in her sleep. But this time she'd been following a programme from Coach Ian in an attempt to try to go faster. I guess the competitive spirit is one of those attributes that stays with you for life. It's certainly the case for Mum.

MUM AND I SUBCONSCIOUSLY WANTED OUR DAY TO BE AS NORMAL AS POSSIBLE IN ORDER TO KEEP THE ANXIETY AND NERVES AT BAY. IF WE KEPT OURSELVES BUSY, WE WOULDN'T HAVE TIME TO OVERTHINK THE RUN.

Anyway, Mum and I seem to have a bit of a habit of walking for miles whenever we go overseas together to do a marathon. Just like that time we decided to walk to the Hollywood sign only two days after running the Chicago Marathon, we spent hours walking around the shops in Tokyo. I wish I'd been wearing my watch, because I'd love to know how many kilometres we'd covered. We stopped for some lunch, and I started to get nervous about how long I had been on my feet.

'Maybe we should head back to the hotel to get a bit of rest?' I suggested.

'You go,' Mum said. 'I want to keep shopping.'

I had my doubts about her orientation competency, but she assured me she'd be all right getting back to the hotel on her own. I left her to it.

Back at the hotel, I lay on my bed fretting. My legs were tingling from all that walking. *You've definitely overdone it*, I kept thinking. As I write this now, I realise how stupid this sounds, but at the time I was quite mad with myself—pre-race nerves and time to start overthinking things will do that to you, I guess.

In order to distract myself, I spent the next hour watching the documentary *Breaking2* on my iPad. I've seen it before. Many times. I find it really inspiring, so it makes perfect viewing the day before an important run. If you haven't seen it, you can watch it on YouTube. I won't tell you what happens, but I will tell you that it was bankrolled by Nike and is all about their quest to get one of the athletes they endorse to break two hours in the marathon. One of the runners is the world's best marathoner, Eliud Kipchoge. At the time of writing, Kipchoge has won three London marathons, two Berlin marathons, one Chicago marathon and an Olympic gold medal for the marathon. Not bad, eh?

Sitting in my hotel room in Tokyo, I paused the doco when Kipchoge says, 'Marathon is life. It is not about the legs, but it's about the heart and mind.' I grabbed a pen and a piece of paper and wrote the quote down, then put the slip of paper in my pocket for the race the next day. I figured it'd be a helpful thing to keep top of mind.

A couple of hours later, Mum knocked on my door. She'd only just made it back to the hotel. She looked a bit sheepish.

'What happened?' I asked.

'Well . . .' she seemed hesitant to fess up. 'I got a bit lost.'

That was the understatement of the century. It turned out she'd got totally disoriented in the middle of an enormous and confusing department store. It had eight floors, and every single floor looked exactly like all the others, so she just couldn't work out how to get back out onto the street. Completely befuddled, she'd ended up bursting into tears in the middle of the store.

It sounds ridiculous . . . and it is. It was also wildly out of character for Mum.

She later decided that it was probably just pre-race nerves, which made sense since she'd trained harder than usual for this event. But, as well as being nervous for herself, I think she might have been a bit nervous for me.

THAT NIGHT, AFTER A good, carb-rich pasta meal, I headed to bed. I got seven solid hours of sleep, but woke up an hour before my alarm was set to go off.

I lay in bed thinking about things. I was nervous as hell, but I also felt a sense of calm and I reminded myself that, no matter what happened, I would still be getting my Six Star Finisher medal at the end of the day.

I thought back over all the training I'd done in preparation for this one run. Based on the times I'd been posting in my training, I knew I could hold the pace required for 30 kilometres. It would be the last hour of the Tokyo Marathon that would determine whether or not I would break three hours.

I leaned over and switched on the bedside light, then read Coach Ian's race plan for the thousandth time. As well as telling me what warm-ups and stretches to do 20 minutes before the run, it also laid out the plan of attack for the marathon itself. In essence, the game plan was to run at 4:10-kilometre pace for the first half, then drop to 4:14-kilometre pace for the second half if I needed to. Then, if I felt great at 37 kilometres, I could dig in for a fast finish—or, if I felt like crap (the most likely scenario), just try to hang on. Oh, and I mustn't forget to take an energy gel every 45 minutes.

I had studied this plan so many times I had it committed to memory. I knew exactly where I needed to be at every stage of the run. The hard bit wasn't knowing the plan; it was going to be executing the plan. Never in all of the marathons I've done have I got to 37 kilometres and felt so good that I can put my head down and pick up the pace.

I HAD STUDIED THIS PLAN SO MANY TIMES I HAD IT COMMITTED TO MEMORY. I KNEW EXACTLY WHERE I NEEDED TO BE AT EVERY STAGE OF THE RUN. THE HARD BIT WASN'T KNOWING THE PLAN; IT WAS GOING TO BE EXECUTING THE PLAN.

After that, I picked up my phone and scrolled through all the good-luck messages from my friends and followers on social media. There was, of course, a message from Coach Ian.

> You've got this, mate! You're stronger than ever— and have done the extra kilometres this time, as well as more work around your race pace to make you stronger for longer, too.
>
> It's natural to feel nervous. Don't worry about it. Remember all the training you have done—and that was in the crazy heat and humidity! Remember how

much stronger you are than last time, when you were so close!

You're going to be sweet, mate. Remember to relax and take the first few kilometres a little bit easier than race pace, and you'll be fine.

Before long, though, I had to stop reading all the messages of support. It was making me too anxious! That is the blessing and the curse of telling people a goal: you get all this wonderful encouragement, but then you also have so many people who will know if you fail. And, in a strange way, you feel like you might let them down as well as yourself.

It was time for me to get out of bed, have a shower and a shave (an integral part of my little OCD pre-race ritual), and go and get some breakfast.

I MET UP WITH Mum at breakfast. Our hotel was just a short walk to the start line, so we had plenty of time. Probably too much time, actually. Waiting to start a marathon is, in lots of ways, the hardest part. Once you start running, all the nerves disappear.

After eating, Mum and I went outside for a nosy around the starting area. Kickoff was still an hour and a half away, but thousands of runners had already started to gather in the freezing cold. Mum and I soon headed back to the warm hotel to wait for as long as possible before we had to venture outdoors again. Anticipating the cold conditions, I had purchased a cheap beanie and gloves before leaving home, the plan being to wear them for the start of the run then toss them to the side of the road once I'd warmed up. After our wee jaunt, though, I decided to wear trackpants and a sweatshirt to the start line as well. I'd then offload these just before the starter's gun sounded. Underneath, I was wearing the gear I'd run in: shorts, a T-shirt, a beanie and not one but two pairs of gloves.

At last, with about half an hour to go before the start of the race, Mum and I left the hotel. We were in different starting blocks, so we parted ways at the starting area, but not before wishing each other good luck.

By the time I got into my starting block, there were only fifteen minutes to go before the start of the race and the block was already crammed with runners. I was happy with my spot, which was about 40 metres back from the start line. For an event of this size, with around 35,000 participants, that is bloody close.

As I stood there among all the other runners, I had flashbacks to the start of the Berlin Marathon. It had been so congested for the first few kilometres of that race, and that had slowed me down early on. I didn't want to make the same mistake here. Nearby, I spied a fleet of spritely Japanese men trailing helium balloons with 'three hours' written on them. The three-hour pace group. The important thing was for me to keep sight of them.

With precisely three minutes until go-time, and with very little room to move, I awkwardly removed my trackpants and sweatshirt. The couple of minutes before the start of a race on a cold morning are really a sight to behold: thousands of garments fly through the air, landing in sorry little heaps on the side of the road.

I was ready to go.

I took a deep breath.

Trust the training.

The starter's gun went off.

CHAPTER 19
THE ELUSIVE SUB-THREE

WHITE CONFETTI SPRAYED EVERYWHERE. I took a few breaths to soak up the atmosphere and enjoy the moment. Then I started shuffling along. Ahead, I could see the guys with the three-hour balloons were already over the start line and running. There was no use in panicking, though. My time wouldn't officially begin until I actually crossed the start mat, so I just had to be patient and wait.

Exactly 22 seconds after the gun had gone off, I crossed the start mat.

At the same moment, I tapped the start button on my watch and started running. Fast.

I got off to a great start, and after the first two kilometres I had caught up to the three-hour pace group. I was ahead of the plan. Coach Ian had wanted me to run the first couple of kilometres really conservatively, but I'd gone a bit faster.

His reasoning was that if I eased into things early on it would help me out later on in the run. I think my nervous energy got the better of me, though. For my own peace of mind, I really wanted to be near those three-hour lads.

I ran with them for a few hundred metres before I realised I was actually pulling ahead of them. These pacers were so disciplined that they were running exact splits for a 2 hour 59 minute marathon. Since I was feeling pretty good, I figured I'd run slightly faster than that so I'd have a bit of time up my sleeve for the final few kilometres, during which I always drop off the pace and lose time. I knew I'd probably see these guys again somewhere after the 35-kilometre mark. Then, as Eliud Kipchoge said, hopefully I'd have enough in my heart and mind to hang on to them until the finish.

At the 5-kilometre sign, I glanced at my watch: 21 minutes and 5 seconds. An average pace of 4:13 per kilometre. Pretty much perfect. I felt great, too. I actually think the freezing-cold conditions were helping. I was still wearing my cheap beanie and two pairs of gloves, and had no intention of discarding either.

In a flash, I was at the 10-kilometre sign. I looked at my watch again: 41 minutes and 47 seconds. An average pace for the last 5 kilometres of 4:08. I was ahead of schedule, and I was still feeling great. I mean, it was hard—but it was comfortably hard. *You should be feeling great*, I reminded myself, trying to keep any excitement in check. *You've only run 10 kilometres. Your work for the day hasn't even started yet!*

At 45 minutes, I took my first gel and it dawned on me that I was only a quarter of the way through. I would need to keep running like this for another 2 hours 15 minutes. That sneaky self-doubt crept in for a moment. *Fucking hell. There's no way you can do that!*

I nipped these negative thoughts in the bud. For the next few minutes, in time with my feet hitting the road, I repeated the mantra over and over in my head: *Trust the training. Trust the training. Trust the training.*

One by one, I passed the signs marking each kilometre. When you see one every four minutes, they seem to pile up quite quickly. I also found it helpful to tackle the run as a shitload of 1-kilometre runs, instead of one big, long 42.2-kilometre run.

At the halfway mark, I glanced at my watch again. I'd been running for 1 hour 27 minutes and 46 seconds. Not much slower than I'd run at the Masters half marathon. The difference with that run was that it had taken everything I had—so much so, that I was vomiting bile at the finish line. Today, though, I'd managed that time, and was still feeling mentally and physically ready for the same distance all over again.

Continuing in this positive vein, I also realised I now had 1 hour 32 minutes and 14 seconds up my sleeve to complete the second half of the marathon in. My pace for the first 21 kilometres had averaged 4:10 per kilometre, and that meant I could afford to run the second half at a pace of 4:22.

Not that I was planning to slow down, though. I was going to keep running this same pace until my body refused to follow orders. Memories of Germany eighteen months earlier crept in. It was at the 27-kilometre mark in Berlin when I'd hit the wall. Physically, I was done. And, mentally, I was too tired to care. That's the thing with a marathon: you can be feeling great one minute, then crap the next. Sometimes the crap feeling passes and you get back on track; sometimes it doesn't, and that's it. As I ran, I waited nervously for the wall to appear.

As I passed the 25-kilometre sign, I realised I'd been running alongside a couple of guys for a few kilometres. We'd been running at exactly the same pace. I decided to drop back and sit right in behind them, figuring it would be good to let them set the pace so I didn't have to worry about constantly checking my watch. Also, they would shelter me from the cold breeze.

I WAS NOW WELL PAST THE POINT WHERE THINGS HAD FALLEN APART FOR ME IN BERLIN, AND I WAS RUNNING STRONG AND STEADY.

This plan worked out great for me—until we hit the 28-kilometre sign. I was feeling restless. I stole a peek at my watch and noticed that the pace was starting to drop. It was only by a couple of seconds each kilometre, but it was definitely getting slower. Maybe the wall had appeared for my anonymous running buddies. It was time for me to say 'Sayonara' to them and carry on running my own race.

I was now well past the point where things had fallen apart for me in Berlin, and I was running strong and steady. I still had a lot of work left to do, but with each kilometre I knocked off I started to feel more and more hopeful. Maybe today was the day. Maybe I really was going to crack three hours.

I got to 30 kilometres in 2 hours 5 minutes. That's an average pace of 4:10 per kilometre, and I was still holding my own. It was definitely getting harder, and I was pushing myself, but my body was responding. Never before, in all of the fifteen marathons I'd done, had I experienced this sort of mental clarity at this stage of a run. It was a remarkable feeling.

I did some quick calculations in my head. Even if my pace dropped back to 4:30 per kilometre, I would still sneak in under three hours. I wouldn't say I was feeling cocky, but I *was* starting to feel cautiously optimistic.

I hit the 35-kilometre mark in 2 hours 26 minutes. Time for some more quick maths: even if my pace dropped right back to 4:43 per kilometre, I would still break three hours. At this point in the Tokyo Marathon, you turn and run back in the direction you've just come for 7 kilometres. After I'd done my one-eighty and was heading back towards the finish line, I passed the three-hour pacers coming in the other direction. I was in front of them by a good couple of minutes.

Even so, I still wasn't getting ahead of myself. There was still a lot of work to be done: the hardest and most important 7 kilometres of my life.

At 37 kilometres, I ran past a couple of paramedics working on a collapsed runner. This guy was sitting in the gutter with a foil emergency blanket round him. He was having an ugly-cry. For him it was game over. Marathons can be so cruel. A whole run can unravel in a matter of minutes. It was a stark reminder that, even though I was still feeling good (well, as good as you can after two and a half hours of hard running), nothing was guaranteed.

Stay focused, I reminded myself. *Keep your head in the game.*

My body was in a world of pain, but it was still running the pace it needed to.

As I passed the 40-kilometre sign, I let my arms hang down and shook them out. I had 2.2 kilometres left to go. Ten minutes of running. All I needed to do was relax, stay calm and keep running.

My legs were burning up. *Dig it in*, I told myself. *The pain will stop as soon as you do. Pain is temporary. Victory is forever.*

I turned on to a cobbled street, and saw the finish line 700 metres away. The crowd thickened and the cheering got louder the closer I got to the finish line. For the first time during the whole run—and, I suddenly realised, for the first time in days—I started to relax. Truly relax. I smiled. Nothing was going to stop me now.

I gave it everything I had. I remembered how at this stage of the London Marathon I'd been so rooted I had to walk. That day, 700 metres had seemed like a daunting distance. Today was totally different.

I got to the 42-kilometre sign. Only 200 metres left to go. Less than a minute of running. It's hard to describe the elation you feel when you see the finish line of a marathon looming. No matter whether you've had an epic run or a disappointing one, finishing is always a euphoric experience. But I have never felt as incredible as I did the day that I crossed the finish line of the Tokyo Marathon.

As I raced across the finish line, I reached down to my wrist and clicked the stop button on my watch.

Two hours 57 minutes and 25 seconds.

Smashed it.

Mission accomplished.

IT'S A STRANGE FEELING when you really want to celebrate, but you have no one to share the moment with. Due to the language barrier, I couldn't tell the very efficient Japanese officials at the finish line my good news, so instead I grinned at them like a very exhausted idiot. Then I took my Tokyo Marathon medal and an emergency blanket from them, and awkwardly hobbled away.

I made my way to the Six Star Finisher tent, where I was

finally presented with my giant medal. As one official placed it round my neck, another took my picture. I threw my arms up in the air and screamed, 'Yeeeeeeeeeeeaah!' The crew laughed, then gave me a round of applause.

I had done it. I was officially a sub-three marathon runner, *and* I had completed all six of the World Marathon Majors. What a bloody cool feeling.

With both medals clinking round my neck, I started the walk to the bag pick-up area. Nobody warns you about this, but after running for 42.2 kilometres in Tokyo you then have to walk another couple of kilometres to a park to pick up your warm clothes and catch the bus back to your hotel. The cold was a killer. As soon as I stopped running, I started to feel it. I would have jogged, but even walking was difficult. At least I had that emergency blanket.

I HAD DONE IT. I WAS OFFICIALLY A SUB-THREE MARATHON RUNNER, *AND* I HAD COMPLETED ALL SIX OF THE WORLD MARATHON MAJORS. WHAT A BLOODY COOL FEELING.

As soon as I got my hands on my bag, I put my jacket on and hobbled over to get on the warm bus. Once I'd made myself comfortable in a seat, I held up my Six Star Finisher medal and studied it more closely. As I did so, I reflected on all the runs I'd done to earn it, and all the work that had gone into them. An inspirational quote I'd seen lurking around the internet sprung to mind: 'Set yourself a goal so big you can't achieve it until you grow into the person who can.'

I'd always thought it was a bit cheesy, but sitting there on that bus I finally appreciated what it meant. I'd had doubts that I was physically capable of achieving my goal of breaking three hours in a marathon. In the end, I'd learned that the capability was always there; I just had to grow into a sub-three marathon runner.

A COUPLE OF HOURS later, I finally made it back to the hotel. I immediately checked my phone, and got on the Tokyo Marathon app to check in on Mum. She had finished in a time of 4 hours 17 minutes. Her fastest marathon in many years. Pretty good for any age, but exceptional for 65! When I saw her later and told her my news, she was ecstatic. We had both done it.

Also on my phone, waiting for me, was a message from Coach Ian.

> Wooooooooooooooooooooooooooo! Awesome, mate! Well done! Bloody good effort. That is so amazing, dude. You should be proud!
>
> You obviously kept your head in the game, as it was a perfect marathon. All those extra kilometres at the end of your training paid off. So much effort over the last six months especially, and it all paid off today!
>
> It must have been hard at the end, but you held in there. Minimal slowdown! Passing people all the way to the end too!

He was excited. Just a little bit. He deserved to be. This wasn't just my victory; it was our victory.

And he was dead right about the extra kilometres in training. I had started to think I was mentally brittle and just not tough enough to break three hours, that maybe my brain was the muscle letting me down. In the end, though, I learned I was tough enough—but, no matter how tough you are, it has to be backed up by great training.

AFTERWORD

BEFORE RUNNING TOKYO, I spent a lot of time wondering how it would feel if I ever managed to achieve my goal of breaking three hours in a marathon. Part of me had worried that it might be a bit underwhelming, but I needn't have bothered.

It was most definitely not underwhelming. It felt bloody awesome.

I'm also pretty sure that a huge part of the reason it felt so great was that I'd had to work so damn hard to achieve it. The bigger a goal, the more satisfying it is when you reach it.

When I first wrote this book, a big part of my motivation was to try to inspire my teenage son, by showing him that if you set big goals and work bloody hard anything is possible. This book was first published after I'd run Berlin, but before I ran Tokyo, so I wrote it having fallen short of my sub-three marathon goal. Back then, I finished the book by saying that the outcome of my run at Berlin was an unforeseen blessing, and I stand by that now.

Life is not always fair. Sometimes your best is not quite good enough. Sometimes you work really bloody hard and still fall short. That's life. It's better to give something a go and fall short than to never try in the first place.

However, just because you don't succeed the first time round—or even the second time, or the tenth, or the hundredth—that doesn't mean you should stop trying. Life throws all sorts of hurdles in the way of big dreams, but that doesn't mean you should give up. And, even when you think you've given something 100 per cent, you will more than likely find there's still room for improvement the next time.

You might not realise it right now, but you're capable of a lot more than you believe.

MY NAME IS DOMINIC HARVEY. I am a marathon runner.

I have never been first, and I have never been worst (yet).

I always try my hardest, and I hope that I always will.

I might not ever be the best, but I will always be the best I can be.

#BETHEBESTYOUCANBE

MY RUNNING TIMELINE

FEBRUARY 1973: I was born.

1982: At the age of nine, I did a 'fun run' from Feilding to Palmerston North. It was 18 kilometres . . . and I ran it in bare feet.

1984: I ran the Steinlager Manawatu Half Marathon (21.1 kilometres). Sadly, the race officials decided I was too young to get a can of the sponsor's product when I crossed the line.

1987: Aged fourteen, I ran my first full marathon (42.2 kilometres) in just under four hours.

1988–2004: For over a decade, I did my very best to avoid exercise altogether. I dabbled in some weightlifting and had a crack at cycling, but Lycra didn't agree with me and my gooch didn't agree with saddle sores so I spent a large portion of this time drunk, stoned or eating potato fritters.

2004: At the age of 31 and the weight of 115 kilograms, I took up running again.

2005: Just over twenty years after my first marathon, I ran my second! I finished the Gold Coast Marathon in 3 hours 53 minutes.

2005: I ran the first 4 kilometres of the Auckland Marathon . . . then collapsed and was rushed in an ambulance to hospital, where I had a bad-ass tumour taken out.

2007: I ran the Auckland Half Marathon.

2010: I ran the Christchurch Marathon in my best-ever time: 3 hours 14 minutes. Fast enough to qualify for the famous Boston Marathon . . . by five seconds!

2012: I ran the Boston Marathon in 3 hours 22 minutes.

2013: I was going to run the New York Marathon . . . until it was cancelled due to a hurricane!

2014: I ran the London Marathon in 3 hours 24 minutes, and the New York Marathon (second time lucky!) in 3 hours 21 minutes.

2015: I teamed up with a coach to try to make myself faster. I ran the Chicago Marathon in 3 hours 10 minutes.

2016: After training harder than I have ever trained before, I ran the Berlin Marathon in 3 hours 5 minutes 43 seconds.

2018: At long last, I cracked the sub-three marathon in Tokyo with a finishing time of 2 hours 57 minutes 25 seconds. I also finally got my Six Star Finisher medal for completing all six of the World Marathon Majors.

SOME CELEBRITY MARATHON TIMES

PAMELA ANDERSON: 2013 New York City Marathon 5:41:03

SEAN 'P DIDDY' COMBS: 2003 New York City Marathon 4:14:52

BRYAN CRANSTON: 1985 New York City Marathon 3:20:45

WILL FERRELL: 2003 Boston Marathon 3:56:12

FLEA (FROM THE RED HOT CHILI PEPPERS): 2012 Los Angeles Marathon 3:41:49

KATIE HOLMES: 2007 New York City Marathon 5:29:58

RONAN KEATING: 2008 London Marathon 3:59:33

ALICIA KEYS: 2015 New York City Marathon 5:50:52

SHIA LABEOUF: 2010 Los Angeles Marathon 4:35:31

PIPPA MIDDLETON: 2015 Safaricom Marathon, Kenya 3:56:33

ALANIS MORISSETTE: 2009 Bizz Johnson Trail Marathon 4:17:03

GORDON RAMSAY: 2004 London Marathon 3:30:37

RYAN REYNOLDS: 2008 New York City Marathon 3:50:22

OPRAH WINFREY: 1994 Marine Corps Marathon 4:29:20

CAROLINE WOZNIACKI: 2014 New York City Marathon 3:26:33

EXAMPLE TRAINING PROGRAMMES

WHEN I ASKED HIM to put together three simple example training programmes for this book, Coach Ian Kostrzewa kindly obliged with the ones on the following pages. They cover three separate distances—10 kilometres, a half marathon and a full marathon. Ian runs Competitive Edge Sport Science (cesports.co.nz) and specialises in tailor-made programmes, but these offer a good starting point.

10-kilometre training programme (12 weeks)

	MONDAY	TUESDAY	WEDNESDAY	THURSDAY	FRIDAY	SATURDAY	SUNDAY
WEEK 1	Run/Walk: Run for 30 seconds, then walk for 30 seconds. Repeat for 10 minutes.		Run/Walk: Run for 1 minute, then walk for 30 seconds. Repeat for 10 minutes.		Run/Walk: Run for 30 seconds, then walk for 30 seconds. Repeat for 10 minutes.		Run/Walk: Run for 1 minute, then walk for 30 seconds. Repeat for 15 minutes.
WEEK 2	Run/Walk: Run for 30 seconds, then walk for 30 seconds. Repeat for 15 minutes.		Run/Walk: Run for 1 minute, then walk for 30 seconds. Repeat for 20 minutes.		Run: Run for 10 minutes continuously—only walk if you have to.		Long Run: Run for 20 minutes—only walk if you have to.
WEEK 3	Run/Walk: Run for 1 minute, then walk for 30 seconds. Repeat for 15 minutes.		Sprints: Sprint as fast as you can for 10 seconds, then walk for 20 seconds. Repeat for 10 minutes.		Run/Walk: Run for 30 seconds, then walk for 30 seconds. Repeat for 20 minutes.		Hill Run: Run for 30 seconds up a moderately steep hill, the walk back down. Repeat 5 times.
WEEK 4	Run: Run for 10 minutes continuously—only walk if you have to.		Run/Walk: Run for 1 minute, then walk for 30 seconds. Repeat for 20 minutes.		Run/Walk: Run for 1 minute, then walk for 30 seconds. Repeat for 20 minutes.		Long Run: Run for 5 km—only walk if you have to.

WEEK 5	Run: Run for 15 minutes—only walk if you have to.		Sprints: Sprint as fast as you can for 10 seconds, then walk for 20 seconds. Repeat for 10 minutes.		Run/Walk: Run for 1 minute, then walk for 30 seconds. Repeat for 25 minutes.		Hill Run: Run for 30 seconds up a moderately steep hill, then walk back down. Repeat 5 times.
WEEK 6	Run/Walk: Run for 1 minute, then walk for 30 seconds. Repeat for 25 minutes.		Run: Run for 15 minutes—only walk if you have to.		Run/Walk: Run for 1 minute, then walk for 30 seconds. Repeat for 30 minutes.		Long Run: Run for 6 km with no walking breaks.
WEEK 7	Run: Run for 20 minutes—only walk if you have to.		Run/Walk: Run for 1 minute, then walk for 30 seconds. Repeat for 40 minutes.		Sprints: Sprint as fast as you can for 10 seconds, then walk for 20 seconds. Repeat for 15 minutes.		Hill Run: Run for 60 seconds up a moderately steep hill, then walk back down. Repeat 5 times.
WEEK 8	Sprints: Sprint as fast as you can for 10 seconds, then walk for 20 seconds. Repeat for 15 minutes.		Run/Walk: Run for 1 minute, then walk for 30 seconds. Repeat for 25 minutes.		Run: Run for 30 minutes—only walk if you have to.		Long Run: Run for 8 km with no walking breaks.

	MONDAY	TUESDAY	WEDNESDAY	THURSDAY	FRIDAY	SATURDAY	SUNDAY
WEEK 9	Run: Run for 30 minutes—only walk if you have to.		Long Sprints: Sprint as fast as you can for 20 seconds, then walk for 20 seconds. Repeat for 15 minutes.		Run/Walk: Run for 1 minute, then walk for 30 seconds. Repeat for 50 minutes.		Hill Run: Run for 30 seconds up a moderately steep hill, then walk back down. Repeat 10 times.
WEEK 10	Run: Run for 40 minutes—only walk if you have to.		Long Sprints: Sprint as fast as you can for 20 seconds, then walk for 20 seconds. Repeat for 20 minutes.		Run/Walk: Run for 1 minute, then walk for 30 seconds. Repeat for 60 minutes.		Long Run: Run for 10 km with no walking breaks.
WEEK 11	Run: Run for 35 minutes—only walk if you have to.		Run/Walk: Run for 1 minute, then walk for 30 seconds. Repeat for 60 minutes.		Run: Run for 25 minutes—only walk if you have to.		Hill Run: Run for 60 seconds up a moderately steep hill, then walk back down. Repeat 10 times.
WEEK 12	Easy Run: Run at a slow pace for 35 minutes.		Easy Run: Run at a slow pace for 20 minutes.		Rest Day.		Your 10-km event!

Half-marathon training programme (16 weeks)

	MONDAY	TUESDAY	WEDNESDAY	THURSDAY	FRIDAY	SATURDAY	SUNDAY
WEEK 1	Run/Walk: Run for 30 seconds, then walk for 30 seconds. Repeat for 10 minutes.		Run/Walk: Run for 1 minute, then walk for 30 seconds. Repeat for 10 minutes.		Run/Walk: Run for 30 seconds, then walk for 30 seconds. Repeat for 10 minutes.		Run/Walk: Run for 1 minute, then walk for 30 seconds. Repeat for 15 minutes.
WEEK 2	Run/Walk: Run for 30 seconds, then walk for 30 seconds. Repeat for 15 minutes.		Run/Walk: Run for 1 minute, then walk for 30 seconds. Repeat for 20 minutes.		Run: Run for 10 minutes—only walk if you have to.		Long Run: Run for 20 minutes—only walk if you have to.
WEEK 3	Run/Walk: Run for 1 minute, then walk for 30 seconds. Repeat for 15 minutes.		Sprints: Sprint as fast as you can for 10 seconds, then walk for 20 seconds. Repeat for 10 minutes.		Run/Walk: Run for 30 seconds, then walk for 30 seconds. Repeat for 20 minutes.		Hill Run: Run for 30 seconds up a moderately steep hill, then walk back down. Repeat 5 times.
WEEK 4	Run: Run for 10 minutes—only walk if you have to.		Run/Walk: Run for 1 minute, then walk for 30 seconds. Repeat for 20 minutes.		Run/Walk: Run for 1 minute, then walk for 30 seconds. Repeat for 20 minutes.		Long Run: Run for 5 km—only walk if you have to.

	MONDAY	TUESDAY	WEDNESDAY	THURSDAY	FRIDAY	SATURDAY	SUNDAY
WEEK 5	Run: Run for 15 minutes—only walk if you have to.		Sprints: Sprint as fast as you can for 10 seconds, then walk for 20 seconds. Repeat for 10 minutes.		Run/Walk: Run for 1 minute, then walk for 30 seconds. Repeat for 25 minutes.		Hill Run: Run for 30 seconds up a moderately steep hill, then walk back down. Repeat 5 times.
WEEK 6	Run/Walk: Run for 1 minute, then walk for 30 seconds. Repeat for 25 minutes.		Run: Run for 15 minutes—only walk if you have to.		Run/Walk: Run for 1 minute, then walk for 30 seconds. Repeat for 30 minutes.		Long Run: Run for 7 km with no walking breaks.
WEEK 7	Run: Run for 20 minutes—only walk if you have to.		Run/Walk: Run for 1 minute, then walk for 30 seconds. Repeat for 40 minutes.		Sprints: Sprint as fast as you can for 10 seconds, then walk for 20 seconds. Repeat for 15 minutes.		Hill Run: Run for 60 seconds up a moderately steep hill, then walk back down. Repeat 5 times.
WEEK 8	Sprints: Sprint as fast as you can for 10 seconds, then walk for 20 seconds. Repeat for 15 minutes.		Run/Walk: Run for 1 minute, then walk for 30 seconds. Repeat for 25 minutes.		Run: Run for 30 minutes—only walk if you have to.		Long Run: Run for 10 km with no walking breaks.

WEEK 9	Run: Run for 30 minutes—only walk if you have to.	Long Sprints: Sprint as fast as you can for 20 seconds, then walk for 20 seconds. Repeat for 15 minutes.	Run/Walk: Run for 1 minute, then walk for 30 seconds. Repeat for 50 minutes.	Hill Run: Run for 30 seconds up a moderately steep hill, then walk back down. Repeat 10 times.
WEEK 10	Run: Run for 40 minutes—only walk if you have to.	Long Sprints: Sprint as fast as you can for 20 seconds, then walk for 20 seconds. Repeat for 20 minutes.	Run/Walk: Run for 1 minute, then walk for 30 seconds. Repeat for 60 minutes.	Long Run: Run for 13 km with no walking breaks.
WEEK 11	Run: Run for 50 minutes—only walk if you have to.	Sprints: Sprint as fast as you can for 10 seconds, then walk for 20 seconds. Repeat for 20 minutes.	Run: Run for 70 minutes—only walk if you have to.	Hill Run: Run for 60 seconds up a moderately steep hill, then walk back down. Repeat 10 times.
WEEK 12	Run: Run for 60 minutes—only walk if you have to.	1-km Sprints: Sprint as fast as you can for 1 km, then walk for 1 minute. Repeat for 35 minutes.	Run: Run for 50 minutes—only walk if you have to.	Long Run: Run for 17 km with no walking breaks.

	MONDAY	TUESDAY	WEDNESDAY	THURSDAY	FRIDAY	SATURDAY	SUNDAY
WEEK 13	Run: Run for 45 minutes—only walk if you have to.		Run: Run for 70 minutes—only walk if you have to.		Long Sprints: Sprint as fast as you can for 20 seconds, then walk for 20 seconds. Repeat for 20 minutes.		Hill Run: Run for 30 seconds up a moderately steep hill, then walk back down. Repeat 15 times.
WEEK 14	Run: Run for 90 minutes—only walk if you have to.		1-km Sprints: Sprint as fast as you can for 1 km, then walk for 1 minute. Repeat for 40 minutes.		Run: Run for 60 minutes—only walk if you have to.		Long Run: Run for 21 km with no walking breaks.
WEEK 15	Run: Run for 45 minutes—only walk if you have to.		Sprints: Sprint as fast as you can for 10 seconds, then walk for 20 seconds. Repeat for 20 minutes.		Run: Run for 50 minutes—only walk if you have to.		Hill Run: Run for 60 seconds up a moderately steep hill, then walk back down. Repeat 15 times.
WEEK 16	Easy Run: Run at a slow pace for 35 minutes.		Easy Run: Run at a slow pace for 20 minutes.		Rest Day.		Your half-marathon event!

Marathon training programme (25 weeks)

	MONDAY	TUESDAY	WEDNESDAY	THURSDAY	FRIDAY	SATURDAY	SUNDAY
WEEK 1	Run/Walk: Run for 30 seconds, then walk for 30 seconds. Repeat for 10 minutes.		Run/Walk: Run for 1 minute, then walk for 30 seconds. Repeat for 10 minutes.		Run/Walk: Run for 30 seconds, then walk for 30 seconds. Repeat for 10 minutes.		Run/Walk: Run for 1 minute, then walk for 30 seconds. Repeat for 15 minutes.
WEEK 2	Run/Walk: Run for 30 seconds, then walk for 30 seconds. Repeat for 15 minutes.		Run/Walk: Run for 1 minute, then walk for 30 seconds. Repeat for 20 minutes.		Run: Run for 10 minutes—only walk if you have to.		Long Run: Run for 20 minutes—only walk if you have to.
WEEK 3	Run/Walk: Run for 1 minute, then walk for 30 seconds. Repeat for 15 minutes.		Sprints: Sprint as fast as you can for 10 seconds, then walk for 20 seconds. Repeat for 10 minutes.		Run/Walk: Run for 30 seconds, then walk for 30 seconds. Repeat for 20 minutes.		Hill Run: Run for 30 seconds up a moderately steep hill, then walk back down. Repeat 5 times.
WEEK 4	Run: Run for 10 minutes—only walk if you have to.		Run/Walk: Run for 1 minute, then walk for 30 seconds. Repeat for 20 minutes.		Run/Walk: Run for 1 minute, then walk for 30 seconds. Repeat for 20 minutes.		Long Run: Run for 5 km—only walk if you have to.

	MONDAY	TUESDAY	WEDNESDAY	THURSDAY	FRIDAY	SATURDAY	SUNDAY
WEEK 5	Run: Run for 15 minutes—only walk if you have to.		Sprints: Sprint as fast as you can for 10 seconds, then walk for 20 seconds. Repeat for 10 minutes.		Run/Walk: Run for 1 minute, then walk for 30 seconds. Repeat for 25 minutes.		Hill Run: Run for 30 seconds up a moderately steep hill, then walk back down. Repeat 5 times.
WEEK 6	Run/Walk: Run for 1 minute, then walk for 30 seconds. Repeat for 25 minutes.		Run: Run for 15 minutes—only walk if you have to.		Run/Walk: Run for 1 minute, then walk for 30 seconds. Repeat for 30 minutes.		Long Run: Run for 7 km with no walking breaks.
WEEK 7	Run: Run for 20 minutes—only walk if you have to.		Run/Walk: Run for 1 minute, then walk for 30 seconds. Repeat for 40 minutes.		Sprints: Sprint as fast as you can for 10 seconds, then walk for 20 seconds. Repeat for 15 minutes.		Hill Run: Run for 60 seconds up a moderately steep hill, then walk back down. Repeat 5 times.
WEEK 8	Sprints: Sprint as fast as you can for 10 seconds, then walk for 20 seconds. Repeat for 15 minutes.		Run/Walk: Run for 1 minute, then walk for 30 seconds. Repeat for 25 minutes.		Run: Run for 30 minutes—only walk if you have to.		Long Run: Run for 10 km with no walking breaks.

WEEK 9	Run: Run for 30 minutes—only walk if you have to.		Long Sprints: Sprint as fast as you can for 20 seconds, then walk for 20 seconds. Repeat for 15 minutes.		Run/Walk: Run for 1 minute, then walk for 30 seconds. Repeat for 50 minutes.	Hill Run: Run for 30 seconds up a moderately steep hill, then walk back down. Repeat 10 times.
WEEK 10	Run: Run for 40 minutes—only walk if you have to.		Long Sprints: Sprint as fast as you can for 20 seconds, then walk for 20 seconds. Repeat for 20 minutes.		Run/Walk: Run for 1 minute, then walk for 30 seconds. Repeat for 60 minutes.	Long Run: Run for 13 km with no walking breaks.
WEEK 11	Run: Run for 50 minutes—only walk if you have to.		Sprints: Sprint as fast as you can for 10 seconds, then walk for 20 seconds. Repeat for 20 minutes.		Run: Run for 70 minutes—only walk if you have to.	Hill Run: Run for 60 seconds up a moderately steep hill, then walk back down. Repeat 10 times.
WEEK 12	Run: Run for 60 minutes—only walk if you have to.		1-km Sprints: Sprint as fast as you can for 1 km, then walk for 1 minute. Repeat for 35 minutes.		Run: Run for 50 minutes—only walk if you have to.	Long Run: Run for 17 km with no walking breaks.

	MONDAY	TUESDAY	WEDNESDAY	THURSDAY	FRIDAY	SATURDAY	SUNDAY
WEEK 13	Run: Run for 45 minutes—only walk if you have to.		Run: Run for 70 minutes—only walk if you have to.		Long Sprints: Sprint as fast as you can for 20 seconds, then walk for 20 seconds. Repeat for 20 minutes.		Hill Run: Run for 30 seconds up a moderately steep hill, then walk back down. Repeat 15 times.
WEEK 14	Run: Run for 90 minutes—only walk if you have to.		1-km Sprints: Sprint as fast as you can for 1 km, then walk for 1 minute. Repeat for 40 minutes.		Run: Run for 60 minutes—only walk if you have to.		Long Run: Run for 21 km with no walking breaks.
WEEK 15	Run: Run for 45 minutes—only walk if you have to.		Sprints: Sprint as fast as you can for 10 seconds, then walk for 20 seconds. Repeat for 20 minutes.		Run: Run for 50 minutes—only walk if you have to.		Hill Run: Run for 60 seconds up a moderately steep hill, then walk back down. Repeat 15 times.
WEEK 16	Run: Run for 100 minutes—only walk if you have to.		1-km Sprints: Sprint as fast as you can for 1 km, then walk for 1 minute. Repeat for 45 minutes.		Run: Run for 70 minutes—only walk if you have to.		Long Run: Run for 25 km with no walking breaks.

WEEK 17	Run: Run for 50 minutes—only walk if you have to.		Sprints: Sprint as fast as you can for 10 seconds, then walk for 20 seconds. Repeat for 20 minutes.		Tempo Run: Run at a fast pace for 40 minutes.		Hill Run: Run for 30 seconds up a moderately steep hill, then walk back down. Repeat 15 times.
WEEK 18	Run: Run for 115 minutes—only walk if you have to.		Long Sprints: Sprint as fast as you can for 20 seconds, then walk for 20 seconds. Repeat for 20 minutes.		Run: Run for 75 minutes—only walk if you have to.		Long Run: Run for 30 km with no walking breaks.
WEEK 19	Run: Run for 50 minutes—only walk if you have to.		Sprints: Sprint as fast as you can for 10 seconds, walk for 20 seconds. Repeat for 20 minutes.		Run: Run for 100 minutes—only walk if you have to.		Hill Run: Run for 60 seconds up a moderately steep hill, then walk back down. Repeat 15 times.
WEEK 20	Run: Run for 120 minutes—only walk if you have to.		1-km Sprints: Sprint as fast as you can for 1 km, then walk for 1 minute. Repeat for 40 minutes.		Run: Run for 75 minutes—only walk if you have to.		Long Run: Run for 34 km with no walking breaks.

	MONDAY	TUESDAY	WEDNESDAY	THURSDAY	FRIDAY	SATURDAY	SUNDAY
WEEK 21	Run: Run for 55 minutes—only walk if you have to.		Sprints: Sprint as fast as you can for 10 seconds, then walk for 20 seconds. Repeat for 20 minutes.		Tempo Run: Run at a fast pace for 45 minutes.		Hill Run: Run for 30 seconds up a moderately steep hill, then walk back down. Repeat 20 times.
WEEK 22	Run: Run for 130 minutes—only walk if you have to.		1-km Sprints: Sprint as fast as you can for 1 km, then walk for 1 minute. Repeat for 45 minutes.		Run: Run for 90 minutes—only walk if you have to.		Long Run: Run for 38 km with no walking breaks.
WEEK 23	Run: Run for 75 minutes—only walk if you have to.		Long Sprints: Sprint as fast as you can for 20 seconds, then walk for 20 seconds. Repeat for 20 minutes.		Tempo Run: Run at a fast pace for 45 minutes.		Hill Run: Run for 60 seconds up a moderately steep hill, then walk back down. Repeat 20 times.
WEEK 24	Run: Run for 90 minutes—only walk if you have to.		Run: Run for 60 minutes—only walk if you have to.		Easy Run: Run at a slow pace for 70 minutes.		Rest Day.
WEEK 25	Easy Run: Run at a slow pace for 60 minutes.		Easy Run: Run at a slow pace for 50 minutes.		Rest Day.		Your marathon event!

ACKNOWLEDGEMENTS

THANKS TO MY PARENTS. If you guys were not runners, chances are I may never have gravitated towards the marathon distance.

Thanks to Ian Kostrzewa at Competitive Edge Sport Science (cesports.co.nz). With Ian's knowledge, I have been able to go faster than I ever thought possible.

Thanks to the fantastic team at Allen & Unwin, in particular Kimberley Davis. She took my incoherent rambles about running and transformed them into this thing you are holding now. When they suggested I write a book about running, I told them I was worried it would be bloody boring but they assured me it wouldn't be. I hope I have been proven wrong.

ABOUT THE AUTHOR

Dom Harvey is a top-rating, award-winning broadcaster. His radio show on The Edge, with co-hosts Megan Annear and Clinton Randell, is New Zealand's most listened-to breakfast show.

This is Dom's third book. He has also written the bestsellers *Bucket List of an Idiot* and *Childhood of an Idiot*.

He was born in Levin and raised in Palmerston North, but now calls Auckland home.

@DomHarveyGroup

@DomHarvey

@DomHarveyNZ

@TheDomHarvey

Want ideas for what to read next, competitions and news about your favourite authors?

Join us at:

Facebook
www.facebook.com/AllenAndUnwinNZ

Instagram
www.instagram.com/AllenAndUnwinNZ

Twitter
www.twitter.com/AllenAndUnwinNZ

ALLEN&UNWIN
www.allenandunwin.co.nz